ASIAN TEXTS — ASIAN CONTEXTS

SUNY series in Asian Studies Development

Roger T. Ames and Peter D. Hershock, editors

ASIAN TEXTS — ASIAN CONTEXTS

Encounters with Asian Philosophies and Religions

Edited by

David Jones
and
E. R. Klein

SUNY PRESS

Published by State University of New York Press, Albany

© 2010 State University of New York

For information, contact State University of New York Press, Albany, NY
www.sunypress.edu

Production by Kelli LeRoux
Marketing by Anne M. Valentine

Library of Congress Cataloging-in-Publication Data
Asian texts, Asian contexts : encounters with Asian philosophies and religions / edited by David Jones and E. R. Klein.
    p. cm. — (SUNY series in Asian studies development)
Includes bibliographical references and index.
ISBN 978–1–4384–2675–4 (hardcover : alk. paper)
ISBN 978–1–4384–2676–1 (pbk. : alk. paper)
1. Philosophy, Asian. 2. Asia—Religion.
I. Jones, David Edward. II. Klein, Ellen R.
B5005.A85 2009
181—dc22   2009017053

10 9 8 7 6 5 4 3 2 1

Contents

Introduction

In our age of globalization, the world appears to be getting increasingly smaller each day. We are better informed, better connected, and have greater access to information about one another than ever before. In the face of the "war on terror," understanding not only motives or loyalties of other cultures, but also their social and cultural norms has become a primary challenge for Americans. The horrific events on an otherwise ordinary September morning forever changed the way Americans view the world and themselves; this new view, if anything, is the gift of our collective tragedy. It is now painfully clear that our collective ignorance of the world around us must end—it must end if for no other reason than to spare future generations from experiencing similar tragedies. The *9/11 Commission Report* not only documented heroism and villainy, but also offered Americans a chance to better understand themselves. Although not the intent of the report, it nevertheless punctuates the lack of understanding Americans have of the diversity of the world's cultures. Despite the villainous motives of those who attacked, their knowledge of American culture enabled them to blend in for so long. They were the world's "cosmopolitans."

Keeping an eye out for future terrorist attacks is certainly an important reason for us to become more cosmopolitan, but it is not the only reason. Nor is it the purpose of this volume. Our purpose is, rather, one of understanding and appreciation, and as we know, true understanding and appreciation are always multifaceted and complex. To simplify is simply simple-minded, and it has deleterious consequences. Given the diversity and complexities of cultures that have emerged on this planet over the millennia, understanding one another is our greatest challenge, and could quite possibly be a question of our survival as a species.

This vision of understanding and its celebration was quietly realized in 1936 on a distant island in the Pacific. In the year in which Hitler broke the Treaty of Versailles and sent troops to the Rhineland,

Charles A. Moore and Wing-tsit Chan founded the first comparative philosophy program in the world at the University of Hawaii, not so far from Pearl Harbor. Their vision was to bring together Western and Asian philosophers in a discourse of diverse cultures and traditions in hope of creating spaces for understanding. As Moore has written, "Understanding is a very complicated matter. Genuine understanding must be comprehensive, and comprehensive understanding must include a knowledge of all the fundamental aspects of the mind of the people in question. Philosophy is the major medium of understanding, both because it is concerned deliberately and perhaps uniquely with the fundamental ideas, ideals, and attitudes of a people, and also because philosophy alone attempts to see the total picture and thus includes in its purview all the major aspects of the life of a people."[1] The present collection of accessibly written essays is a modest attempt to contribute to the dissemination of Charles Moore's vision of understanding and to those who continued his work over the generations, and to those who continue it today. Such a vision leads to cooperation and the sustainability of humanity.

Global cooperation in business, medical research, human rights law, and even the future of space exploration depends on knowing about and truly understanding the ideas and ideals of each and every culture on the globe. Such a task is, of course, herculean, but the attempt to deal with a smaller portion of it—that concerning the Asian countries of China, India, and Japan—is precisely the mission we set for our authors.

Our first set of authors was given the theoretical challenge to offer reasons why it is that all undergraduate professors—in community colleges, four-year colleges, and universities—across America should take seriously their duty to guide their students into cosmopolitanism in general and the study of Asian thought and culture in particular. Both handled this task in a way specific to their own areas of specialization.

The philosopher John M. Koller, in "The Importance of Asian Philosophy in the Curriculum," addresses this issue head-on when he argues that "understanding basic Asian values and ideas is crucial for survival in an interdependent world . . . [and] necessary for a deeper understanding of ourselves and our own society. . . ." But Koller does not simply make the theoretical case. In addition, he offers prospective teachers, especially those delving into this area of pedagogy for the first time, eleven important guidelines for valuable text selection and techniques for responsible leadership.

Roger T. Ames, the comparative philosopher and specialist on Chinese culture, begins his argument with an interesting thought-experiment: Imagine seeing the whole of the world through the eyes of Chinese imperialism. Imagine what the curriculum in the United States would look like if the Eurocentric philosophies of Descartes and Kant were replaced by the teachings of Confucius and where Shakespeare and Bach were viewed as exotica. With a different historical worldview, argues Ames, one would view the contemporary world quite differently. Given that the Chinese begin their investigation of the universe, humanity, knowledge, and the interconnection between the three with basic presuppositions that Ames claims are profoundly different from those in the West, one cannot help but agree that in order to be a cosmopolitan one cannot avoid studying China and Confucianism.

For studying to be the most fruitful, however, requires guidance from a teacher. And teaching has never been easy. Teaching undergraduate students to understand a culture alien from their own is even more difficult. Taking the difficulty of this task seriously, we decided to ask experts in various fields of Asian studies—specifically those involving India, Japan, and China—to help others infuse Asian philosophies and religions into their specific curricula by documenting both the foundations and pedagogical techniques they have found helpful and insightful throughout their teaching careers.

The remainder of the book—parts 2 and 3—is devoted to the two main ways in which scholars approach the teaching of Asian philosophies and religions in the undergraduate classroom: texts and contexts. By concentrating on texts, scholars offer undergraduate professors new to the mainstreaming of Asian thought and culture creative practical guides to the introduction of great texts such as the *Bhagavad Gītā* and the *Daodejing* into their Western curriculum. Professors of history, literature, philosophy, political science, and religion (just to name a few) will find part 2 eminently readable and useful. Part 3 will offer transglobal contexts in philosophy, religion, history, and art, such as Chinese landscape painting as a way of approaching a better understanding of Asian thought and culture and of our own, as well as the need for more intercommunication between the two.

Part 2 is divided into treatment of three geographical areas—India, China, and Japan—so that burgeoning teachers of Asian thought and culture can pick and choose what they want to teach, either by general area or by specific text. In the first section of Part 2, the *Bhagavad Gītā*—the story of an ethical struggle on a battlefield taken from the great Indian epic the *Mahabharata*—is the focus of the piece by philosopher and feminist Vrinda Dalmiya. Dalmiya is able to draw out a beautiful account of the story itself from the intricate tapestry of Indian philosophy more broadly, all with an eye toward traditional Western analyses of ethics and ethical decision-making. Lessons drawn from the text include those learned from struggling with the knowledge of one's duty, conflicts of duty, and the overall problem of moving from theory to praxis within the context of ethical decision-making. Dalmiya's piece is a sophisticated treatment of the text that is nonetheless eminently accessible; it is pedagogically invaluable if one wants to incorporate the *Bhagavad Gītā* into a standard syllabus.

The next piece, "Vimalakirti's Triumphant Silence," by the Asian scholar Jeffrey Dippmann, focuses on the classic Indian sutra (Sanskrit for "string"), the *Vimalakirti Nirdesa Sutra*. Dippmann focuses on this specific text because he believes that it helps one "bridge the gap between Indian and Chinese Buddhism" and because it has particular interest to students due to its "physical" nature and, one could argue, racy content. As college and university students often find themselves struggling, on the one hand, with the need to focus on academics in order to have a good life in the long run, and, on the other, with the immediate desire to partake in the more decadent "good life" that is a part of campus life, this timeless sutra about struggle can easily be made pertinent to most traditional students. Dippmann explains how it is one can adopt this text to show both the differences between Asia and the West as well as the similarities of the human condition that haunt all persons.

In "The Things of This World Are Masks the Infinite Assumes: Introducing Samkhya and Yoga Philosophy," the philosopher Tom Pynn begins his essay by discussing an important 9/11 date from the year 1893 when, in Chicago, many American scholars first realized the beauty, power, and diversity of Asian thought and culture. The texts Pynn believes can best teach this power are the *Yoga Sutras* and any of the Samkhya texts and commentaries, such as Iswara Krishna's *Samkhya Karika*. With the help of detailed commentary, Pynn offers the first-time user of such texts a comprehensive and comprehensible flow chart of the differences and similarities between Yoga and Samkhya philosophies, as well as their convergences with and divergences from Western philosophers such as Plato, Aristotle, and Descartes. Pynn ends his chapter with a general comparison between the philosophies of Asia and the West via the interesting and very popular subject of subjectivity.

Many developments of Asian thought and culture have their chronological beginnings in India; its ideas and ideologies later migrated into China, where they were reinvented and changed forever. From China, these ideas went on to be discovered by the rest of East Asia. Through this process of appropriation, they were again influenced by indigenous beliefs and ways of understanding. Our text retraces this historical path, and it is to the great texts of China that the second section of part 2 now turns. The first article on China is by the philosopher Ronnie Littlejohn and deals with one of the most widely read Asian texts, the *Daodejing*. The *Daodejing* is one of the great classic texts of Chinese religion and philosophy, and Littlejohn offers the novice teacher of the *Daodejing* a step-by-step guide to its use in the classroom. In addition, Littlejohn helps the reader understand the depth and breadth of the *Daodejing*, a book that he claims in "Too Twisted to Fit a Carpenter's Square" is so intricate and rich that its "gnarly fiber" makes it impermeable to the tools of modern analysis and interpretation, and thereby retains its historical dignity.

The *Daodejing*, in conjunction with the *Zhuangzi* and the *Sunzi* (*The Art of War*), is taken under the pedagogical wing of the philosopher Robin R. Wang. Wang offers suggestions for teaching these fascinating texts separately and in concert so as to show how the Chinese mind "participates in the deeper inquiry about the nature of philosophy, especially what it means to be doing philosophy." Her goal is not only to help with the introduction of the texts into the Western classroom, but also to show how such an introduction transforms the classroom itself by "creating a space between teacher and learners" that will alter the way the text and learning are perceived and performed. Wang's article suggests that welcoming the *Daodejing*, the *Zhuangzi*, and the *Sunzi* into the classroom will create an environment that teaches *about* Asian thought and culture by providing a space for a small part of it to come alive through the process of learning itself.

The last piece in the China subsection of "Texts" is by Xinyan Jiang and concentrates on the fourth-century BCE Confucian thinker Mengzi (Mencius). The *Mengzi*, argues Jiang, provides readers with a "systematic elaboration of Confucianism" and puts forward "novel ideas" (that were later widely accepted) on the foundations of Neo-Confucian thought. Given that Confucianism and Neo-Confucianism are both the historical foundations and contemporary cornerstones of Chinese thought and culture, anyone studying this genre of ideas cannot avoid reading Mengzi. The title of Jiang's contribution, "Mengzi: Human Nature is Good," makes it clear that the *Mengzi* focuses on the essence of humanity, which makes it of special interest for students of psychology and sociology as well as religion, philosophy, ethics, and all areas of applied ethics including, for example, business ethics. Mengzi, according to Jiang, begins with the presupposition that "human nature is good" and that one need only contemplate one's own feelings—of commiseration, shame, deference, and of right and wrong—if one wants to understand oneself and others. In a similar vein to that of Aristotle in the *Nicomachean Ethics*, Mengzi argues that the seeds of goodness are inherent in humankind and that what people need is the proper environment in which to grow into virtuous citizens. Although not explicitly stated, Jiang suggests a parallel between Mengzi and the students who read him. If students of Asian thought and culture come to the material with the "seeds of goodness," and if they are given the proper environment in the classroom—in this case, the opportunity to read Mengzi—their concern for humanity as a whole will take root and flourish.

From China we move to Japan. In this section the classical texts being proposed for the classroom are not discussed individually but rather as one part of a large whole or "school of thought." The comparative philosopher Brian Schroeder addresses the problems and prospects of teaching Zen texts, focusing on those texts written by and about the great Zen master Eihei Dōgen. Zen, Schroeder begins, is often thought to be the "very antithesis" of Western thought and culture, but through the work of Dōgen and the Soto Zen sect of Zen Buddhism that he founded, the obtaining of "Zen mind" through ordinary experiences such as cooking or walking on the beach is something that is open and available to everyone. Schroeder suggests Dōgen's own biography, specific readings, interesting anecdotes, and various meditative exercises are ways of introducing Western students to Japan and to the "way" of Zen.

There are a variety of Buddhist schools in Japan, and it is the work of the Kyoto School founder Nishida Kitarō that is, according to the comparative religions thinker Gereon Kopf, the best way to introduce Japanese thought and culture to the undergraduate philosophy classroom. In his entry "The Absolute Contradictory What: On How to Read the Philosophy of Nishida Kitarō," Kopf argues that the best way to understand the work of Nishida is as a response to the philosophical standpoints akin to that of Advaita Vedanta. Kopf stresses the need to see Nishida's philosophy as one of "nondualism" stressing a "three-world model . . . that accommodates different ways of thinking as the alternative between two mutually exclusive paradigms."

Part 2 of our collection is concluded with the work of the philosopher Jason M. Wirth, who takes even a broader approach to the teaching of Japanese thought and culture by presenting the Kyoto School—especially the work of Nishida Kitarō, Suzuki Daisetz, and Tanabe Hajime—in comparison to German idealism, which paralleled its development and was also an independent invigorating force within the Japanese Buddhist tradition. In so doing, Wirth frames the Kyoto School as one of the most important intellectual "spaces" from which one can understand the major philosophical foundations of both Asia and the West that profoundly affect contemporary thought and culture on both sides of the Pacific. Wirth stresses the Kyoto philosophers' use of language and tradition as a means by which the most profound and primordial aspects of Asian philosophies and religions have been rescued from the obscurity and indignity to which they have been consigned as Western ideals have grown more popular.

When the historical, artistic, philosophical, or religious implications and foundations of Asian thought and culture were viewed to be more fundamental to the pedagogical style of particular scholar-teachers than any specific text or a particular writer or school of thought, we included their work in part 3, "Contexts." Part 3 serves the purpose of incorporating a broader range of pedagogical tools for the mainstreaming of Asian philosophies and religions into undergraduate curricula and classrooms.

The first section of part 3 categorizes three suggestions for such mainstreaming under the broad and general category of "frameworks."

The first suggestion is made by a historian of Japan, John A. Tucker, who argues that if one is to be educated to become a cosmopolitan, then one's historical perspective cannot be simply Western in origin or approach. As scholar-teachers, we have a duty to offer our students a historical perspective that is "grounded in 'world systems'" so that it "affirms a more global" account of intellectual "systems" for properly understanding human history. With respect to the scope of this volume—India, China, and Japan—Tucker offers a "systems through texts" approach in which he suggests professors use many of the texts mentioned in the first section, as well as other classic volumes such as the literary, philosophical, sociological, religious, and, most especially, historical contexts from which to introduce Asian philosophies and religions into any undergraduate classroom.

Francis Brassard, an Asian scholar and Buddhologist, begins his pedagogical piece by offering the reader a global perspective of human thought and culture—specifically via the great religious traditions—so as to better frame the need for the study of Asian contexts to properly understand and teach the great classical texts of the region. According to Brassard, without first understanding the global context of human nature and what is taken to be the ultimate reason for being across cultures, one is unable truly to see the power of the Buddhist canon. And, in turn, if one is unable to see the historical and cultural framework of Buddhist thought that now extends to all parts of the world, then readers of Asian texts will never grasp the power and profundity of any of the works that grow out of it. According to Brassard, a mainstream understanding of the texts first requires a mainstream understanding of the contexts.

But what if the context in question suggests a complete denial of itself? This is the conundrum addressed by the philosopher and logician Shigenori Nagatomo in "A Sketch of the *Diamond Sutra*'s Logic of Not." Nagatomo argues that certain Asian texts—for example, the *Diamond Sutra*—argue from a context that emerges from contradiction, including its own self-denial when it states: "*A* is not *A*, therefore it is *A*." What would be viewed by most Western thinkers as nonsensical (at worst) or paradoxical (at best) is within the scope of Asian philosophies and religions as one of the many tools for understanding problems, including those theoretical issues that often lead thinkers into paradox. Nagatomo claims that the "dualistic, either-or egological stance" presented in works such as the *Diamond Sutra* present both Asian and Western thinkers with certain theoretical difficulties. However, this stance also presents an unusual framework from which one can rethink the questions and answers that are used to "understand one's self, the relationship between 'I' and 'other,' and our ecological relation with nature."

The scholars above offer a variety of theoretical frameworks for the more novice professors of Asian thought and culture so as to provide them with secure scaffolding from which they can appropriately and securely renovate their Western curriculum to better support more diverse contexts of thought and culture. In addition, for the reader more familiar with Asian texts, the above authors provide interesting and innovative ways of understanding the wisdom of India, China, and Japan in various contexts. Other scholars have worked at making these new contexts more accessible.

Art has always held a special place in the human heart and soul, and the next set of authors believes works of art are the best entrée into alien contexts we can offer our undergraduate students. The humanities scholar and interdisciplinary thinker Harriette D. Grissom claims that one can best understand the thought and culture emerging from the Indian subcontinent through the study of art, specifically religious art. Grissom suggests beginning with the Kailashanta Temple at Ellora, the entire architecture of which is "hewn from a mountain" and is rife with "archetypal, religious, and philosophical symbolism." By examining this mammoth "sculpture," one can reach a greater understanding of Indian ideas of self, their construction of the perennial struggle between the material and spiritual, and their notion of *purusha*, or the "cosmic body."

Art and artists, according to the Chinese art historian Stephen J. Goldberg, offer society something more than the products of their genius. A Chinese artwork and its creator offer students (and professors) a chance to access the most fundamental aspects of Asian thought and culture. With respect to Chinese visual art, the very essence of which, according to Goldberg, may be "politicized" so as to act to challenge the "sociocultural authority and power in traditional China," studying art gives those of us who are more distant "in geography and generation" to traditional China a chance to close the gap and "attend" to and appreciate the subject matter and contemporary import of Chinese Confucian philosophy.

As we move from different artistic contexts—from the temples of India to the textured landscape paintings of China—we once again mirror some of the cultural borrowing throughout Asia. The last category of part 3 is certainly not the least, and it is an area of focus that many scholars consider to be the heart of Asian culture and thought: philosophy and religion. The first contribution in this section is by the comparative philosopher Mary I. Bockover and is called "Teaching Chinese Philosophy from the Outside In." Bockover is a self-proclaimed "outsider" and believes that such an acknowledgment is actually pedagogically useful when trying to get "into" another context. Her introductory remarks will make even the most novice users of Asian texts comfortable with the project of "infusion." From her comparison of different translations of the *Daodejing* to her insight into the problems and apprehensions that the new scholar/teacher may experience, Bockover offers one a comfortable first look at a text that opens the door to the understanding of Chinese culture and the interconnectedness between ancient Chinese culture and the mind of contemporary Chinese Americans (many of whom are our students). Finally, Bockover offers a template for exciting students—many of whom feel the need for political activism as opposed to contemplative meditation—into becoming both more philosophical and more cosmopolitan.

Though many scholars, even those who specialize in comparative philosophy, warn the Western reader to behave parsimoniously with respect to trying to juxtapose the philosophies and religions of Asia with those of the West, the analytic philosopher James Peterman believes that some comparison is healthy and pedagogically efficacious. He suggests using Plato's *Euthyphro* and Confucius's *Analects* in the same introductory course, since both texts "help define and inaugurate the path of their respective, quite different traditions." As such, urges Peterman, traditional students in the Western classroom are introduced to the thought and culture of Asia through a range of topics and approaches to philosophy and religion. He also suggests that the give-and-take of methodological contexts will enable students to truly grasp the point of comparative studies by exposing them to the need for a more cosmopolitan attitude.

From the outset, this project recognized the serious need for a volume with both content and pedagogical focus to assist college and university professors wishing to introduce Asian philosophies and religions—or, more generally, thought and culture—into their courses. Following the premise that teaching requires a solid content base as well as pedagogical methodologies, this collection of essays offers contemporary, yet accessible, interpretations of primary philosophical and religions texts from India, China, and Japan both for Asia-trained professors and for newcomers. The book is designed to appeal to those outside the disciplines of religion and philosophy as well as to those in those disciplines who wish to incorporate Asia-related materials into their standard Western courses. While providing content assistance, the anthology also offers pedagogical ways of incorporating Asian philosophies and religions into other humanities courses. Philosophy and religion play an important role in the development and preservation of culture, and we believe Asian histories and cultures should be understood through the foundation of their religions and philosophies.

Religion, and later philosophy's crucial emergence from it, is found at the taproot of all cultures' growth and evolution. When human consciousness raises itself to more reflective and critical levels, philosophy emerges as the primary human thinking activity that gives birth to other human endeavors. Although religion and philosophy ought to have more prominent roles, given their central places in human evolution, both disciplines have struggled, and continue to struggle, to eke out a living on the margins of contemporary education. One aspiration of this book, voiced by its contributors from within those disciplines and from without, is to articulate the need to position religion and philosophy in a more central location in educational discourse and practice, and to punctuate their contribution to the complexities of understanding and to the creation of a more cosmopolitan comportment by Americans.

On a more practical note, we seek to offer non-Asian-specialty teaching professors from the humanities and social sciences a means to begin deciphering for themselves and delivering to their students some of the fundamental philosophical and religious texts of Asia. Piggybacking on this aspiration is a more specific one that offers nonspecialists in Asian philosophies and religions ways to begin thinking about the integration and infusion of Asian philosophical and religious materials into various Western philosophy and religion courses.

The authors in this volume are experts in a variety of fields; some are primarily Asianists, many are philosophers and religion specialists. In all cases, our authors are exemplary teachers and scholars, and for this reason, they were chosen as contributors, and we are grateful for their contributions. Not only do we trust this collection of essays will serve a useful purpose and be interesting in its own right for those already familiar with the thinking and cultures of Asia, but also we trust that it provides a modest mechanism by which the complexities of understanding will lead to more cooperation and the possibility of a more humane future by creating more "citizens of the cosmos."

Ellen Klein, Washington D.C.
David Jones, Atlanta

Note

1. Charles A. Moore, ed. *The Indian Mind: Essentials of Indian Philosophy and Culture*, (Honolulu: East-West Center Press, 1967), 2.

1

Encountering Asian
Philosophies and Religions

John M. Koller

The Importance of Asian Philosophy in the Curriculum

Most college and university philosophy departments in the United States have no courses at all in Asian philosophy. And only a few departments have more than a few token courses. And while some courses in Asian philosophy are taught in departments of religion or departments of religious studies, for the most part the emphasis in those departments is not on philosophy, but on religion.

This situation suggests that, in the competition for scarce dollars, most colleges and universities have decided that Asian philosophies are not sufficiently important to be included in the curriculum. Can we make the case that the study of Asian philosophies is of such importance that it should be included? This is the case that I would like to begin to make by exploring four reasons why the study of Asian philosophies should be included in the curriculum.

Reasons for Studying Asian Philosophies

The first reason is that understanding basic Asian values and ideas is crucial for survival in an interdependent world. Today, it is clear that our very survival depends on cooperation among people whose lives are guided by diverse values and ideas. But this cooperation is impossible unless we understand the basic ideas and values that shape the cultures and guide the societies of the peoples with whom we must cooperate. Because these ideas and values are rooted in the philosophical and religious thought that underlies every society's institutions and practices, it is necessary to come to an understanding of at least the major philosophical traditions of the world. And because the majority of the people in the world today are Asian, it makes sense to include at least some studies of Asian philosophies in the curriculum.

What are the main ideas that have shaped Asian cultures? What are the fundamental values that have guided the lives of Asian peoples over the millennia? How have the great philosophical thinkers of Asia thought about these ideas and values?

The basic human ideas and values that shape our personal and cultural identities as well as our social practices and institutions derive from answers to fundamental questions about existence and human life. People everywhere, whether Asian or Western, seek to answer the same basic questions: Who am I? How should I live? What is real? How do we come to know something? What is the right thing to do? What is good? However, these questions arise in different contexts and assume different forms for people living at different times and in different places, and the answers given vary accordingly. But these questions, sometimes arising out of wonder, sometimes arising out of human suffering, or sometimes arising out of the efforts to improve the conditions of human existence, are questions that every reflective person, in every time and place, seeks to answer. And the answers to these questions provide the fundamental ideas and values that guide the development of whole cultures as well as the lives of individual persons.

By studying the philosophical traditions of Asia, it is possible to understand these traditions' carefully considered answers to these questions, answers that are supported by profound insights and good reasons. Because these answers have guided the thought and action of the peoples of Asia over the centuries, they provide the basic clues to understanding the guiding ideas and values of Asian societies today. And in today's world, where the very future of humankind depends upon understanding and cooperation among people with diverse values and ideas, it is imperative that these values and ideas be understood.

A second reason for including the study of Asian philosophies in the curriculum is that it can contribute significantly to the central aim of education—namely, the development of self-understanding, both individual and social. There can be no doubt that our self-understanding develops only in the context of understanding the other. In our attempts to understand the Asian other in terms of the fundamental ideas and values that shape their identities, we come, through the same processes of understanding, to understand ourselves and our own society, seeing the ideas and values that shape our personal, social, and cultural identities.

A third reason for studying Asian philosophies is that such study provides rich resources for developing one's own philosophy. One of the marks of an educated person is his or her ability to transform self-understanding into a personal philosophy of life. As each of us tries to creatively develop our own philosophy to guide and direct our lives, we can benefit enormously from an understanding of the different ways that the basic questions of life have been asked and answered by philosophers in the Asian traditions. Furthermore, in the inevitable comparing and contrasting of Asian and Western philosophers required to understand Asian philosophies, we gain new perspectives that enable us to understand Western philosophies in more insightful and profound ways. For example, Joel Kupperman, in *Learning from Asian Philosophy*, demonstrates how Asian philosophies can be helpful in thinking about Western views of what it is to be a self and what it means to acquire moral character.[1] And Eliot Deutsch's work on aesthetics and on becoming persons shows how comparative philosophy can deepen our understanding of our most fundamental human activities.[2]

A fourth reason for including Asian philosophies in the curriculum is that their study is extremely helpful in developing abilities to imagine alternative ways of life and to think clearly and rigorously about alternative ideas. In the process of thinking along with, and against, the great Asian philosophers, one not only gains skill in thinking clearly and deeply about important issues, but also learns how to critically examine received answers and raise new questions. Sometimes the life story of a philosopher whose mind is immersed in both Western and Asian philosophy can be revealing of the riches encountered in moving between culturally different philosophical questions and answers; such is the case with J. Mohanty's autobiographical account of his philosophical life.[3]

Characteristics of Asian Philosophies

Asian philosophical thought, while it is also self-critical, tends to emphasize as its chief characteristics insight into and understanding of reality and its importance as a guide to life. Indeed, the Indian philosophical traditions are called "visions [of reality]" (*darshana*), and the Chinese philosophical traditions are called "way [of life]" (*dao*). One consequence of this Asian tendency to see philosophy in practical terms, as concerned with human transformation, is the widespread recognition of the relevance of philosophy to life. Philosophy in Asia has not been viewed as ivory tower speculation, something separate from the concerns of daily life. Rather, it has been seen as one of life's most basic and most important activities.

Indian Philosophies

In India, for example, home to one-fifth of the world's people, it is the philosophies of Hinduism that have provided and articulated the major ideas and values that guide the life choices and social practices of most of the people. If we are to understand India, the world's largest democracy, a major nuclear power, and home of some of the world's greatest spiritual traditions, we must study its philosophical traditions.

It is in her philosophical traditions that we find how India has answered the fundamental questions about existence and human life: Who am I? What is real? How do we know? What is the right thing to do? What is the ultimate goal of life? For three thousand years Indian thinkers have been exploring these questions and examining various answers to them in their efforts to find ways of life that satisfy the deepest needs of a person. Building on the visions of the great thinkers of the Vedas and Upanishads dating from 1500 to 500 BCE, India's philosophers have produced nine enduring philosophical traditions in their efforts to answer the fundamental questions of human life.

These philosophical traditions articulate India's visions of reality in systematic ways that focus on how to understand the self, the highest reality, causality, knowledge, ethics, and spiritual liberation. For example, there has been widespread agreement concerning the importance of fulfilling one's moral duties, especially the duty to avoid hurting other living beings. At least part of the reason why living a moral life is so important is the widespread agreement that all human actions are governed by the principle of karma, which says, roughly, that because every action inevitably produces its effects, therefore it is our actions that make us the kinds of persons we become. To become good we must engage in morally good actions. Performing bad actions will make us into bad persons. Through the study of such ideas we can see and learn from the beautiful tapestry of the Indian way of life that the philosophical traditions have created.

Buddhism

One of the traditions that originated in India twenty-five hundred years ago was Buddhism, a tradition that soon spread north, south, and east, becoming an important influence throughout almost all of Asia. The basic problem of life, according to Buddhism, is that of overcoming suffering. The essential teachings of the Buddha revolve around the questions, What is suffering? On what conditions does it depend? How can these conditions be eliminated? What path should one follow to eliminate suffering?

These questions, however, cannot be answered without inquiring into the nature of the self that suffers and the nature of the world that constitutes a source of suffering for the self. The question, How is suffering caused? led to a general theory of causation that shapes the theories of self and reality that constitute Buddhist metaphysics. The problems of justifying the claims made about the nature of the self and the nature of reality led to theories of logic and knowledge. And the problem of how to overcome suffering led to the development of understanding about morality and mental discipline as well as a new understanding of consciousness. Thus, the eminently practical problem of finding a way to overcome suffering provoked the reflections that constitute the Buddhist philosophical tradition, a tradition that comprises many subtraditions.

Many of the Buddhist traditions began in India as a result of differing interpretations of the Buddha's teachings and different emphases within those teachings. But many traditions began in Tibet, China, Korea, and Japan, for example, as a result of interactions between Buddhism and indigenous philosophical traditions.

Chinese Philosophy

The three enduring philosophical traditions in China are Confucianism, Daoism, and Buddhism. Confucianism, which began with the teachings of Confucius in the sixth century BCE, incorporated important features of competing traditions such as Legalism, Mohism, the School of Names, and yin yang thought, as it developed. Daoism, which began at about the same time, provided not only a counterbalance to Confucian thought, but also provided much of the philosophical framework and vocabulary necessary for Buddhism to take hold in China and become the third great tradition fifteen hundred years ago.

Before the development of Chinese Buddhism, philosophical thought was concerned primarily with the ways of moral, social, and political life, or with understanding the ways of nature. The central problems of Chinese philosophy are reflected in the Confucian question, How can I achieve harmony with humanity? and in the Daoist question, How can I achieve harmony with nature? For two thousand years, the Confucian writings comprised the core curriculum of the imperial university system and the basis of the civil service exams, making Confucianism the official ideology of China. That Confucian thought could be taken as the basis for social and political practice was possible because of the Chinese tendency to regard thought and practice as inseparable from each other.

As philosophy developed in China, there was an increasing tendency to see human nature in terms of natural processes. To the extent that this identification took place, the problem of achieving harmony with nature was the problem of being in harmony with oneself. In turn, being in harmony with oneself was regarded as the necessary basis for achieving a harmony with other persons. Being in harmony with oneself, being in harmony with humanity, and being in harmony with heaven and earth constitute the highest good in Chinese philosophy. Because human nature is seen as essentially moral, the dominant concern of Confucian and Neo-Confucian philosophy has been morality. The Confucian questions, How can I be good? and What is the basis of goodness? are basic questions throughout the history of Chinese philosophy, as is the Daoist question, How can I achieve harmony with the Dao?

The development of Chinese Buddhism in the fourth and fifth centuries BCE fostered an interest in metaphysical questions about the nature of the self and reality and about the relationship of knowledge to liberation, causing Confucian and Daoist thought to become more involved with these issues. At the same time, Confucian concerns with fostering the way of humanity and social harmony and Daoist concerns with the workings of nature, allowed Buddhism to develop in new ways in China.

Interactions and Shared Concerns

Although Buddhism was the main vehicle of interaction between Indian thought and the thought of East and Southeast Asia, it turned out that the influence was largely one-way, from India to the rest of Asia, with India experiencing little influence in return. The most notable external influences on Indian thought came from the Greeks, who came to India with Alexander the Great; another influence was from the Muslims, who came to India between the eighth and eleventh centuries, and ruled India from the thirteenth to the nineteenth centuries; and of course, the last influence was from the Europeans, who colonized most of Asia in the nineteenth century.

There are many differences between the philosophies of India, China, and Buddhist Asia, but they all share the practical concern of how to live better. There is shared agreement that the development of moral virtue is an important ingredient of a successful way of life, and that the well-being of the individual cannot be separated from the well-being of the family and the larger social community. They also agree that to follow the way to a better life we must have a deep understanding of the world and ourselves.

Because it is concerned with the fundamental ideas and values of the people, philosophy has been of primary importance in Asian cultures. Therefore, in order to understand the life and the attitudes of the peoples of Asia, it is necessary to understand their philosophies. And in order to understand their philosophies, it is necessary to look at the traditions in which these philosophies developed and through which they continue to nourish the cultures of Asia.

Issues in Learning and Teaching

Turning to a discussion of issues concerned with how to include the study of Asian philosophies in the curriculum, it should be noted that whether the strategy is to create whole programs of Asian philosophy, specific courses, or modules in other core courses, the crucial issue is which texts to choose for study and how to approach these texts. It is important, then, to understand the issues involved in the choice of texts that we use with our students.

The most urgent question for teachers, especially those putting together anthologies and writing textbooks, is, Which issues and texts are appropriate for students of Asian philosophy? This question is especially acute because many of our students are not grounded either intellectually or existentially in any of the Asian traditions. Based on my experience in studying and teaching Asian and comparative cultures and philosophy for more than thirty years, including the preparation of *A Sourcebook in Asian Philosophy*,[4] *The Indian Way*,[5] and five editions of *Asian Philosophies*,[6] I would like to suggest that a teacher should ask the following questions about the texts and issues being considered for courses dealing with Asian traditions:

1. Are the texts representative of the tradition?
2. Did they have a significant role in shaping the tradition?
3. Do they provide entry into other issues and texts?
4. Are the texts relatively free of technical jargon and unspoken assumptions?
5. Are the issues, as presented in the texts, grounded in human experience familiar and accessible to students?
6. Do they address questions of contemporary interest?
7. Are the translations accurate, reliable, and accessible?
8. To what extent do the texts invite comparisons across traditions and eras?
9. Are good interpretive studies of these texts available that will help students inquire into the issues presented by the texts?
10. Are the texts congenial to my own experience and style of teaching?
11. Are the texts appropriate for the learner's level and for the amount of time available?

Each question can be seen as a criterion, and each is problematic in various ways. The following discussion helps to illuminate some of these problems and overcome them. I explain each criterion and its significance, and I give a relevant example. Viewing criteria as sorting devices, I envision each criterion as embodying a central test question that will guide us in accepting or rejecting a proposed text.

Depending on their own experiences, the kinds of students they have, and the level of the course, answers to these questions as well as the order of their importance will vary. Trying to keep in mind variations in teachers, students, and levels of preparation, I will attempt to answer each of these questions.

The first criterion, "Are the texts representative of the tradition?" concerns the extent to which the texts focus on what is central and dominant within the tradition. Do they represent the concerns, and ways of thinking about these concerns, that have shaped the tradition? Have they been the focus of controversy and discussion over an extended period of time? Does the tradition's own canon include these thinkers and texts? For example, do the texts include (portions of) the *Shijing, Rig-Veda, Daodejing, Arthasastra, Analects, Bhagavad Gītā,* and so forth?

The second criterion, "Did the texts have a significant role in shaping the tradition?" asks not merely whether the text is representative, but how seriously the tradition itself took these texts. Many texts are representative of a tradition without being significant. Many of the so-called minor Upanishads are representative of the central tradition, but are not regarded as especially significant, and therefore would not belong in a basic anthology. On the other hand, we might argue that Wang Yangming's commentary on the *Great Learning* is not representative of Confucius's approach to learning, but we would have to agree that the Confucian tradition itself took this text seriously, giving it great prominence. Usually it is helpful to see where philosophical texts fit in the larger canon of a culture's classical literature; this enables us to help students see connections between art, literature, politics, and history. Although this is difficult for many of us because our own education was not sufficiently broad, there are many helpful aides that we can seek out, such as de Bary's *Guide to the Oriental Classics*.[7]

The third criterion, "Do these texts provide entry into other texts and issues?" reflects a strong pedagogical concern. We want our study and teaching to give us a sense of the whole of a tradition, an understanding that allows us to fit the various pieces of the puzzle together into a picture that maps the territory constituting the intellectual tradition being examined. To this end we look for texts that provide a foundation for understanding a tradition and that become pathways to other issues and texts in the tradition in a kind of natural progression.

For example, I agree with Zhu Xi 's recommendation that the *Great Learning* is the place to begin one's study of the Confucian way, because it provides the foundation for studying the *Analects*, *Central Harmony*, and *Mencius*. I used to begin always with the *Analects*, because it not only leads to the issues dealt with in the other three books, but also has the advantage of standing at the beginning of the Confucian tradition. Since discovering Zhu Xi 's advice, however, I have found the *Great Learning* an excellent point of entry. Students find it closer to their own experience and learning than the *Analects* or *Central Harmony*. They can compare existentially their own values and ideas with this brief text with a minimum of help. It provides a foundation in a dominant theme and leads easily to *Analects*, *Mencius*, and *Central Harmony*, and from there to Neo-Confucianism. It also can be used to contrast with Legalist, Moist, and Daoist thought. So I would be inclined to have my students begin their study of the Confucian tradition by reading Wang Yangming's *Inquiry on the Great Learning* before reading the *Xiaojing* (*Classic of Filial Piety*) or the *Analects*.

The fourth criterion, "Are the texts relatively free of technical jargon and unspoken assumptions?" is related pedagogically to students' need to enter into the inquiry on their own terms. Unless students can find either an existential or intellectual basis for entering into the inquiry within their own experience, they are unlikely to find enthusiasm or energy to pursue genuine learning. Texts with excessive technical vocabulary and difficult unspoken assumptions make it arduous for students to enter into the inquiry and have no place in an introductory course.

The fifth criterion, "Are the issues represented in the texts grounded in human experience familiar and accessible to students?" is an extension of the fourth criterion, moving the consideration from texts to issues, and reflects my conviction that we use texts to get at issues. Conceptual issues that may be of great intellectual significance to those of us working in the field may be of little interest to students who lack the requisite intellectual experience. This may be true for many philosophical, religious, aesthetic, and literary issues. On the other hand, most students are familiar with issues involving authority and freedom, moral choice, and political action, and such issues allow entry into some of a tradition's classical texts. The point of this criterion is to meet the students where they are experientially and intellectually, finding issues and texts to which they can relate, in order to move their inquiry and understanding to a deeper level.

I do not regard the teacher primarily as a person who passes on knowledge to the student, but rather as a person who leads a student on a path of inquiry and understanding, enabling the student to actively inquire and learn. Like other kinds of leaders, as leaders of learning sometimes we are out in front, showing by example and explaining what we are doing; other times we are behind, pushing or encouraging. But if we get more than a step ahead, we lose students; and if we get more than a step behind, they may not advance. If the issues and texts are too many steps beyond where the students are, they cannot take the first step of the inquiry journey and remain where they started (except now they may also be confused and discouraged).

The sixth criterion, "Do the texts address questions of contemporary interest?" recognizes that contemporary issues excite most students. Texts dealing with issues of only antiquarian interest are too far from their own interests to engage them actively. Because the deepest contemporary issues arise from the deepest existential issues of life in society, and because the truly foundational texts of every culture reflect on fundamental existential issues of life, this criterion seeks to ensure use of texts that enable us as teachers to build the bridges from our students' existential and intellectual interests to the cultural issues and texts into which we want them to inquire.

To see how this criterion works, let us take as a test case the *Bhagavad Gītā*, by any criterion a classic and a foundational text of Indian culture. Because the central issue of reconciling conflicting dharmas in the *Gītā* is far removed from the contemporary interests of our students, it might appear that the *Gītā*'s inclusion would fail to meet the test of this criterion. But this is not the case, for in another sense the *Gītā* is quite contemporary; it is about how to deal with conflicting obligations, and we all face conflicting obligations. Therefore, it is rather easy to show the relevance of the *Gītā* to existential issues our students face in trying to meet conflicting demands.

The seventh criterion, "Are the translations accurate, reliable, and accessible?" points to the need for good translations. Those of us who read Sanskrit, Chinese, Tibetan, and so forth, often know texts that would work well for students, but for which no good translation exists.

Sometimes we translate these texts for our students, but often we lack the necessary skills or time. For the most part we all rely on translations by others—not only for the languages we do not read, but also for those that we do. Good translations have to be accurate without being pedantic. The language into which they are translated must be reasonably contemporary, and the style must be inviting and engaging. Although occasionally translations from fifty, or even a hundred, years ago have not yet been surpassed, usually more recent advances in scholarship have resulted in new translations that are superior to the older translations. For example, while Arthur Waley's translation of the *Daodejing* of sixty years ago is wonderfully smooth and polished, Victor Mair's recent translation is more accurate and more accessible.[8]

The eighth criterion, "To what extent do the texts invite comparisons across traditions and eras?" looks primarily to comparative study. This criterion assumes that the previous criteria have been met, and that when we have a choice between texts that meet all the previous criteria we give preference to texts that lend themselves to useful comparisons, in this case comparisons across cultures.

The ninth criterion, "Are good interpretive studies available that will help students inquire into the issues of the texts selected?" recognizes that issues and texts do not teach themselves and that understanding issues and texts from a different cultural tradition requires special help for teachers as well as students. When we have a choice between a bare text, no matter how good the translation, and a text that is helped by one or more good interpretive studies, we should choose the latter. For example, over the years I tried using Chan's translation of the *Analects* (it has some helpful, though very brief commentary) as well as D. C. Lau's translation. But even though I had H. G. Creel's excellent study available, I always had trouble getting students excited about this text until Ames and Hall's interpretive study *Thinking Through Confucius* appeared.[9] Similarly, Wei-ming Tu's study of the *Central Harmony* revealed this text for me and my students far beyond anything available previously.[10] In this case, I continue to use Chan's translation, but with Tu's interpretive study available, students can inquire much more deeply into the central issues. More recently the same thing happened with Daniel Gardner's translation and study of the *Great Learning*.[11] Not to mislead here, let me try to be clearer about the use of interpretive studies. In advanced courses students can work directly with these interpretive studies, but in beginning courses it is we, as teachers, who need these interpretive studies to transform our own understanding and teaching of issues in selected texts. As teachers (that is, leaders of learners) we are first learners and then teachers; and when we cease being learners, we inevitably cease being teachers.

The tenth criterion, "Are the texts congenial to my own experience and style of teaching?" emphasizes the importance of the teacher's enthusiasm. Some issues are more richly informed by our own experience, and some texts lend themselves better to our teaching styles than others. No matter what the so-called intrinsic values of a particular issue or text may be, if the teacher is not enthusiastic about it the usual result will be a poor learning experience for students. Our own excitement and enthusiasm inspire students more than most of us (and certainly more than most administrators!) realize. Selecting texts and issues that we are excited about energizes our teaching and inspires our students.

Zhuangzi has been one of my favorite authors since I discovered him in 1963, and I have used the first few chapters of his book many times. Some years ago I gave two students Kuang-ming Wu's *The Butterfly as Companion* as primary reading for an independent study course in Daoism.[12] Wu's obvious love for and excitement about this text as a primary vehicle of his own learning, along with my own enthusiasm, invited these students into Zhuangzi's world as we read this book together. They studied and played there for two months, calling it the best learning experience of their lives. Wu's meditations on the first three chapters of this text led us into realms of inquiry and excitement far beyond anything we had experienced before. That we did not read the *Laozi* (as planned) did not seem to matter; students were transformed (to a greater extent than any previous students) by a chance encounter with a text that their teachers (Wu, through his book, and Koller, through direct conversations) were deeply excited about. I reiterate, excitement counts for a great deal in teaching and learning. When possible, we should choose texts and issues that genuinely engage us.

The eleventh criterion, "Are the texts appropriate to the learner's level and the time available?" encourages us to consider the students' level of knowledge and ability and the time we have to build on this base. What is appropriate for a general studies course for first-year undergraduates, where three weeks is allotted for the study of Chinese thought, will, of course, be different from what is appropriate for a first-year graduate course for philosophy students where an entire semester is devoted to Chinese philosophy. And it would be far different for a graduate program in Chinese philosophy where ten different courses in Chinese philosophy are offered.

The general principle remains the same: In every case more issues and texts will be ignored than will be selected for study. What we are looking for are criteria that will enable us to make these difficult choices as wisely as possible. All of the foregoing criteria will have to be mediated by the criterion of appropriateness. Thus, if I had only three weeks to introduce Chinese thought in a general studies course, such as my Eastern Religions course or my course Asian Worldviews, I would not focus on the logical issues raised by Gongsun Long, or Mozi's conception of universal love, because they are not as fundamental as *ren* and *li*, and not as accessible as the *Great Learning*.

Notes

1. Joel J. Kupperman, *Learning from Asian Philosophy* (New York: Oxford University Press, 1999).
2. Eliot Deutsch, *Studies in Comparative Aesthetics* (Honolulu: University Press of Hawaii, 1975); Deutsch, *Essays on the Nature of Art* (Albany: State University of New York Press, 1996); Deutsch, *Persons and Valuable Worlds: A Global Philosophy* (Lanham, MD: Rowman & Littlefield, 2001).
3. Jitendranath Mohanty, *Between Two Worlds, East and West: An Autobiography* (New York: Oxford University Press, 2002).
4. John M. Koller and Patricia Koller, *A Sourcebook in Asian Philosophy* (New York: Macmillan, 1991).
5. John M. Koller, *The Indian Way: An Introduction to the Philosophies and Religions of India*, Second Edition (Upper Saddle River, NJ: Pearson/Prentice Hall, 2006).
6. John M. Koller, *Asian Philosophies*, Fifth Edition (Upper Saddle River, NJ: Prentice Hall/Pearson, 2007).
7. W. T. de Bary, A. T. Embree, and A. V. Heinrich, eds., *A Guide to Oriental Classics*, Companions to Asian Studies (New York: Columbia University Press, 1989).
8. V. H. Mair, trans., *Tao Te Ching: The Classic Book of Integrity and the Way* (New York: Bantam Books, 1990).
9. David L. Hall and Roger T. Ames, *Thinking Through Confucius* (Albany: State University of New York Press, 1987).

10. Wei-ming Tu, *Centrality and Commonality: An Essay on Confucian Religiousness* (Albany: State University of New York Press, 1989).
11. Daniel K. Gardner, *Chu Hsi and the "Ta-hsueh": Neo-Confucian Reflection on the Confucian Canon* (Cambridge, MA: Harvard University Press, 1986).
12. Kuang-ming Wu, trans., *The Butterfly as Companion: Meditations on the First Three Chapters of the "Chuang Tzu"* (Albany: State University of New York Press, 1990).

Roger T. Ames

The Confucian Worldview: Uncommon Assumptions, Common Misconceptions

In thinking through the Confucian worldview, we might begin by playing with a thought-experiment. What would the history of the relationship between the Chinese Empire and the outside world have looked like if China had had its own imperialist aspirations? What would the world have looked like if indeed China had ravaged Europe and America rather than the other way round?

We certainly had our Columbus, our Cabot, our Cook, and our Vancouver. But imagine instead Chinese explorers beginning with Zheng He searching through the waterway systems of the "new world," mapping the coastline, and planting the Manchu flag at Jiujinshan (San Francisco) to declare "New Canton" for His Majesty Kangxi and the empire.

In the late sixteenth century, Jesuit missionaries began Rome's calculated attempt to convert the Chinese people, a population corrupted by superstitions and false ideas. For the next century, the Rites Controversy raged in Rome, where clerics debated the extent to which the Chinese mission could accommodate traditional Chinese culture in the conversion of Chinese Christians. But imagine instead Chinese missionaries penetrating deep into the European subcontinent from the southern ports of Iberia, brandishing their superior technologies to demand respect for Eastern learning in schools and temples, and debating in the high courts of Beijing whether European culture could be accommodated in the spread of Chinese ancestor reverence, or whether it must be eradicated to keep the Chinese culture free of Judeo-Christian superstitions.

Just as Rome was formally condemning the accommodationist strategies of the Jesuit missionaries in the eighteenth century, the East

India Company kindled an incipient opium trade that, in the nineteenth century, would ignite to become the world's most valuable single commodity trade. But imagine instead Chinese merchant ships, under the protection of the emperor's navy, plying between China's colonies in the Indian subcontinent and Europe to trade for gold their cargo of "sweet poison" craved by the dissolute European aristocracy, and returning to China only to offload the bullion and *objets de curiosité* such as German musical instruments and Belgian lace.

The use of Chinese silver to finance England's colonization of India, and the use of the Indian fleet of British warships to coerce concessions from Beijing, inevitably led to contests between the superior English percussion-lock muskets and the obsolete Chinese matchlocks. But imagine instead Chinese gunships plowing up the Thames, the Rhine, and the Volga to deal the backward European victim a third humiliating defeat in a period of less than twenty years.

The Eurocentric focus of the curriculum in our colleges today—sociology is the Euro-American family experience, philosophy is Descartes to Kant, and so on—is being challenged by advocates of an inclusive international curriculum that more adequately reflects the roots of non-European Americans and the richness of the world's high cultures. But imagine instead a resolutely Sinocentric America, under pressure from students reflecting recent demographic changes that have brought waves of immigrants from Europe, having reluctantly to reevaluate undergraduate education in its seats of learning and to take into account exotica such as Shakespeare and Bach in the definition of American civilization.

Is this alternative scenario of recent human history—an imperialist China bringing Europe and America to their knees—unthinkable? I think the answer is yes—at least, it did not occur to the Chinese.

Chinese civilization established an early lead over the rest of the world in the development of her material culture—textiles, iron casting, paper, maritime arts, pottery, soil sciences, agricultural and water technologies, and so on. We must allow that as recently as the beginning of the Industrial Revolution in the late eighteenth century, it was China rather than Europe that, by most standards, was the arbiter of science and civilization on this planet. This gestaltist exercise of imagining an alternative pattern of world development over the past several centuries, then, requires us to probe into those features of the formidable Chinese civilization that inhibited its spread beyond its East Asian sphere of influence. And the answers to "why didn't China?" posited by scholars familiar with the contest between China and the European powers are many and wonderful, ranging from the question-begging simple superiority of Western imperialism to curious psychological diagnoses proposed by Western modernization theorists: apparently, on some readings, the Chinese are "thalassophobic" (they dread oceans).[1]

China for the Western powers has been, and in large degree remains, a paradox—a Chinese puzzle. Why didn't China under Zheng He and his armada of hundreds of treasure ships colonize the Americas? Why hasn't China, a culture that places its highest value on community, ever been a member of the international community? Why does China send cooks rather than missionaries, and build restaurants rather than churches?

The prominent French sinologist Jacques Gernet argues that when the civilizations of China and Europe, having developed almost entirely independently of each other, first made contact in about 1600, the seeming ineptitude of the Chinese for understanding Christianity—and more importantly, the philosophic edifice that undergirded it—was not simply an uneasy difference in the encounter between disparate intellectual traditions. It was a far more profound difference in mental categories and modes of thought, and particularly, a fundamental difference in the Chinese conception of human agency.[2] Much of what Christianity and Western philosophy had to say to the Chinese was, for the Chinese, nonsense. Given their own philosophic commitments, they simply could not think it. The Jesuits on their part interpreted this difference in ways of thinking as a Chinese ineptness in reasoning, logic, and dialectic.[3]

And Europe fared little better in its opportunity to appreciate and to appropriate Chinese culture. In fact, it fared so badly that the very word "Chinese" in the English language has come to connote "confusion," "incomprehensibility," "impenetrability"—a sense of order inaccessible to the Western person.[4] The degree of difference between our dominant sense of order and the aesthetic order prevalent in the Chinese worldview has plagued our encounter with this antique culture from the start. Seeking corroboration for our own universal indices in the seventeenth century, we idealized China as a remarkable and curious land requiring the utmost scrutiny.[5] Our esteem for this "curious land," however, plummeted from these Cathay idealizations to the depths of disaffection for the inertia of what, in the context of our own Industrial Revolution, was cast as a moribund, backward-looking, and fundamentally stagnant culture.

To explore Chinese ways of thinking and living, then, we will, at the very least, have to recognize that we are dealing with a fundamentally different worldview. And the more distant Chinese thinking is from our own conceptions, the more likely it is that our own languages will have difficulty in accommodating our discussion of it.

In Chinese there is an expression, "We cannot see the true face of Mount Lu because we are standing on top of it." Although virtually all cultural traditions and historical epochs are complex and diverse, there are certain fundamental and often unannounced assumptions on which they stand that give them their specific genetic identity and continuities. These assumptions, extraordinarily important as they are for understanding the culture, are often concealed from the consciousness of the members of the culture who are inscribed by them, and become obvious only from a perspective external to the particular tradition or epoch. Often a tradition suspends within itself competing and even conflicting elements that, although at odds with one another, still reflect a pattern of importance integral to and constitutive of its cultural identity. These underlying strands are not necessarily or even typically logically coherent or systematic, yet they do have a coherence as the defining fabric of a specific and unique culture.

Within a given epoch, even where two members of a tradition might disagree in some very basic ways—the classical Confucian and Daoist, for example—there are still some common assumptions more fundamental than their disagreements that identify them as members of a specific culture, and that have allowed for meaningful communication to occur between them.

Looking at and trying to understand elements of the classical Chinese culture from the distance of Western traditions, then, embedded as we are within our own pattern of cultural assumptions, has both advantages and disadvantages. One disadvantage is obvious and inescapable. To the extent that we are unconscious of the difference between our own fundamental assumptions and those that have shaped the emergence of classical Chinese thought, we are sure to impose upon China our own presuppositions about the nature of the world, making what is exotic familiar, and what is distant near. On the other hand, a clear advantage of an external perspective is that we are able to see with greater clarity at least some aspects of "the true face of Mount Lu"— we are able to discern, however imperfectly, the common ground on which the Confucian and the Daoist stand in debating their differences, ground that in important measure is concealed from them by their own unconscious assumptions.

Perhaps the only thing more dangerous than identifying and making such generalizations about complex cultural epochs and traditions is failing to do so. Assumptions, although always changing, are also persistent. In pursuit of an understanding of both the classical and the contemporary Chinese world—both Confucius and Mao Zedong—we have no choice but to attempt to identify and excavate these uncommon assumptions, and to factor them into our reading of the tradition. Some of the differences between the classical Chinese worldview and those classical Greek, Roman, and Judeo-Christian assumptions that had persisted and grounded the Western narrative are fundamental and might be drawn in broad strokes in the following terms.

We can call the worldview that, by the time of Plato and Aristotle had come to dominate classical Greek thinking, a two-world theory. Later, with the melding of Greek philosophy and the Judeo-Christian tradition, this dualistic mode of thinking became firmly entrenched in Western civilization as a dominant underlying paradigm. In fact, this way of thinking is so much a matter of second nature to us in the Judeo-Christian narrative that we do not have to be professional philosophers to recognize ourselves reflected in its outline. A significant concern among the most influential Greek thinkers and later the church fathers was to discover and distinguish the world of reality from the world of change, a distinction that fostered both a two-world theory and a dualistic way of thinking about it. These thinkers sought that permanent and unchanging first principle that had overcome initial chaos to give unity, order, and design to a changing world, and that they believed makes experience of this changing world intelligible to the human mind. They sought the "real" structure behind change—called variously Platonic Ideas, natural or divine law, moral principle, God, and so on—that, when understood, made life predictable and secure. The centrality of metaphysics in classical Greek philosophy, the science of these first principles, reflects a presumption that there is some originative and independent source of order that, once discovered and understood, will provide a coherent explanation for the human experience.

There were of course many diverse answers to the basic question: What is the One behind the many? What is the *uni* that brings everything together as a "universe?" What—or who—has set the agenda that makes human life coherent, and thus meaningful? For the Jewish prophets and scribes, and later for the Christian church fathers, it was the existence of the one transcendent Deity who, through Divine Will, overcame the formless void and created the world, and in whom truth, beauty, and goodness reside. It is this One that is the permanence behind change, and that unifies our world as a single-ordered universe. It is this One that allows for objective and universal knowledge, and guarantees the truth of our understanding. Because this One is permanent and unchanging, it is more real than the chaotic world of change and appearances that it disciplines and informs. The highest kind of knowledge, then, is the discovery and contemplation (*theoria*) of what is in itself perfect, self-evident, and infallible. It is on the basis of this fundamental and pervasive distinction between a permanently real world and a changing world of appearance, then, that our classical tradition is dominated by a two-world theory.

Another way of thinking about this two-world view that has its origins in classical Greece begins from a fundamental separation between that which creates and that which is created, between that which orders and that which is ordered, and between that which moves and that which is moved. There is an assumption that there exists some preassigned design that transcends the world it seeks to order. The contrast between the real One—the First Cause, the Creator, the Good—and the less real world of change is the source of the familiar dualistic categories that we appeal to in order to organize our experience of the world: reality/appearance, knowledge/opinion, truth/falsity, Being/Nonbeing, Creator/creature, soul/body, reason/experience, cause/effect, objective/subjective, theory/practice, agent/action, nature/culture, form/matter, universal/particular, logical/rhetorical, cognitive/affective, masculine/feminine, and so on.

What is common among these binary pairs of opposites is that the world defined by the first member is thought to stand independent of, and to be superior to, the second. This primary world, defined in terms of "reality," "knowledge," and "truth," is positive, necessary, and self-sufficient, while the derivative world, described by the second members as "appearance," "opinion," and "falsity," is negative, contingent, and dependent for its explanation upon the first. After all, it is reality that informs and explains what only appears to be the case, and that allows us to separate the true from the false, fact from fiction. On the other hand, appearances are shadows—the false, the fictive. And like shadows, they are at best incidental to what is real; at worst, they not only are of no help to us in arriving at clear knowledge, but also further obscure it from us. Because the secondary world is utterly dependent on the first, we can say that the primary world is necessary and essential, the *Being* behind the *beings*; and the secondary world is only contingent and passing, with the *beings* derived from *Being*. There is a fundamental discontinuity in this worldview between what is real and what is less so.

It is because the first world determines the second that the first world is generally construed as the originative source—a creative, determinative principle, easily translatable into the Judeo-Christian Deity that brings both natural and moral order out of chaos. Hence, our early tradition tends to be both cosmogonic (meaning that it assumes some original act of creation and initial beginning) and teleological (meaning that it assumes some final purpose or goal, some design to which initial creation aspires). God created the world, and human life is made meaningful by the fact that God's creation has some design and purpose. It is from this notion of determinative principle that we tend to take an explanation of events in the world to be linear and causal, entailing the identification of a premise behind a conclusion, a cause behind an effect, some agency behind an activity.

Perhaps a concrete example will help bring this dominant Western worldview into clearer definition. The way in which we think about the human being serves this need, because in many ways humanity is a microcosm of this two-world universe. From many of the Western traditions, we might generalize in the following terms. A particular person is a discrete individual by virtue of some inherent nature—a psyche or soul or mind—that guarantees a quality of reality and permanence behind the changing conditions of the body. The human being, as such, straddles the two worlds, with the soul belonging to the higher, originative, and enduring world and the body belonging to the realm of appearance. The soul, being the same in kind as the permanent principles that order the cosmos, has access to these principles through reason and revelation, and thus can make claim to knowledge. It is through the discovery of the underlying order that the universe becomes intelligible and predictable for the human being.

Turning to the dominant worldview of classical Confucian China, we begin not from a two-world theory, but from the assumption that there is only the one continuous, concrete world that is the source and locus of all of our experience. Order within the classical Chinese worldview is emergent and site-specific—growing and transforming within things themselves—like the grain in each unique piece of wood, like striations in stone, like the cadence of the surf, like the veins in a leaf. The classical Chinese believed that the energy of creativity resides in the world itself, and that the order and regularity this world evidences are not derived from or imposed upon it by some independent, activating power, but inhere in the world as a source of reconstrual. Change and continuity are equally "real."

The world, then, is the efficient cause of itself. It is resolutely dynamic, auto-generative, self-organizing, and, in a real sense, alive. This one world is constituted as *qi*, psychophysical energy that disposes itself in various concentrations, configurations, and perturbations as one thing transforms to become something else. The intelligible pattern of experience that can be discerned and mapped from each different perspective within the world is *dao*, a "pathway" that can, in varying degrees, be traced out to make one's place and one's context coherent. *Dao* is, at any given time, both *what* the world is and *how* it is. In this tradition, there is no final distinction between some independent source of order and what it orders. There is no initial, determinative beginning or ultimate, teleological end. The world and its order at any particular time are self-causing—spontaneously "so-of-itself" (*ziran*). It is for this reason Confucius would say: "It is human beings who extend order in the world (*dao*), not order that extends human beings."[6] Truth, beauty, and goodness as standards of order are not "givens" as much as they are historically emergent, something done, a cultural product.

The two-world order of classical Greece has given our tradition a theoretical basis for objectivity—the possibility of standing outside and taking a wholly external view of things. Objectivity allows us to decontextualize things as "objects in our world." By contrast, in the this-world view of classical China—world as such—instead of starting abstractly from some underlying, unifying, and originating principle, we begin from our own specific place within the world. Without objectivity, objects dissolve into the flux and flow, and existence becomes a continuous, uninterrupted process. Each of us is invariably experiencing the world as one perspective within the context of many. Since there is only the one world, we cannot get outside of it. From the inherently unique place one always occupies within the cosmos of classical China, one interprets the order of the world around one as contrastive "this's" and "that's"—"this person" and "that person"—more or less proximate to oneself. Since each and every person or thing or event in the field of existence is perceived from some position or another, and hence is continuous with the position that entertains it, each thing is related to and a defining condition of every other.

All human relationships are continuous from ruler and subject to friend and friend, relating everyone as an extended family. Similarly, all "things," like all members of a family, are correlated and interdependent. Everything is what it is at the pleasure of everything else. Whatever can be predicated of one thing or one person is a function of a network of relationships, all of which conspire to give it its role and to constitute its place and its definition. A father is "this" good father by virtue of the quality of the relationships that locate him in this role and the deference of "these" children and "that" mother, all of whom are intrinsically related to him.

Because all things are unique, there is no strict notion of identity in the sense of some self-same identical characteristic that makes all members of a class or category or species the same. There are no natural kinds in the Aristotelian sense. For example, there is no essential defining feature—no divinely endowed soul, universal rational capacity, or natural locus of rights—that makes all human beings equal. In the absence of such equality that would make us essentially the same, the various relationships that define one thing in relation to another tend to be hierarchical and contrastive: bigger or smaller, more noble or more base, harder or softer, stronger or weaker, more senior or more junior. Change in the quality of relationships between things always occurs on a continuum as movement between such polar oppositions. The general and most basic language for articulating such correlations among things is metaphorical: in some particular aspect at some specific point in time, one person or thing is overshadowed by another—that is, *yin* to another's *yang*. Literally, *yin* means "shady" and *yang* means "sunny," defining in the most general terms those contrasting and hierarchical relationships that constitute order and regularity.

It is important to recognize the interdependence and correlative character of the *yin/yang* kind of polar opposites, and to distinguish this contrastive tension from the dualistic opposition implicit in the vocabulary of the classical Greek world we explored above, where one primary member of a set, such as the Creator, stands independent of and is more "real" than the world he creates. The implications of this difference between dualism and correlativity are fundamental and pervasive.

One such implication is the way in which things are categorized. In what came to be a dominant Western worldview, categories are constituted analytically by an assumed formal and essential identity—all human beings who qualify for the category "human beings" are defined as having an essential *psyche* or soul. All just or pious actions share some essential element in common. The many and diverse things or actions reduce to one essential identical feature or defining function.

In the dominant Chinese worldview, "categories" (*lei*) are constituted not by essences, but by analogy. One thing is associated or disassociated with another thing by virtue of the contrastive and hierarchical relations that set it off from other things. This particular human being evokes an association with other similar creatures in contrast to other less similar things, and hence gathers around himself or herself a collection of analogous particulars as a general category. "This" evokes "that"; one evokes many. Coherence in this world, then, is not so much analytic or formally abstract. Rather, it tends to be synthetic and constitutive—the pattern of continuities that lead from one particular phenomenon to some association with others. It is a concrete coherence that begins from the full consequence of the particular itself and carries on through the category that it evokes.

If we were going to compare these two senses of "categorization," instead of the set of objects "hammer, chisel, screwdriver, saw" being defined as "tools" by the assumption of some identical formal and abstract function, we are more likely to have a Chinese category that includes "hammer, nail, board, strike, blister, band-aid, house, whitewash"—a category of "building a house" constituted by a perceived interdependence of factors relevant to the process of successfully completing a given project. Whereas the former sense of category, defined by abstract and objective essences, tends to be descriptive (what something *is*), the latter category is usually prescriptive and normative (what something *should be* in order to be a successful "this" or "that").

The relative absence in the Chinese tradition of a Western-style teleology that assumes some given end has encouraged the perception among some historians that the Chinese, with libraries of carefully recorded yet seemingly random detail, are inadequate chroniclers of their own past. There seems to be little concern to recover an intelligible pattern from what seriously threatens to remain formless and meaningless. Jorge Luis Borges captures this perception in his well-known citation of "a certain Chinese encyclopedia" in which the category "animals" is divided into: (i) belonging to the Emperor, (ii) embalmed, (iii) tame, (iv) sucking pigs, (v) sirens, (vi) fabulous, (vii) stray dogs, (viii) included in the present classification, (ix) frenzied, (x) innumerable, (xi) drawn with a very fine camel-hair brush, (xii) et cetera, (xiii) having just broken the water pitcher, and (xiv) that from a long way off look like flies.[7] From the perspective of a more rationalistic worldview, the penalty the Chinese must pay for the absence of that underlying metaphysical infrastructure necessary to guarantee a single-ordered universe is what we take to be intelligibility and predictability. The compensation for this absence in the Chinese world is a heightened awareness of the immediacy and wonder of change, and one's complicity in it—the motive for revering the *Book of Changes* as the ultimate defining statement of the tradition, and as an apparatus for shaping a propitious world.

For the classical Greek philosophers, knowledge entails the discovery and grasping of the defining essences, forms, or functions behind elusively changing appearances. Hence the language of knowing includes "concept," "conceive," and "comprehend." Reality is what is permanent, and hence its natural state is inertia. The paradigm for knowledge, then, is mathematics, and more specifically, geometry. Over the door of Plato's Academy was written: "Let none who have not studied geometry enter here." Visual and spatial language tends to predominate in the philosophical vocabulary, and knowledge tends to be understood in representational terms that are isomorphic and unambiguous—a true copy impressed on the mind of that which exists externally and objectively.

In the classical Chinese model, knowledge is conceived somewhat differently. Form is not some permanent structure to be discovered behind a changing process, but a perceived intelligibility and continuity that can be mapped within the dynamic process of experience itself. Spatial forms—or "things"—are temporal flows. Things and events are mutually shaping and being shaped, and exist as a dynamic calculus of contrasting foci emerging in tension with one another. Changing at varying degrees of speed and intensity, the tensions constitutive of things reveal a site-specific regularity and pattern, like currents in the water, sound waves in the air, or weather systems in the sky. Etymologically, the character *qi*—"the vital stuff of existence"—denotes an acoustic as well as a physical sensibility, making resonance and tensions a particularly appropriate way of describing the relations that obtain among things. In contrast with the more static visual language of classical Greek thought typified by geometry, classical Chinese tends to favor a dynamic aural vocabulary, where wisdom is closely linked with communication—with that keenness of hearing and those powers of oral persuasion that will enable one to encourage the most productive harmony out of relevant circumstances. Much of the key philosophic vocabulary suggests etymologically that the sage orchestrates communal harmony as a virtuoso in communicative action.

Reason is not a human faculty independent of experience that can discover the essences of things, but a palpable determinacy that pervades both the human experience and the world experienced. Reason is coherence: the dynamic intelligibility of things and their functions. Rational explanation does not lie in the discovery of some antecedent agency or the isolation and disclosure of relevant causes, but in mapping out the local conditions that collaborate to sponsor any particular event or phenomenon. And these same conditions, once fully understood, can be manipulated to influence and anticipate the next moment. Such is the foreknowledge of the sage.

An important factor in classical Chinese knowing is a putative comprehensiveness. Without an assumed separation between the source of order in the world and the world itself, causal agency is not so immediately construed in terms of relevant cause and effect. All conditions interrelate and collaborate in greater or lesser degree to constitute a particular event as a confluence of experiences. Knowing is thus being able to trace out and manipulate those conditions far and near that will come to affect the shifting configuration of one's own place and time.

There is a direct and immediate affinity between the human being and the natural world, so that no firm distinction is made between natural and man-made conditions—they are all open to cultivation, articulation, and manipulation. In fact, it is because of the fundamental continuity between the human pattern and the natural pattern that all of the conditions, human and otherwise, that define a situation can be brought into sharp focus. In the absence of a severe animate/inanimate dualism, every situation, from the stew pot to the battlefield, with its complex of conditions, is very much vibrant and alive.

The inventory of philosophical vocabulary used in classical China to define this kind of knowing tends to be one of tracing out, unraveling, penetrating, and getting through. Knowing entails "undoing" something, not in an analytic sense to discover what it essentially is, but rather tracing out the connections among its joints and sinews to discern the patterns in things, and, on becoming fully aware of the changing shapes and conditions of things, to anticipate what will ensue from them. The underlying metaphor of "tracing a pattern" is implicit in the basic epistemic vocabulary of the tradition, such as "treading a pathway, a way" (*dao*), "figuring an image or model" (*xiang*), "unraveling and undoing" (*jie*), "penetrating" (*tong*), "breaking through" (*da*), "naming and inscribing" (*ming*), "ritualizing" (*li*), "inscribing" (*wen*), and so on. In contrast with its classical Greek counterpart where knowing often assumes a mirroring correspondence between an idea and an objective world, Chinese knowing is resolutely participatory, pragmatic, and creative—"tracing," in both the sense of etching a pattern and of following it. To know is to realize, to "make real." The path is not a given, but is made in the treading. Thus, one's own actions are always a significant factor in the shaping of one's world.

Because this emergent pattern invariably arises from within the process itself, the tension that establishes the line between one's own focus and one's field gives one a physical, psychological, social, and cosmological skin, a shape—a continuing, insistently particular identity. This dynamic pattern is reflexive in the sense that one's own dispositions are implicit in and affect the shaping of one's environment. One's own shape is constantly being reconstructed in tension with what is most immediately pressing in upon one, and vice versa.

To continue with the personhood example from our discussion of the classical Greek worldview, generally in classical Chinese philosophy a particular person is not a discrete individual defined in terms of some inherent nature familiar in recent liberal democratic theory, but is a fluid configuration of constitutive roles and relationships: Yang Dawei's father, An Lezhe's teacher, Gao Daren's neighbor, a resident of Yonghe village, and so on. These roles and relationships are dynamic, constantly being enacted, reinforced, and ideally deepened through the multiple levels of communal discourse: embodying (*ti*), doing (*xing*), ritualizing (*li*), speaking (*yan*), playing music (*yue*), and so on. Each of these levels of discourse is implicit in every other, so there is a sense in which a person can be fairly described as a calculus of specific patterns of discourse. By virtue of these specific roles and relationships, a person comes to occupy a place and posture in the context of family and community. The human being—or better, "human becoming"—is not shaped by some given design that underlies natural and moral order in the cosmos, a design that stands as the ultimate objective of human growth and experience. Rather, the purpose of the human experience, if it can be so described, is more immediate: to coordinate the various ingredients that constitute one's particular world here and now, and to negotiate the most productive harmony out of them. Simply put, it is to get the most out of what you've got here and now.

Creativity also has a different place in the classical Chinese world. Again, in gross terms, the preassigned design and ultimate purpose assumed in classical Greek cosmology means that there is a large investment of creativity "up front" in the birth of a phenomenon—a condition reflected rather clearly in the preestablished Ideas of Plato that have to be "recollected," in the potentiality/actuality distinction of Aristotle, or in the Creator/creature dualism of the Judeo-Christian tradition. For the Confucian worldview, in the absence of an initial creative act that establishes a given design and a purpose governing change in the cosmos, the order, regularity, and meaning of the world emerge from the productive juxtapositions of different things over the full compass of their existence. No two patterns are the same, and some dispositions are more fruitfully creative than others. For this reason, human knowledge is fundamentally performative—one knows a world not only passively in the sense of recognizing it, but also in the active shaping and realizing of it. It is the capacity to anticipate the patterned flow of circumstance, to encourage those dispositions most conducive to a productive harmony, and ultimately to participate in negotiating a world order that makes best advantage of its creative possibilities. Harmony is attained through the art of contextualizing.

A major theme in Confucius and in Confucianism is captured in the phrase, "the exemplary person pursues harmony (*he*), not sameness."[8] This Confucian conception of harmony is explained in the classical commentaries by appeal to the culinary arts. In the classical period, a common food staple was *geng*, a kind of millet gruel in which various locally available and seasonal ingredients were brought into relationship with one another. The goal was for each ingredient—the cabbage, the turnip, the bit of pork—to retain its own color, texture, and flavor, but at the same time to be enhanced by its relationship with the other ingredients. The key to this sense of harmony is that it begins from the unique conditions of a specific geographical site and the full contribution of those particular ingredients readily at hand—*this* piece of cabbage, *this* fresh young turnip, *this* tender bit of pork, and so on—and relies upon artistry rather than recipe for its success. In the *Spring and Autumn Annals of Master Lu*, cooking as the art of contextualizing is described in the following terms: "In combining your ingredients to achieve a harmony (*he*), you have to use the sweet, sour, bitter, acrid and the salty, and you have to mix them in an appropriate sequence and proportion. Bringing the various ingredients together is an extremely subtle art in which each of them has its own expression. The variations within the cooking pot are so delicate and subtle that they cannot be captured in words or fairly conceptualized."[9]

The Confucian distinction between an inclusive harmony and an exclusive sameness has an obvious social and political application. There is a passage in the *Discourses of the States* (*Guoyu*), a collection of historical narratives probably compiled around the fourth century BCE, that underscores the fertility of the kind of harmony that maximizes difference:

> While harmony (*he*) is fecund, sameness is barren. Things accommodating each other on equal terms is called blending together in harmony, and in so doing they are able to flourish and grow, and other things are drawn to them. But when same is added to same, once it is used up, there is no more. Hence, the Former Kings blended earth with metal, wood, fire, and water to make their products. They thereby harmonized the five flavors to satisfy their palate, strengthened the four limbs to

protect the body, attuned the six notes to please the ear, integrated their various senses to nourish their hearts and minds, coordinated the various sectors of the body to complete their persons, established the nine main visceral meridians to situate their pure potency, instituted the ten official ranks to organize and evaluate the bureaucracy . . . and harmony and pleasure prevailed to make them as one. To be like this is to attain the utmost in harmony. In all of this, the Former Kings took their consorts from other clans, required as tribute those products that distinguished each region, and selected ministers and counselors who would express a variety of opinions on issues, and made every effort to bring things into harmony. . . . There is no music in a single note, no decoration in a single item, no relish in a single taste.[10]

This harmony is not a given in some preassigned cosmic design, but is the quality of the combination at any one moment created by effectively correlating and contextualizing the available ingredients, whether they be foodstuffs, farmers, or infantry. It is not a quest of discovery, grasping an unchanging reality behind the shadows of appearance, but a profoundly creative journey where the quality of the journey is itself the end. Indeed, simply put, it is making the most of any situation.

In summary, at the core of the classical Chinese worldview is the cultivation of harmony—a specifically radial and centripetal harmony. This harmony begins from what is most concrete and immediate—that is, from the perspective of any particular human being—and draws from the outside in toward its center. Hence, there is the almost pervasive emphasis on personal cultivation and refinement as the starting point for familial, social, political, and cosmic order. A preoccupation in classical Chinese philosophy, then, is the cultivation of this centripetal harmony as it begins with oneself, draws inward, transforms, and radiates outward. The cultivation of this radial harmony is fundamentally aesthetic. Just as those specific bits of paint constitute the one and only *Mona Lisa*, so one coordinates those particular details that constitute one's own self and context, and in so doing seeks a harmony that maximizes their creative possibilities.

The Confucian worldview is thus dominated by this bottom-up and emergent sense of order that begins from the coordination of concrete detail. It can be fairly described as an aestheticism, exhibiting concern for the artful and eventful way in which particular things can be correlated efficaciously to thereby constitute the ethos of concrete historical events and cultural achievements. Order, like a work of art, begins with always unique details, from "this bit" and "that bit," and emerges out of the way in which these details are juxtaposed and harmonized. As such, the order is embedded and concrete—the coloration that differentiates the various layers of earth, the symphony of the morning garden, the relief in a wall of stone, the rhythm in the rustling of the autumn leaves, the wind piping through the orifices of the earth, the enacting of rituals and roles that constitute a communal grammar to give community meaning. Such an achieved harmony is always particular and specific—resistant to notions of formula and replication.

Notes

1. Mark Mancall, *China at the Center: 300 Years of Foreign Policy* (New York: Free Press, 1984), 3–4. In fairness to Mancall, his exploration of this question is far more complex and intelligent than this one passage might lead one to believe.
2. Jacques Gernet, *China and the Christian Impact* (Cambridge: Cambridge University Press, 1985), 3–4.
3. Ibid., 242.
4. The examples of such a usage are many and varied: a Chinese puzzle (an intricate maze), Chinese revenge (doing a mischief to oneself to spite another), a Chinese flush in poker (a hand with no discernible sequence or pattern), a Chinese screwdriver (Australian slang for a "hammer"), and the ever popular Chinese fire drill (a college prank: stopped at a traffic signal, students leap from an automobile, run around in circles, and then as the light changes, they reenter the automobile in a different order, much to the perplexity of other motorists).
5. See the introduction to D. E. Mungello's *Curious Land: Jesuit Accommodation and the Origins of Sinology* (Honolulu: University of Hawaii Press, 1985) for a discussion of the "curious (L. *curiosus*)" inquiry of the seventeenth century intellectuals.
6. *Analects* 15.29.
7. See Borges's anthologized "The Analytical Language of John Wilkins," in *Borges: A Reader*, edited by Emir Rodriguez and Alasdair Reid (New York: E. P. Dutton, 1981), [Poges']. Ironically, Chinese categories found in the traditional *leishu* often appear to an outsider as altogether too close to Borges's parody. Michel Foucault's *The Order of Things: An Archaeology of the Human Sciences* (New York: Vintage, 1973) is a self-conscious response to Borges's categories.
8. *Analects* 13.23.
9. Xu Weiyu, *Lushi chunqiu* (Peking: Wenxue guji kanxingshe, 1955), 540.
10. *Discourses of the States (Guoyu)*, sibubeiyao edition (Shanghai: Zhonghua shuju, 1928), 16.4a–b.

II

Texts

INDIA

Vrinda Dalmiya

On the Battlefield of Dharma: The Moral Philosophy of the *Bhagavad Gītā*

The "Song of the Lord" (the literal meaning of *Bhagavad Gītā*) sung for Arjuna on the battlefield of Kurukṣetra thousands of years ago gets inflected in different ways as we eavesdrop on it from multiple philosophical, historical, and sociopolitical "reading (listening) positions." Since it is part of the corpus identified as the Vedānta, which means "essence of the Vedas," philosophers of diverse metaphysical persuasions such as Śaṃkara (Advaita), Rāmānuja (Viśiṣṭādvaita), Mādhavācharya (Dvaita), and Abhinavagupta (Kashmir Śaivism) were all motivated to write commentaries on the *Gītā* emphasizing the conformity of its vision of ethical life with their widely differing metaphysics. Though treated as an independent text of Indian ethics comparable to Western discussions of moral life, it is important to remember that the *Bhagavad Gītā* is really part of the much larger epic, the *Mahābhārata*. The *Mahābhārata,* being an *itihāsa* and a *smṛti*,[1] consciously explores how abstract injunctions of high philosophy play out in human lives lived within messy and complicating situations. Situating the *Gītā* in this context makes it more than a theoretical articulation of the "right" and the "good" and urges us to look for thicker connections of its ethical vision to moral psychology and to the tensions of a social order framing ethical life. The tonality of a song sung in a society rigidly structured by the order of *varṇāsrama* (social strata and stage-of-life) would differ from the notes that find resonance for postcolonial and contemporary authors like Gandhi[2] and Spivak.[3] In short, keeping the politics of reading in mind, it is foolhardy to look for a single interpretation of the message of the *Gītā*.

The "Inner War" of Moral Dilemmas

The improbable setting of the *Gītā*—a philosophical dialogue staged quite literally in the middle of a battlefield—is replete with metaphorical and methodological significance. As is well known, Arjuna, the leading archer of the Pāṇḍavas, went to the front lines with his charioteer, Kṛṣṇa, to survey the enemy formations of the Kauravas on the eve of the great battle of Kurukṣetra. The Kauravas, however, were cousins, and their army was comprised of Arjuna's teachers, friends, and elders. On seeing them poised for combat, Arjuna suffered a moment of existential angst and was overcome by the moral futility of the projected war. The *Gītā* is Kṛṣṇa's attempt to draw Arjuna out of his "faintheartedness" and get him back to fighting like a true warrior.

The juxtaposition of the moral domain with a battlefield is doubly significant. First, the valorization of *mokṣa* (liberation) as the highest aim in classical India, along with the rise of the sramaṇic traditions (like Buddhism) with their emphasis on renunciation, made it possible to debunk the social order as a snare. By casting moral life as a battlefield, a field of constant activity, the *Gītā* served to counter this lazy and dangerous interpretation of the philosophical milieu as a world-denying quietism. Second, combat signifies the methodological importance of clashing moral obligations. It is not merely a conflict between Arjuna's emotional recoil from violence and Kṛṣṇa's dispassionate upholding of the ethical code of the dutiful warrior. But even Arjuna's recoil is depicted as a moral stance. He does not see any good (*sreyas*) in killing kinsmen in battle and considers it a duty to desist from such bloodshed. By centering Arjuna's quandary created by such a conflict of duties—with its attendant emotions of guilt, remorse, and confusion—the dharma ethics expounded by Kṛṣṇa becomes a vision of ethical life as a struggle of practical wisdom when faced with conundrums, rather than a straightforward following of a coherent system of rules of conduct. Scholars like Matilal have underscored the significance of genuine moral dilemmas and the resultant ambiguity in the ethical theorizing of the times.[4] However, to build up to the moral paradox at the heart of the *Gītā*, it is helpful to first step back and consider the concept of *svadharma*.

The robust idea that what we are constrains what can be expected legitimately of us, along with the recognition that different people have different natures, underlies the notion of *svadharma*. "One's own (*sva*) dharma" is the cluster of socioethical obligations that follow from our (different) natures. But the infamous *varṇa* order of Indian society went on to divide "different natures" into the four castes—Brāhmans (priest-scholars), Kṣatriya (governor-warriors), Vaiśya (traders), and Śūdras (laborers)—with the special duties, respectively, of study, governance-defense, trade, and service. Though it is well documented how recognition of such difference gradually ossified into an oppressive hierarchy of birth, it is important to note that the *Gītā* itself vacillates between making caste categorizations hereditary or aptitude-based.[5] However, irrespective of how our caste natures are determined, the fact that obligations flow from our position in the caste system is explicit. Besides caste, the course of a human life is diachronically subdivided into four stages (*āsrama*)—*brahmacarya, gārhasthya, vānaprastha,* and *sannyāsa*—and there are specific obligations (*viśeṣa* dharma) associated with each of these stages: the duties of a student are clearly not those that we expect out of a retiree. Overarching all these are the *sāmānya* or *sādharana* dharmas—duties like truth speaking, not stealing, and not killing—that are universally normative irrespective of the variations of *varṇa* and *āsrama*. The upshot of all this is that the Indian concept of duty is rather different from the Kantian idea of universalizable obligations. What we have is closer to the notion of "my station, my duties," where one's station is fleshed out in terms of location within the grid of *varṇāsrama*, which is itself framed by certain common normative expectations.

In this context, the opening sections of the text can be organized into the argument given below. Arjuna throws down his bow in a gesture of resignation and despair due to the following rationalization:

1. My being a Kṣatriya entails that I fight this war. And not doing my caste duties is a sin.
2. Fighting this war will mean fighting (and killing) my elders, my teachers, and will bring about social chaos. And both of these are sins.
3. I can either fight or not fight this war.
4. Thus, on either option I would have sinned.

This destructive dilemma can be read as signifying the clash between *viśeṣa* dharma (premise 1) and *sāmānya* dharma (premise 2). But then, premise 1 can also be recast as the common duty of upholding truth and righteousness, for to opt out of the specific battle in question would be to allow untruth to prevail. So we could have here a clash between the two *sāmānya* dharmas of *ahiṃsā* (nonviolence) and *satya* (truth). According to Rajendra Prasad,[6] a contemporary Indian philosopher, Arjuna's despair is that of a sensitive, rational agent coming up against an *internal incoherence* in the dharmic ethics of his times. In the light of this, Kṛṣṇa's admonitions to get Arjuna to fight amount to traditional conservatism that ends up upholding caste duties in spite of rational criticisms of it.

It is undeniable that Kṛṣṇa's aim is to urge Arjuna to resume his caste duty of fighting, and I will return later to the issue of whether this is a blind conservatism. But the *Gītā* attempts to address more than this internal incoherence. Remember that the *Mahābhārata* is the story of humankind in all its richness. Thus, Arjuna is really "everyman" and what he points to is a more fundamental problem about the apparent futility of morality per se in the classical Indian ethos, rather than of any specific articulation of it. Such a thickening of Arjuna's/the *Gītā*'s central problem relies on two further concepts—those of *karma* and *mokṣa*.

The doctrine of karma is an expression of acute ethical naturalism—the belief that whatever happens to us is "deserved" as the consequence of what we have done in the past and that there is a complex causal linkage between our actions and the hedonic tone of our lives. Every action has a twofold effect: a *phala* (the direct result) and a *saṃskāra* (a disposition, potency, or seed). The latter can be understood as moral energy that enables the deferral of the hedonic fruit of an act to later times. Thus, a murderous act has the direct result (*phala*) of removing the hated person from our lives, but it need not immediately be followed by punishment (for prosperous villains, after all, surround us). However, even in such apparently unjust situations, the law linking good and bad actions to happiness and distress, respectively, remains in place because the initial act of murder generates a sadness-producing potency or *saṃskāra*. The murderer, for example, meets with unhappiness when this (negative, in this case) energy is activated. If it is not activated in this life, the energy is carried over to the next. Similarly, apparently random happinesses and sadnesses of our present life are "explained" as the causal consequences of *saṃskāras* produced by good and bad actions in previous births. The law of karma is thus said to be a postulate to ensure long-term justice without theistic intervention. It brings in the ideas of rebirth to keep in place our basic moral intuition that we reap what we sow.

In the concept of *mokṣa*, we move from the realm of duties, obligations, and the right to that of value, ideals, or the good. The philosophical milieu of the time hosted a plurality of legitimate aims of life. The system of *puruṣārthas* (human goals) spoke of a hierarchy of values—of *artha* (material prosperity), *kāma* (sensuous and aesthetic pleasure), and *dharma* (moral and social order), culminating in yet another goal, *mokṣa*. Though the metaphysics of *mokṣa* was articulated variously in the different philosophical systems, it minimally referred to a state free from all suffering. Now, given the pervasive belief that human embodied existence can never be free of pain, cessation of the cycle of births becomes the essence of *mokṣa*. Thus, the highest aim of life is to transcend or get off the wheel of embodiment/rebirth. This links up in an interesting way with the karma doctrine. As we saw, the logic of karma led to rebirth. For *saṃskāras* to bear fruit, we need embodiment; if the karmic potencies are not all exhausted in this life, then we must be reborn in order to suffer/experience the hedonic consequences of our actions (think also of the *saṃskāra* produced by the last act before we die). Thus, if *mokṣa* is cessation of rebirth, it is also transcending the law of karma. Bondage is being fettered by the law of karma.

With these conceptual props in place, the stage is set for a generalized version of Arjuna's problem as everyman's dilemma. Following the lead of A. L. Herman,[7] this can be stated as a general "dilemma of action" in the following form:

1. If I perform right actions, *saṃskāras* are produced and I am bound.
2. If I perform wrong actions, *saṃskāras* are produced and I am bound.
3. I can perform either right or wrong actions.
4. Thus, in either case, I am bound.

What we have here is an *external tension* between the right and the good, between morality and *mokṣa*. Arjuna as everyman despairs of ethical life because it contradicts the supreme goal of human life, and the *Gītā*'s message is relevant for abetting such moral nihilism or quietism.

The Space between the Horns

The logical structure of Kṛṣṇa's solution regards Herman's premise 3 as flawed. Doing right and doing wrong in their conventional senses do not exhaust the sphere of action. There is a third possibility, variously called "ethical action," "skilled action," or simply *yoga*. This is action that does *not* generate *saṃskāra* (unlike conventionally right and wrong acts) and hence, is not binding. The *Gītā* famously goes on to articulate this option as the category of *niṣkāma* karma, literally "desireless action," where "desireless" means "without attachment for *results* of the action." The ethical injunction is therefore "Without attachment perform ever the work that is to be done; for by doing work without attachment man attains to the highest" (3.19).[8] Note that the destructive dilemma made Arjuna and everyman want to give up or renounce (*tyāga*) all *action*. The *Gītā* counters with the logical impossibility of and the bad faith behind that wish—the natural order requires some activity or other simply to stay alive—but points to the possibility and desirability of a deeper renunciation: the giving up of *attachment* to the consequences of our action. Thus, the attempt here is to steer us toward a higher form of *tyāga* and a category of ethical or true action defined in terms of a motivational shift that distinguishes it from conventional actions (whether good or bad). The text puts this point paradoxically as "He who in action can see inaction and can see action still continuing in cessation from works, is the man of true reason and discernment among men; he is in Yoga and a many-sided universal worker" (4.18). Now, if ethicality lies in a certain *way* of acting (i.e., desirelessly), it might be feared that we would lose all content to the distinction between right and wrong—serial killers would, for example, be moral as long as they went about their business in a detached manner! To avoid this counterintuitive result, it should be underscored that the *Gītā complicates* rather than abandons dharma ethics. Some commentators read it as echoing the dictum of "duty for the sake of duty." But note that the content of our duties, a determination of *what* actions should be performed in a desireless manner, is determined by dharma ethics as spelled out earlier. Thus, Kṛṣṇa maintains that we should do actions specified by our *varṇāsrama* dharma but without any desire for the fruits of those actions.

Once again, the point here is that such actions neutralize karmic bondage because they do not produce (or they burn up) *saṃskāras*. The link between desirelessness and nonproduction/destruction of *saṃskāras* is interesting and slippery. The basic idea is that the more we identify with our agency and the more we covet the consequences of the act as "mine," the tighter becomes the link between the self, the action and the action's moral consequences (basically, punishment and praise). Moral responsibility is understood ordinarily as entitlement to these moral results, because we freely claim the action as ours; we identify with it. *Saṃskāras* are merely the postulated links between the agent and the (sometimes long-term) consequences of actions. The *Gītā,* however, tries to drive a wedge between *causal* agency and *moral* agency. To the extent that the agent distances herself from the action and its direct results (*phala*) through the strategy of desirelessness, she loosens her moral responsibility and, to that extent, the consequences of the action do not taint her. The text, therefore, describes the ideal agent as follows: "Having abandoned all attachment to the fruits of his works, ever satisfied without any kind of dependence, he does nothing though (through his nature) he engages in action. He has no personal hopes, does not seize on things as his personal possessions . . . performing action by the body alone he does not acquire[9] sin" (4. 20-21). The philosophical complications of this core doctrine become clearer in responding to obvious objections against it—some of which are raised in the text itself. I shall briefly consider three of them here.

Desireless action is psychologically impossible: The motive of action is desire for its intended result. To act intentionally presupposes a desire for the goal. Consequently, giving up desire for the result/goal undercuts the very spring of action, and the *Gītā*'s recommendation makes it psychologically impossible for us to do anything at all.

A response will depend obviously on detailed analyses of motivational structure, and one may even toy with the idea that sometimes the objective pull of normative *facts* rather than psychological desire induces action. For our purposes, however, I will simply spell out the three strategies (or yogas/"meditations") that the *Gītā* suggests to enable performance in the absence of desire, without getting into their fascinating connections with action theory in general. First, we are urged to contemplate the metaphysics of the actor/enjoyer who, according to the *Gītā*, is not the essential self but the lower, empirical ego. Knowing that the "real" me does not enjoy the pleasures/pains of the consequences of actions (which also are not performed by the real me) can help engender a detachment from the results. This is the *Way of Knowledge*.

Second, we are urged to model work on sacrifice. This idea refers to the Vedic sacrificial rituals to please gods. Though on one level such sacrificial rituals were simply barters or exchanges with higher powers for material benefits, a more philosophical interpretation cast them as ritualistic repayment of unconsciously incurred congenital debts. Our existence depends on myriad contributions from the social and natural environment. Rituals are symbolically staged gestures of paying back these eternal and inexhaustible debts. Now, the imperative of repayment (like that of promise keeping) is not necessarily fueled by the desire for some special results. (Yes, the *phala* of repayment is "absence of reprimand," but is that the only motivation for my abiding by those imperatives?) This is the *Way of (Ritualistic) Action*.

Finally, Kṛṣṇa suggests that we model work on worship by "devoting" ourselves to Him as the deity and "giving up" our actions to him. Section 18.57 asserts that in the devotional moment, we perform actions not because *we* (as agents) desire the consequences of the actions, but simply to please our deity, who might want us to do certain things. This is the *Way of Devotion*. Once again, these are alternative models that we are asked to explore in our attempt to break the ordinary habit of acting out of desire for results. Which of these would work best for an individual is dependent on his or her personality.

Desireless action is logically incoherent: The imperative to act without desire reduces to the injunction to *desire* desirelessness. Moreover, the entire theory of *niṣkāma* karma is motivated by the goal of *mokṣa*, and hence, by the *desire* for liberation. Thus, the message of the *Gītā* to give up all desires turns out to be self-contradictory and paradoxical.

A response to this objection would depend on further clarifying the *Gītā*'s notion of desire and of desirelessness. If by desire is meant an intention to act, then clearly we are not required to give it up; and to the extent that a goal/aim differentiates one intentional act from another, an agent cannot be asked to lose sight of the goal of an action either. So what kind of desirelessness is the *Gītā* proposing as an ideal? A clue is provided in 2.48, where giving up desires amounts to "having become equal in failure and success." Now, we can remain calm and unperturbed by either achievement or failure if we give up *attachment* to the results of our actions. Roy Perrett[10] explains this through the distinction between first-order and second-order desires. An agent performing an intentional action such as sitting for an exam has a first-order desire to pass the exam. A second-order desire in this case would be the desire to have that first-order desire—that is, a desire to desire to pass the exam. Moral philosophers like Harry Frankfurt speak of freedom as the coherence between first-order and second-order desires, where a recovering addict is *not* free because she desires drugs on the first level but does not wish to desire them. The *Gītā*'s model of freedom, on the other hand, is to have first-order desires but not to form the corresponding second-order desires. This, according to Perrett, is the *Gītā*'s "unattached desires." It is easy to see how first-order desires in the absence of the corresponding second-order desires can result in equanimity in the face of success or failure. In such cases, though the agent is motivated by x to act, she is "unattached" from that motivation; she does not identify with it nor define herself in terms of it, and thus can be a calm and objective observer of her motivated action and its results.

Given the above theory of structured desires, the desire for *mokṣa* too is not a counterexample to the *Gītā*'s doctrine. Note that *mokṣa* in the tradition is not a "thing," and hence not an object of first-order desires. It is a state of being, and in the context of the *Gītā* is the state of "desirelessness" itself. Thus, attainment of *mokṣa* is a change in our motivational structure, and to wish for *mokṣa* is to wish for the entrenchment of "unattached desires" as explained above. Perhaps it can be described as a *third*-level desire to develop the virtue of second-level desirelessness; and once again, such a third-level desire does not conflict with desirelessness any more than a retention of directly action-inducing first-level desires do.

Desireless action is unattractive as an ideal: The ideal of performing duties without any attachment makes the moral agent into a mechanical robot; desirelessness undercuts enthusiasm, warmth, joy, and energy; consequently, its vision of moral agency is dry and unappealing. Moreover, the *Gītā* ethics is embedded in a framework structured by belief in rebirth, *mokṣa,* and the doctrine of karma. Can its message be transported into contexts where these esoteric beliefs are absent?

Interestingly, the *Gītā* sees no contradiction between nonattachment and enthusiasm. Its picture of the agent is one who is "[f]ree from attachment, free from egoism, full of resolution and zeal . . ." (18.26).[11] In assuming that there can be no initiative without attachment (in the relevant sense), the objection assumes that ownership and possession are the primary sources of joy. But the *Gītā* speaks of a selfhood that is *sullied* by possessions and is joyous to the extent that it can transcend the narrow constructions of "me" and "mine." But then, the critic continues, this is an odd and culture-specific understanding of self and an ethics crafted under its auspices is completely irrelevant in contemporary contexts working with more individualistic notions of personhood. But is this really the case? Perrett strives to retrieve a secular reading of the *Gītā*'s message by distinguishing between a "life of reaction" and a "life of response." Construing *saṃskāras* as habit-forming dispositions, Perrett claims that typically actions tend to become entrenched in our psyche as habits, and hence restrict the possible reaction space of an individual. Desirelessness, by preventing the formation of such dispositions, removes these constraints and makes it possible for us to *respond* creatively to situations beyond the straightjacket of what we might have done in the past. This life of response is the freedom that the *Gītā* gives us and has very little to do with *mokṣa* as the supreme goal of life.

Gītā-Dharma: Deontology? Teleology? Or Virtue?

In this concluding section, it is interesting to try and map the theory outlined above onto the three principal orientations of ethical theorizing in the West. Typically, deontological theories are contrasted with teleological ones. The former define appropriate moral actions in terms of the underlying motives and universalizable maxims irrespective of their consequences, and the latter tie rightness to an evaluation of the consequences of the actions. The *Gītā* is hard to locate within this binary. On the one hand, the doctrine of *niṣkāma* karma is clearly deontological, defining ethical actions in terms of motivational structure (desirelessness), but then the whole point of *Gītā*-dharma is to attain *mokṣa*, and a course of action is deemed appropriate if it has this consequence.

Arindam Chakrabarti has attempted to solve this problem by drawing on the familiar distinction between "act" and "rule" versions of deontological and teleological theories.[12] Thus, the *Gītā* urges us to perform our dharma simply because it is our duty, without weighing and balancing consequences. On the level of individual actions then, the *Gītā* is clearly deontological. But what is the justification for urging this attitude on us? *Why* should we do our dharma for the sake of duty alone? An answer to this question—to the query why the injunction or rule of doing actions desirelessly is appropriate—is given in terms of *mokṣa*. Thus, the *Gītā*'s theory is layered; it is, as Chakrabarti puts it, "act deontological, but rule teleological."

It is clear, then, that the *Gītā* ethics has both elements of deontology and teleology. But what about virtue? The notion of a "sthitaprajña" articulates the notion of an ideal person as someone who has equanimity, and there are many verses in the text that foreground the acquiring of a list of virtues as the primary ethical goal. Thus, "He who neither desires the pleasant and rejoices at its touch nor abhors the unpleasant and sorrows at its touch, who has abolished the distinction between fortunate and unfortunate happenings . . . he is dear to Me. Equal to friend and enemy, equal to honour and insult, pleasure and pain, praise and blame, grief and happiness, heat and cold . . . silent, content and well-satisfied with anything and everything, not attached to person or thing, place or home, firm in mind . . . that man is dear to Me" (12.18-19).

However, a virtue ethics emphasizes *character* as the primary object of moral evaluation and makes the moral quality of *actions* dependent on the moral qualities of the person performing them. Deontological and teleological theories, on the other hand, follow the opposite strategy of primarily judging specific *actions* to be right or wrong and then making evaluations of character. Given that we seem to have both these elements in the *Gītā*, how do we locate its teachings on our conceptual map?

Once again, the text navigates this tension in a creative way. From the point of view of the ideal, the *Gītā* often points to character traits and moral exemplars (among whom Kṛṣṇa is primary) very much in the spirit of virtue ethics. But from the point of view of moral pedagogy and guidance on how to become moral, it emphasizes the performance of predetermined duties in a specific manner. Acting in a desireless manner is a training to acquire a certain character. Thus, for "a sage who is ascending the hill of Yoga, action is the cause; for the same sage when he has got to the top of the Yoga self-mastery is the cause" (6.3). Clearly morality involves both character and actions—and their primacy depends on where we are situated vis-à-vis moral progress.

Introducing the elements of virtue helps us to address the conservatism of the *Gītā* raised in the first section of this essay, while enabling us to bring it more in line with the general orientation of the *Mahābhārata*. Typically, having a virtuous character does not entail performance of a fixed repertoire of actions, and a sage is guided by his or her conscience in determining the best course of action. Such flexibility is in keeping with the curious mix of moral realism and epistemological humility that we find in the *Mahābhārata*, which features numerous episodes condoning the breaking of rules prescribed by tradition. It also explicitly says, "There are different Vedas, even the *dharmaśāstras* vary from one another. There is not a single *muni* (teacher-sage) whose view is not different (from that of other teachers). The truth of dharma lies hidden in the (dark) cave. (But) the way (leading to dharma) is the one *mahājana* had followed."[13]

Thus, an experimentalism and pluralism regarding the actual content of our duties inspired by sensitivity to context is not unheard-of. The *Gītā*'s explicit upholding of caste dharma in this context may seem an anomaly. But if we remember that acting according to received dharma is a stepping-stone to the acquisition of a virtuous character, the tension can be dissipated. Of course, once we have "climbed to the top"—like Yudhiṣṭhira and Kṛṣṇa—as a *mahājana* (virtuous/good person), we have the liberty to choose what our enlightened conscience dictates. But for most of us, struggling up the ladder of Yoga, the course of action set by society and its elders is binding. What we seem to have here is an anti-individualistic traditionalism. We, as individuals, are required to do what our social station enjoins. But nevertheless, there is space for the *tradition* to be self-reflective and self-correcting.

The actual content of socially determined duties is determined by the reflection and self-reflection of virtuous *mahājanas* who certainly can (and often do) go against the received concept of what is right. Thus, whether or not the *Gītā* served to solidify a conservative order of its own sociopolitical time, there is enough scope to reinterpret it in order to cast a critical look at our contemporary social order.

Notes

1. *Smṛti* texts are distinguished from *śruti* in having a mortal author and one of their functions is to articulate abstract philosophical concepts to ordinary people. *Itihāsa* literally means "history" but is used here in the sense of a "history of humankind"— that is, the story of humanity in its diversity.
2. M. K. Gandhi, *Anāsakti-Yoga,* in *The Gospel of Selfless Action: The Gītā According to Gandhi*, by Mahadeva Desai (Ahmedabad: Navajivan Publishing House, 1946).
3. Gayatri Chakravorty Spivak, *A Critique of Post-Colonial Reason* (Cambridge, MA: Harvard University Press, 1999).
4. Bimal Krishna Matilal, *Collected Essays: Ethics and Epics*, edited by Jonardon Ganeri (New Delhi: Oxford University Press, 2002).
5. See alternative glosses of *Bhagavād Gītā* 4.13.
6. Rajendra Prasad, *Varṇadharma, Niṣkāma Karma and Practical Morality: A Critical Essay in Applied Ethics* (New Delhi: D.K. Printworld, 1999).
7. A. L. Herman, *An Introduction to Indian Thought* (Englewood Cliffs, NJ: Prentice Hall, 1976).
8. The translations of the *Gītā* that I have used here are from Sri Aurobindo, *Essays on the "Gītā": With Sanskrit Text and Translation of the "Gītā"* (Pondicherry: Sri Aurobindo Ashram, 1972). Book and chapter numbers of the *Gītā* are henceforth cited parenthetically in the text.
9. I have changed the translation here to capture the Sanskrit term *na āpnoti*.
10. Roy Perrett, *Hindu Ethics: A Philosophical Study* (Honolulu: University of Hawaii Press, 1998).
11. I have altered the translation here to better capture the original Sanskrit term *dhṛtyutsāhasamanvitah*.
12. Arindam Chakrabarti, "The End of Life: A Nyaya-Kantian Approach to the *Bhagavadgītā*," *Journal of Indian Philosophy* 16 (1998): 327–34.
13. Quoted in Matilal, *Collected Essays*, 167. Matilal clarifies that the untranslated term *mahājana* can mean either "a great person" or "a great number of people."

Jeffrey Dippmann

Vimalakīrti's Triumphant Silence: Bridging Indian and East Asian Buddhism

Having studied Laozi's Daodejing, *Sengzhao (c.378-413) sighed: "It is indeed beautiful, but I have yet to discover that place where my spirit can settle and I can sever all worldly ties." In time he read the* Vimalakīrti-nirdeśa Sūtra *and was overcome with happiness and joy. Turning to it repeatedly, he savored its flavor and exclaimed, "At last I have found my home."*

—*Biographies of Eminent Monks*

The *Vimalakīrtinirdeśa Sūtra* (*VNS*) has traditionally been one of the most popular Mahāyāna texts in China and Japan. Composed in Sanskrit sometime prior to the first century of the common era, it has been translated into Chinese at least seven times, and was the subject of one of Prince Shōtoku's three sutra commentaries in Japanese. Revered by the Tiantai and Chan Buddhist schools, the *VNS* is an eloquent exposition of Mahāyāna ideals, praxis, and wit.

The best recent translations of the *VNS* introduce and explicate the most important doctrinal aspects of the text such as nonduality, the nature of *śūnyatā*, and the centrality of the bodhisattva in Mahāyāna philosophy.[1] In addition, others have pointed out some of the more obvious ways in which the sutra generally appealed to the Chinese gentry.[2] For example, the dialogue that runs throughout, and in particular a lively tête-à-tête between Vimalakīrti and Mañjuśrī in chapter 5,[3] clearly resonates with the "pure conversations" of the third and fourth centuries. Vimalakīrti's life of wealth, commerce, and familial relations greatly appealed to a Chinese gentry class reluctant to abandon traditional life for the seemingly foreign practices of renunciation and monkhood. The sutra's irrepressible humor,[4] often at the expense of

Gautama's wisest of disciples, Śāriputra, reminds one of the sardonic swipes taken at Confucius and the whimsical imagery within the pages of the *Zhuangzi*.[5] It has even been suggested that the *VNS*'s use of miraculous interludes is reminiscent of the magic demonstrations employed during court debates waged between Buddhists and Daoists in the early medieval period.[6]

Rather than putting old, finely wrought wine into a new wineskin, this chapter instead focuses on two interrelated pedagogical devices. Each represents an important philosophical theme, while simultaneously serving as a useful framework for the teaching of the text in the classroom and as another intermediary through which we can bridge the gap between Indian and Chinese Buddhism. The first theme, *upāya* or "skillful means," finds expression in the sutra's opening hymn and is employed continuously throughout the text. In fact, it by no means exaggerates its role to observe that the entire work is *upāya* in action. The second theme, in many ways, to my mind, is the most important, but wholly overlooked, aspect of the text. I believe that the *VNS* conveys its message directly through Vimalakīrti himself, who, far more than preaching the dharma in a philosophically sophisticated manner, embodies it and illustrates it through his actions. This insight helps illuminate such famous images as Vimalakīrti's feigned illness (chapter 2) and thunderous silence (chapter 9).

After working with the *VNS* for a number of years, I have come to regard it as a very "physical" text. By this I mean that the import of its doctrinal message and the text's enduring appeal come not from its philosophically sophisticated pronouncements and compendia-like nature, but instead from its concrete, this-worldly, and everyday manifestation of Buddhist dharma. The compelling narrative draws us along precisely because the dharma is being acted out rather than spoken, lived rather than discussed.

In this way, the *VNS*'s success in China, and subsequently in Japan, can be traced directly to the character and life of its central character, the layman Vimalakīrti. While his philosophical pronouncements, or lack of response, in the famous ninth chapter are insightful and doctrinally important, they can be found in any number of Mahāyanā sutras and *śastras*. What is both unique and narratively compelling is Vimalakīrti himself. Fully embodying the dharma, Vimalakīrti lives out, on a daily basis, the ramifications and promise of enlightenment.

Thereby, his life and mere physical presence serve as daily reminders of and a model for dharma truths. From this perspective, he is remarkably similar to the Chinese sage, and his concrete, this-worldly approach to religious practice is like that emphasized in Japan. This worldview will subsequently culminate in Dōgen's famous pronouncement that "attainment of the Way is indeed achieved through the body as well as the mind . . . only when one lets go of the mind and ceases to seek an intellectual apprehension of the Truth is liberation attainable."[7]

In fact, Vimalakīrti himself alludes to this in an encounter with the hapless Śāriputra in the bodhisattva's sickroom. Chastising Śāriputra for worrying about how the grand assembly would find comfort and sit during the encounter between Mañjuśrī and himself, the bodhisattva inquires as to whether the disciple came "for the sake of the Law [dharma], or [was simply] looking for a place to sit." With great umbrage, Śāriputra retorts that he indeed came for the dharma. Vimalakīrti then explains that seeking the dharma has nothing to do with either sensual comforts or intellectual speculation regarding the Four Noble Truths. Declaring that the dharma seeker does not look for it in the Four Noble Truths (and subsequently anything at all), Vimalakīrti concludes: "Why? Because the Law [dharma] has nothing to do with idle theorizing. To declare that one must recognize suffering, renounce attachments, realize how to reach extinction, and practice the Way is mere idle theorizing, not seeking the Law."[8] Comprehending the dharma cannot be an intellectual exercise. Reason ultimately fails insofar as it relies on discriminative conceptualization, falsely carving up the world into this and that, here and there, and I and other. Seeking the dharma is done with equanimity and equality, seeing things from a nondualistic perspective and, most importantly, living out of that perspective. To focus on the depictions of Vimalakīrti's life rather than fixating on the text's doctrinal pronouncements is beneficial. In this way we can see the application of Zhuangzi's dictum: "The fish trap exists because of the fish; once you've gotten the fish, you can forget the trap. The rabbit snare exists because of the rabbit; once you've gotten the rabbit, you can forget the snare. Words exist because of meaning; once you've gotten the meaning, you can forget the words. Where can I find a man who has forgotten words so I can have a word with him?"[9]

With this in mind, we can turn to a brief examination of the VNS's two primary themes. The first finds expression in the manifold implications associated with the concept of *upāya*. Translators render the Sanskrit in a variety of ways, including "skill-in-means," "skillful means," and "expediency." However, whereas most examples of *upāya* emphasize the appropriate tailoring of philosophical pronouncements, the *VNS* upholds the ideal of embodied expediency, a dharma-filled life "in the world but not of it."

The key to *upāya,* and the basic theme in the text, is found in the opening paean to the Buddha: "Each sees the World-Honored One standing right before him—such are the Buddha's transcendental powers, his unshared properties. The Buddha preaches the Law with a single voice, but each living being understands it according to his kind."[10] Several important features of this verse need to be pointed out. To begin with, the section opens with visual imagery: "Each *sees* the World-Honored One standing before him" (emphasis added). The assembly neither simply hears the words of the Buddha nor relies on merely reading them; there the Law stands, "big as life." While preaching a single message, with a single voice, its effectiveness is such that all who hear it, hear it in a manner conducive to their particular circumstances. Just as the earliest tradition held, to those who cling to pleasures the Buddha will teach the ugliness of death; to those fixated on words he teaches the emptiness of language and concepts.

Even before we encounter Vimalakīrti, the text's main protagonist and exemplar of *upāya*, the Buddha effectively illustrates in the first chapter its dual nature as a verbal and material instrument. In explaining the nature of the purified mind, Śākyamuni presses his toe onto the earth, instantaneously transforming it from a land of defilement to one of jewel-encrusted beauty and splendor. This true vision of the Buddha's land is hidden from ordinary perception, and only the pure of mind can partake of its actual beauty. The everyday world is a world of appearance, one which is in keeping with those who are "lowly and inferior"; its provisional appearance is a manifestation of the Buddha's *upāya*, his desire to fashion a world conducive to the salvation of all in need. Words alone are not enough to teach poor Śāriputra; effective pedagogy includes a visual, material component as well.

It also bears noting that this scene provides further corroboration for my contention that this is a very physical text. As the narrative draws to a close, we learn that upon the revelation of the pure world, five hundred rich sons grasped the truth of birthlessness and eighty-four thousand people set their minds on attaining perfect enlightenment; once the Buddha allows the land to transform back to its prior state, thirty-two thousand beings attained the Dharma-eye and eight thousand monks put an end to their outflows and attained freedom of mind. As Edward Hamlin has already pointed out, most of the *VNS*'s salvific denouements come on the heels of magical demonstrations; it is after the assembly has "seen" that it "awakens."[11]

The true embodiment of the expedient life is introduced in the second chapter, fittingly entitled "Expedient Means." Here we encounter the layman Vimalakīrti, as powerful and transcendent as any Buddha,[12] while simultaneously dwelling in the world. In this way, he represents and again embodies the Mahāyāna conception of the two truths. According to this theory, the Buddhas understand and, through *upāya*, teach the truth at two levels. From the conventional perspective, "I" understand that "I" am responsible for liberating "myself" from the round of samsara; from the ultimate perspective, there is neither "I" nor "myself." The ultimate truth, as exemplified by Vimalakīrti's silence, is inexpressible and ineffable. However, those who have awakened apprehend its reality and are thus enabled to live in the world of convention without contamination. Chapter 8 of the work presents an eloquent exposition of the two truths being lived out, effectively demonstrating the juxtaposition of appearance and reality, conventional and ultimate truth. And yet, as Mañjuśrī observes, it is only within this flawed and muddied world that the Buddha's Law can be apprehended. Just as "the lotus grows in the mud and mire of a damp low-lying place . . . [so too] it is only when living beings are in the midst of the mire of earthly desires that they turn to the Buddha Law."[13]

Indeed, Vimalakīrti comes across as an individual who not only lives in the world, as any good saint does, but who at the same time lives this life to the fullest while assiduously avoiding entanglement. Rather than simply earning a living, he is a prosperous businessman; while devoted to the religious life, he nevertheless maintains family relations and does not shun the brothels and taverns of his hometown; an accomplished bodhisattva, and clearly a follower of the Buddha, Vimalakīrti nevertheless is well-acquainted with both secular literature and that of other religious traditions; honored by all classes and both genders, he epitomizes the complete fulfillment of a dharma life and thereby reflects the tangible ideals of the Chinese sage.

Found in both indigenous Chinese traditions, Confucianism and Daoism, the figure of the sage (*sheng* 聖) or perfected one (*zhi ren* 至人) dominates the religious and philosophical landscape. As Rodney Taylor points out, the character for *sheng* consists of the radical *er* 耳, connoting hearing, and the phonetic *cheng* 呈, which Karlgren glossed as "to manifest."[14] Consistent with this imagery, the sage primarily teaches through example, with most of the "recognized" sages leaving behind few, if any, writings. From the perspective of Confucius, the legendary kings Yao and Shun epitomize sagehood. Primarily known through their deeds, little is recorded of either Yao or Shun's "teachings." A typical depiction appears in the *Analects* 15.5: "The Master said, 'If there was a ruler who achieved order without taking any action, it was, perhaps, Shun. There was nothing for him to do but to hold himself in a respectful posture and to face due south.'"[15]

In the *Mencius* 7A.40, effective teaching is done in five different ways: "The first is by a transforming influence like that of timely rain. The second is by helping the student to realize his virtue to the full. The third is by helping him to develop his talent. The fourth is by answering his questions. And the fifth is by setting an example others not in contact with him can emulate."[16] Only one of these involves what could be deemed oral teachings. The crux of the gentleman's teaching centers on actions, deeds, and providing a living representation of Confucian ideals. Tu Wei-ming has argued that traditional education in the six arts (ritual, music, archery, charioteering, calligraphy, and mathematics) focused on the entire self, cultivating body, mind, and spirit as one indivisible unity. As he notes, "[E]xemplary teaching (*shen-chiao* 身嗷), which is superior to teaching by words (*yen-chiao* 言嗷), literally means to teach by one's body."[17] Ritualizing the body necessarily trains and cultivates the intellect and life force in chorus. By the same token, teaching is "an embodying act . . . undertaken by the whole person." Indeed, "[p]ersonal exemplification is the most authentic and therefore the most effective pedagogy. The Way must be lived and lived well to be truly efficacious, and good teachers embody the form of life they advocate."[18] Further justification for this comparison can be found in a cursory comparison of the initial description of Vimalakīrti in chapter 2, and the ways in which Confucius is described in the *Analects*. In both cases, the authors take great delight and care in describing the daily activities of their subjects. What they do, and the manner they do it, is in many ways more important than any pearls of wisdom. Chapter 10 of the *Analects*, in particular, gives a detailed description of the Master's life, not unlike that found in the second chapter of the *VNS*.

We also find a very strong emphasis in the Confucian tradition on the progressive nature of the sage's path. There is no theory of sudden enlightenment, whereby the sage in an instant achieves realization and thereby becomes perfected. Rather, it entails an ongoing, gradual struggle stretching across one's life span. The example of Confucius himself serves as the locus classicus for this process. As *Analects* 2.4 records: "The Master said, 'At fifteen I set my heart on learning; at thirty I took my stand; at forty I came to be free from doubts; at fifty I understood the Decree of Heaven; at sixty my ear was atuned [*sic*]; at seventy I followed my heart's desire without overstepping the line.'"[19]

While confined to one's mortal existence, in keeping with Confucian metaphysics, the education and refinement of a gentleman parallels in many respects the path of the bodhisattva, whose graduated ascension through the ten stages (*daśabhūmi*) may take tens of thousands of incarnations. Accordingly, Vimalakīrti emphasizes a progressive apprehension of dharma truth. It is the path that comes into focus throughout the text. Little attention is paid to ontological discussions; there is virtually no discourse on the nature of nirvāna, for example, anywhere in the dialogue. One telling example is the continuous refrain following revelatory pronouncements or corporeal demonstrations; none of the audience "attains enlightenment." Instead, multitudes "set their minds on attaining *anuttara-samyak-sambodhi*."

The *VNS* invokes the physical characteristic of teaching in numerous significant ways. Of the many images that could be discussed, let me choose two that I think capture the *VNS*'s spirit and intent best: Vimalakīrti's feigned illness and his silence on the question of nonduality. Other potential examples that instructors may want to explore are the encounter between Śāriputra and the goddess,[20] the various episodes of magical manipulation scattered throughout the text, and the nature of the fragrant rice from the country of Many Fragrances.[21] Each represents a slightly different way in which the text emphasizes an embodied teaching.

The text introduces us to Vimalakīrti as a rich resident of Vaiśali who has chosen to feign sickness as an expedient method of bringing well-wishers to his home, whereupon he can then expound the dharma. His illness, once brought to the Buddha's attention, prompts Śākyamuni to dispatch Mañjuśrī, in the company of the great assembly of bodhisattvas and disciples, gods and celestial beings, to inquire after the layman's health. In this episode, we both see and have verbally revealed the truth about samsaric existence. We are bound by an ephemeral body, subject to countless ills and utterly unreliable. The illness that has confined Vimalakīrti to his bed, while invisible to the naked eye (we have no indications from the text what the particular illness is), incapacitates the seemingly indefatigable sage. Similarly, our own actions and attachments, desires, and "needs" work imperceptibly to bind us and confine us to the continuous round of samsaric existence. In my own teaching about *dukkha* (suffering), I downplay the obvious physical parallels in deference to the psychosocial aspects as a way of alerting students to the profoundly radical nature of the concept. Yet at the same time, the visually compelling nature of Vimalakīrti's sickbed provides the perfect context for elucidating the nature of the phenomenal world. To "see" the effects, in the person of the most well respected man in Vaiśali, is to apprehend the truth at a profound level. Our response goes beyond the intellectual and approaches the visceral.

While Vimalakīrti uses the occasion of his illness to illustrate graphically the nature of samsaric existence, he also uses it as a means of demonstrating the great work and compassion of the bodhisattva. In explaining his illness to Mañjuśrī and the assembly, Vimalakīrti reveals that the bodhisattva path is not simply one of returning to samsara and teaching all living beings. Instead, the bodhisattva, from the depths of compassion, takes on the suffering of others, embodies the illness of others, and accrues great merit for the benefit of others. Once again, the visual "evidence" is profoundly important. It is one thing to say that bodhisattvas suffer in their compassion; it is quite another to be witness to the sickness that encumbers them. In this respect, it is often instructive to reflect upon the iconographic representations of bodhisattvas, which are typically glorious, and the image of the suffering saint depicted here.

I am also convinced that Vimalakīrti's famous "thunderous silence" can be explored profitably as an example of the embodiment of dharma truth. Much ink already has been spilled on the philosophical and religious implications of Vimalakīrti's silent response (along with countless undergraduate attempts to duplicate that silence as evidence of profundity). In another light, I have recourse to the argument that I have been developing here—namely, that this silence is made all the more profound when considered from a physical standpoint. Certainly, the author(s) of the *VNS*, the *Daodejing*, and numerous Zen texts were conscious of the philosophical implications of wordless teachings and the inexpressibility of ultimate truths, given the limitations of human language. However, I also ask students to imagine the scene laid out before them: an innumerable assembly of gods, humans, celestial beings, monks, disciples, and bodhisattvas; a single question: "How does the bodhisattva go about entering the gate of nonduality?"; thirty-two bodhisattvas providing increasingly profound (and philosophically "correct") responses. Following his answer, Mañjuśrī inquires of Vimalakīrti as to his explanation. As the question is posed, what is the assembly doing? They are most certainly not sitting with closed eyes, heads turned to the side to better hear the response, or reading a text. Imagine the assembly, as one, looking at, staring at, intently contemplating the figure before them, eagerly awaiting his word. And what do they experience? Vimalakīrti himself—no words, no explanation, no profundity, simply a life. To borrow the words of another tradition, they experience the "Great I AM." The truth of nonduality is indeed inexpressible. As Mañjuśrī accurately notes, "Excellent! Excellent! Not a word, not a syllable—this truly is to enter the gate of nonduality."[22] Vimalakīrti's exemplary life is the capstone. Nothing more needs to be said. Do you want to know the path of the bodhisattva, the truth of equanimity and equality, the benefits of the dharma life? Then take heed of the person in front of you. There it is, in the flesh.

As the Zen tradition will later assert, Vimalakīrti's silence was like a clap of thunder. In a momentous reversal of phenomenal experience, his silence shattered the clamor of voices and pointed to the underlying truth of a fulfilled life. While his words are certainly memorable, and his understanding of Buddhist philosophy unassailable, it is Vimalakīrti's life that speaks the loudest and exerts the most influence. As the *Zhuangzi* put it several centuries earlier, "[W]hile he is profoundly silent, the thunder (of his words) will resound . . . while he is thus unconcerned and does nothing, his genial influence will attract and gather all things round him."[23] Perhaps most importantly of all, the text's timeless quality can be seen in its contemporary relevance for those of us teaching today. As Vimalakīrti, Confucius, and Zhuangzi each agree, the best teacher is the one who lives out his or her ideals, teaching by example, as well as word.

Notes

1. Three recent translations stand out: Charles Luk, trans., *The Vimalakīrti Nirdeśa Sūtra.* (Berkeley, CA: Shambhala, 1972); Robert Thurman, trans., *The Holy Teaching of Vimalakīrti: A Mahāyāna Scripture* (University Park: Pennsylvania State University Press, 1976); Burton Watson, trans., *The Vimalakirti Sutra* (New York: Columbia University Press, 1997). In terms of readability and overall accuracy, I prefer Watson's translation of the Kumarajiva text. Thurman's excellent rendition of the Tibetan version brings home the work's stately nature, although I find the wording somewhat stiff and inaccessible to undergraduates. Luk's version, also from the Chinese, most effectively captures the text's whimsical nature. All citations from the *VNS* in the text are from Watson.
2. Among the best surveys is Richard B. Mather's "Vimalakirti and Gentry Buddhism," *History of Religions* 8, no. 1 (1968): 61–73.
3. "Vimalakirti said, 'Welcome Manjushri! You come without the marks of coming, you see me without the marks of seeing me.' Manjushri said, 'Just so, layman. What has already come can hardly be coming. And what has departed can hardly be departing. What do I mean? What comes has nowhere it comes from, what departs has nowhere it goes, and what is seen cannot be further seen. But let us put that aside for the moment.'" Watson, *Vimalakirti Sutra*, 65.
4. See Jay G. Williams, "The Vimalakīrtinirdeśa-sūtra: The Comedy of Paradox," *Pacific World*, n.s., 6 (1990): 89–95, for an interesting study on the *VNS*'s humor.
5. See, for example, chapter 14 of the *Zhuangzi* for several encounters between Confucius and Laozi.
6. See Ning Qiang, "Buddhist-Daoist Conflict and Gender Transformation: Deciphering the Illustrations of the *Vimalakirti-nirdesha* in Mediaeval Chinese Art," *Orientations* 27, no. 10 (1996): 50–60, esp. 54–55.
7. From Dōgen's *Shōbō genzō zuimonki*, translated in *Sources of Japanese Tradition*, vol. I, edited by Ryusaku Tsunoda, W. Theodore De Bary, and Donald Keene (New York: Columbia University Press, 1964), 249.
8. Watson, *Vimalakirti Sutra,* 75.
9. *Zhuangzi*, chap. 26; from Burton Watson, trans., *The Complete Works of Chuang Tzu* (New York: Columbia University Press, 1968), 302.
10. Watson, *Vimalakirti Sutra,* 23–24.
11. Edward Hamlin, "Magical *Upāya* in the *Vimalakīrtinirdeśa-sūtra*," *Journal of the International Association of Buddhist Studies* 11 (1988): 89–121.
12. In fact, Hamlin makes a compelling argument that the text records some of the ambiguity concerning the shift in the tradition's understanding of the Buddha— from ordinary human to metaphysical saint, increasingly removed from the aspirations of the common adherent and slowly being replaced by the model exemplified in the person of Vimalakīrti. See especially ibid, 115–16.

13. Watson, *Vimalakirti Sutra,* 95.
14. Rodney L. Taylor, "The Sage as Saint: The Confucian Tradition," in *Sainthood: Its Manifestations in World Religions,* edited by Richard Kieckhefer and George D. Bond (Berkeley and Los Angeles: University of California Press, 1988), 219.
15. D. C. Lau, *The Analects,* by Confucius (London: Penguin Books, 1979).
16. D. C. Lau, trans., *Mencius* (London: Penguin Books, 1970).
17. Tu Wei-ming, "The Human in Mencian Thought: An Approach to Chinese Aesthetics," in *Theories of the Arts in China,* edited by Susan Bush and Christian Murck (Princeton, NJ: Princeton University Press, 1984), 61.
18. Tu Wei-ming, "The Confucian Sage: Exemplar of Personal Knowledge," in *Saints and Virtues,* edited by John Stratton Hawley (Berkeley, CA: University of California Press, 1987), 84.
19. Lau, *Analects,* 63
20. Found in *Vimalakirti Sutra,* chapter 7. This episode is certainly one of the most delightful in terms of humor and the Mahāyāna views on the inherent equality of men and women.
21. *Vimalakirti Sutra,* chapters 10 and 11. When eaten, the rice remains undigested until certain spiritual attainments are achieved. Its fragrance, meanwhile, also remains until digested, and has the power to induce *samadhi.*
22. Watson, *Vimalakirti Sutra,* 111.
23. *Zhuangzi,* chap. 11, in James Legge, trans. *The Texts of Taoism, Sacred Books of the East,* vol. 39, edited by F. Max Müller (Oxford: Oxford University Press, 1891), 294.

For Further Reading and Research

English Translations

Lamotte, Etienne. *The Teaching of Vimalakirti (Vimalakirtinirdesa),* from the French translation with introduction and notes (*L'enseignement de Vimalakirti*), rendered into English by Sara Boin. London: Pali Text Society; distributed by Routledge and K. Paul, 1976. This translation from the Tibetan and Chinese is the most sophisticated in terms of providing detailed technical apparatus for specialists. It would not, however, be appropriate for an undergraduate course.
Luk, Charles, trans. *The Vimalakīrti Nirdeśa Sūtra.* Berkeley, CA: Shambhala, 1972.
Thurman, Robert, trans. *The Holy Teaching of Vimalakīrti: A Mahāyāna Scripture.* University Park: Pennsylvania State University Press, 1976.
Watson, Burton, trans. *The Vimalakirti Sutra.* New York: Columbia University Press, 1997.

Secondary Studies

Hamlin, Edward. "Magical *Upāya* in the *Vimalakīrtinirdeśa-sūtra.*" *Journal of the International Association of Buddhist Studies* 11 (1988): 89–121.
Mather, Richard B. "Vimalakirti and Gentry Buddhism." *History of Religions* 8, no. 1 (1968): 61–73.

Pye, Michael. *Skilful Means: A Concept in Mahayana Buddhism.* London: Duckworth; distributed in the United States by Southwest Book Services, 1978. The fifth chapter, "Skilful Means in the Teaching of Vimalakīrti," is devoted exclusively to an analysis of *upāya* in the *VNS.*

Williams, Jay G. "The *Vimalakīrtinirdeśa-sūtra*: The Comedy of Paradox." Pacific World, n.s., 6 (1990): 89–95.

Tom Pynn

The Things of This World Are Masks the Infinite Assumes: Introducing Samkhya and Yoga Philosophy

When the World Parliament of Religions convened on September 11, 1893, in Chicago, many Americans came face-to-face for the first time with the plurality of Asian philosophical and religious traditions. Already, however, some of America's literary, religious, and philosophical figures had been exploring the images and texts from Vedic culture and Buddhism: Ralph Waldo Emerson had been fascinated with Indian philosophy and religion; Henry David Thoreau had been cultivating an interest in Buddhist texts, particularly the *Lotus Sutra*; and William James had included Buddhism in his groundbreaking study of religious experience. Since the more widespread introduction of Americans to Asian philosophies in 1893, interest in Asian philosophical traditions in general and Indian philosophy in particular has continued to grow. Witness, for instance, the continuing fascination with Buddhism and an increasingly popular interest in yoga. An encounter with the rich and complex traditions of Indian thought offers all of us the twofold opportunity, as Charles A. Moore has written, "to understand the country and its people," and "to enlarge the scope of philosophy and to broaden the horizons of philosophers by attending seriously to the important contributions that Indian philosophy and philosophers have made to the totality of philosophical knowledge and wisdom."[1] Introducing students to classical Indian philosophy presents challenges that enrich a traditionally Western-oriented classroom.

One of the first challenges that Indian philosophy in general and Samkhya and Yoga philosophy in particular poses is indicated by the title of this chapter: "The Things of This World Are Masks the Infinite Assumes," which comes from a phrase written by Huston Smith for the documentary he collaborated on with Elda Hartley entitled *India and the Infinite*.[2] If we focus entirely on the use of "infinite," we are likely to miss the relationship that has been the heart of much Western and Indian metaphysics: What *is* the relation between the finite (visible phenomena) and the infinite (invisible noumena)? If we focus exclusively on the infinite, we are likely to come away with the presumption that Indian philosophy is reducible to religious philosophy or spirituality. As some recent work shows, this is misleading and does an injustice to the complexly variegated history of Indian thought. Complicating matters is the fact that there is not an exact Indian concept for the Western term "philosophy." There are, however, two Sanskrit words often used that roughly correspond to what philosophers tend to do: *tattva* ("thatness" or "reality") and *darsana* ("vision" or "sight," and "point of view," the latter especially when referring to specific philosophical perspectives such as Samkhya, Nyaya, and Carvaka).

At the same time, the controversy over what constitutes the corpus of Indian classical philosophy provides an opportunity to discuss how cultures tend to foreground and background aspects of human experience in the drive to develop comprehensive and consistent worldviews. One place to begin an investigation into the constituent elements of a given culture's worldview is to inquire into the kinds of questions that social groups tend to find interesting. For instance, Westerners have tended to find the question "What can I know about reality?" an interesting question, and its presuppositions and responses have formed a large part of the Western worldview. By contrast, Indian thought has been less interested in this question and, instead, has focused, at least in part, on the question "How can a human being attain his/her greatest good?" The difference in these questions is a difference in worldviews. Acknowledging the difference in questions cultures pose to themselves can lead to an examination of the way presuppositions inform constructions of worldviews and how these same presuppositions can lead to bias. The projection of one's presuppositions onto the other obscures the other's worldview by substituting a kind of straw man that prevents the emergence and fulfillment of commerce, the kind of genuine interchange between cultures Immanuel Kant imagined would be one of the elements necessary in bringing about perpetual peace. A recent work

that develops a theory of foregrounding and backgrounding in the construction of worldviews is Thomas Kasulis's *Intimacy or Integrity:
Philosophy and Cultural Difference.*[3]

The subtitle of this chapter, "Introducing Samkhya and Yoga
Philosophy," indicates another important concern when introducing
students to the history of thought in India. Portraying ancient Indian
thought as primarily orthodox has been the default position since at
least Heinrich Zimmer's *Philosophies of India* and Charles A. Moore's
The Indian Mind. Both were encouraged by the *moksa*-driven or spiritual interpretation of Indian philosophical and religious history given
by Sarvepalli Radhakrishnan in his studies of Indian thought.[4] At the
very least, it can be argued that Zimmer and Radhakrishnan's emphasis
on the orthodox traditions of Indian thought privileges a Hindu-centered
reading that tends to downplay the significance of heterodox perspectives in the history and development of Indian philosophy. Recent scholarship, such as J. N. Mohanty's *Classical Indian Philosophy*, is opting
for the term "classical" to describe a much more expansive Indian philosophical history.[5] Classical Indian philosophy is an *inclusive* category
that defines Indian thought as all those traditions and perspectives that
are pre-Aryan (such as yoga);[6] as Vedic (Aryan), a synthesis of the pre-
Aryan and Vedic; as orthodox (such as one may read in the *Bhagavad
Gītā*), and non-Vedic; or as heterodox (Buddhism, Jainism, Loyakata)—
that is, all ancient Indian points of view or *darsanas*.

One way to classify the types of philosophy in ancient India is to
divide the *darsanas* into the following two categories according to their
relationship to the ancient texts known collectively as the Vedas: (1)
Nastika, or schools of Indian philosophy that do not use the Vedas to
establish their own authority; some of the Nastika schools are Loyakata
(Carvaka), Buddhism, and Jainism; and (2) Astika, or schools of Indian
philosophy that use the Vedas to establish their own authority. Astika is
also referred to as orthodox as opposed to the heterodox *darsanas* of the
Nastika. However, as Arvind Sharma pointed out in a review of Daya
Krishna's *Indian Philosophy—A Counter Perspective*, what eventually
came to be understood by the term "Veda" was not simply a set of texts,
but rather an authoritative point of view.[7] While the traditions, in general, tend not to change greatly, perspectives on/within traditions do.
Thus, a perspective can become authoritative and be known as Veda.

Orthodox Indian philosophy, on the other hand, can be defined as an *exclusive* category primarily consisting of six *darsanas* that, to varying degrees, accept philosophy as a specialized learning directed to the attainment of a higher state of being: the Divine. These *darsanas* are Nyaya, Vaisesika, Samkhya, Yoga, Mimamsa, and Vedanta. Hence, a comprehensive study of Indian philosophy will be representative of the history of Indian thought and not reduced to an unrepresentative sampling. Few of us, however, have the time in a given term to cover the full scope of Indian thought, and so we scale down according to whatever parameters we design for our courses. For purposes of this chapter, then, I focus on introducing students to the Samkhya and Yoga *darsanas*.

Samkhya and Yoga are complementary *darsanas*, each one lending to the other what the other in some sense lacks. Quite often, as in the *Mahabarata*, the two are presented as a unified system by the hyphenated phrase *samkhya-yoga*. In his recent translation and commentary of Patanjali's *Yoga Sutras*, Ashok Malhotra writes, "[O]ne of the main reasons for this juxtaposition is the fact that the Samkhya philosophers offer a metaphysical view of reality, which is eagerly adopted by the Yoga system, whereas the Yoga thinkers provide a step-by-step method to achieve enlightenment, which is accepted by the Samkhya system. Since one offers a theory while the other a practical method, they complement each other and are studied as a complete system."[8] One way to introduce students to Yoga philosophy is to present corresponding themes. The following quatrain, *sahki*,[9] is by the North Indian poet Kabir (1398-1448):

> Mind-ocean, mind-born waves—
> Many unconscious ones drown.
> Kabir says, he is saved
> Whose heart can discern.[10]

The symbolic presentation of the ocean and its waves as the human mind disturbed by the fluctuations of consciousness echoes the first important theme in the *Yoga Sutras*: "Yoga is the stilling of all mental fluctuations."[11] Because we often fail to discriminate between the psychophysical self and Purusa, the transcendental self, we "drown" in the disruptive impressions. To become conscious is to understand the essential difference between the two distinct entities Purusa and Prakriti (the source of the material world). The soteriological function of discernment, and Yoga methodology in general, is introduced in the final couplet: discernment by the "heart," the higher mind's will to truth, leads to liberation from ignorance. To experience liberation there must be a stilling of the mental fluctuations so that the higher mind is undisturbed by the lower mind's sensing of the external world and the profound grasping of the I's self-interest. The result is tranquility, which allows the higher mind to be absorbed in the Purusa at the culmination of involution.

Since the *Yoga Sutras* make several direct references to Samkhya metaphysics, using only the *Yoga Sutras* is recommended (although, one could easily combine a reading of the *Yoga Sutras* with any of the Samkhya texts and commentaries, such as Iswara Krishna's *Samkhya Karika*). I use the *Yoga Sutras* and then speak to the convergences and divergences between these complementary systems by referring to the "Samkhya Metaphysics and Yoga Practice" chart, which is in the appendix to this essay. This chart is a composite that I have constructed from a variety of sources, including George Feuerstein's *Yoga: The Technology of Ecstasy*, the *Yoga Sutras*, and several of Meher Baba's essays from the *Discourses*.[12] This chart, as a visual aid, clarifies some of the difficult points in Samkhya and Yoga, and is comprised of some of the important elements that form the convergence and divergence of Samkhya philosophy and Yoga methodology.

The basic structure of the chart displays the categories of Samkhya metaphysics, the proximity of Purusa and Prakriti, what evolves from Prakriti, and, by arrows, the dynamic processes of evolution and involution of consciousness away from and toward Purusa, respectively. Three important questions can be addressed regarding this basic structure: (1) What is the relationship between Purusa and Prakriti? (2) What are the *gunas*? (3) What are the constituent parts of what John Koller calls the "psychophysical self," and what is their relation to one another?[13]

The first question indicates a weak point in the Samkhya system. All the sources I have studied indicate there is some kind of relationship obtaining between Purusa and Prakriti, but the status of their interaction is inadequately explained. Malhotra, for instance, writes, "[B]ecause of their close proximity, Purusa looks at Prakriti. This witnessing of Purusa upsets the balance of the three qualities in the heart of Prakriti and is responsible for starting the process of evolution."[14] Swami Virupakshananda's translation and commentary on Krishna's *Samkhya Karika* states, "[B]irth is the connection of the Spirit with a particular aggregate of a special group of body, sense-organs, mind, I-Principle, Great Principle and experiences."[15] Later on in the text, he writes that the relation is a "union" that "by itself would not suffice either for enjoyment or for liberation if *Mahat* and the rest were not there; hence the act of union itself brings about the evolution for the sake of enjoyment and liberation."[16] Richard Thompson, in his video *Simulated Worlds*, compares and contrasts the Samkhya system with artificial intelligence and suggests that the relation may be understood as a projection.[17] In any case, whether the relation between Purusa and Prakriti is stated as "witnessing," "union," or "projection," one is still left wondering how these two distinct entities interact.

One of the ongoing controversies in Samkhya and Yoga philosophy concerns the identity of the *gunas*. In the second chapter of the *Bhagavad Gītā* Krishna tells Arjuna that no one, even for an instant, can remain inactive, due to the impulsion of the *gunas*. While it is clear that the *gunas* form the basis of Prakriti, or the transcendental ground of nature, their ontic status is unclear. Are they qualities, as Malhotra translates *gunas*, or are they entities within an encompassing Prakriti with their own essences, as suggested by Krishna's *Samkhya Karika*? Sri Vacaspati Misra, in his commentary on Krishna's *Samkhya Karika*, writes that the *gunas* are "attributes" of Prakriti (also known as Pradhana and the Primordial). Feuerstein's *Encyclopedia of Yoga* translates *gunas* as "strand" or "quality" and states that the term has many connotations, including the two most common: "quality" and "constituent."[18] David Jones has pointed out to me that "tendency" is a stronger philosophical translation, because the *gunas* function affectively rather than effectively, coloring the psychophysical self rather than determining it in any way. It is typical of qualities, characteristics, or essences to function effectively.

Questions about the *gunas* can serve to illuminate important differences between qualities and essences in the language of metaphysics in general and the differences between these concepts in Indian thought and in the history of Western philosophy in particular. However their ultimate identity is conceived, they function in the process of evolution and involution by producing movement or change. When we act in ignorance of the true self—that is, when we get out of the lower mind and the will/higher mind directed to self-interest—*sanskaras* (impressions or instincts) are formed. The configuration of one's *sanskaras* directly affects reincarnation. In the newborn psychophysical self, the sanskaras, or impressions, "are deposits of previous experiences and become the most important factors in determining the course of present and future experience."[19] This is not to suggest that *samkhya-yoga* is deterministic. While we cannot alter the consequences of past formations of impressions, we can change our present accumulation of *sanskaras* and directly affect future consequences and rebirths. The tying and untying of a knot in a length of rope is a good simile to convey that as we act out of self-interest, we increase sanskaras (tightening of the knot), and as we act unselfishly (without the desire for the fruits of action, as the *Gītā* puts it) *sanskaras* are diminished (loosening of the knot). Understanding one's psychophysical self is necessary to bring about the unwinding of *sanskaras*.

On the *samkhya-yoga* view, to have a direct effect on the configuration of one's impressions one must understand the core structure of the psychophysical self (*mahat*, *ahamkara*, and *manas*) and how these elements are generated out of the contact between Purusa and Prakriti. Swami Prabhavananda in his commentary on the *Yoga Sutras* offers a lighthearted explanation of the three main elements of the psychophysical self:

> *Manas* is the recording faculty which receives impressions gathered by the senses from the outside world. [*Mahat*] is the discriminative faculty that classifies these impressions and reacts to them. *Ahamkara* is the ego sense that claims these impressions for its own and stores them up as individual knowledge. For example, *manas* reports, "A large animate object is quickly approaching." [*Mahat*] declares, "That's a bull. It is angry. It wants to attack someone." *Ahamkara* screams, "It wants to attack me, Patanjali. It is *I* who see this bull. It is *I* who am frightened. It is *I* who am about to run away." Later, from the branches of a nearby tree, *ahamkara* may add: "Now I know that this bull (which is not I) is dangerous. There are others who do not know this; it is my own personal knowledge, which will cause me to avoid this bull in the future.[20]

In this illustration, theories of both causation and relation are implied in the evolutionary relationship between the parts of the psychophysical self. Misra explains the evolution of the constituents of the psychophysical self and their relation to one another in this way: "The Great Principle (*Mahat* or *Buddhi*) is the cause of *Ahamkara* (I-Principle), while it is itself (being) the product of the Root evolvent [Prakriti]. Similarly, the Principle of Ahamkara is the cause of the five Primary elements (*Tanmataras*) and (eleven) sense organs (*Indriyas*), itself being the effect of *Buddhi*. In the same way, the five Primary elements are the causes of gross elements like the ether, while they are themselves the evolutes of *Ahamkara*."[21] This causal and relational theory, *satkaryavada*, rests upon the notion that something cannot emerge out of nothing. The cause is present in the effect, and the effect is already, in some sense, present in the cause. "On this theory," as Mohanty shows, "causal production is not bringing into being a new entity, but making explicit what was already implicit, rendering actual what was already there, or giving the preexistent stuff a new form."[22] Recalling the earlier discussion of *sanskaras* and their relation to reincarnation, *sanskaras* can be understood as "causing" certain experiences, because these experiences are already *in potentia* in one's previous experiences.

Once the basic metaphysical theory is addressed, it is time to bring yoga into the discussion: What is yoga's place in all of this metaphysical theorizing? Rooted in the practice of meditation, yoga is understood by all the other *darsanas* to provide the most satisfactory method of accomplishing liberation. The boxed arrow on the bottom left of the chart indicates the place where Patanjali's Raja Yoga (the combination of Kriya Yoga—comprised primarily of *jnana*, yoga of intellectual acuity; *karma*, yoga of selfless action; and *bhakti*, the yoga of devotion[23]—and Ashtanga Yoga) comes into the picture. If the basic problem is that the Purusa has gotten so wrapped up in enjoying Prakriti, then yoga purports to be the way of breaking Purusa's false identification with it. On the chart in the appendix, the arrow is placed between the *mahat* and the *ahamkara* to indicate that the higher mind or will (*mahat*) must be directed away from the lower mind (*manas*) and self-interest (*ahamkara*) and then reoriented toward Purusa. To do this, a system of discipline leading to a rehabituation of the intellectual, physical, and ethical dimensions of the psychophysical self must take place.

The upward curving arrow on the left side of the chart indicates the process of involution, the yogic movement of consciousness through the three stages of one-pointed concentration and their corresponding transformations of consciousness.

Patanjali outlines the internal stages of meditation in sutras 3.1–3.8. Concentration (*dharana*), in sutra 3.1, "is the spontaneous directing of consciousness towards an object." Meditation (*dhyana*) "is the uninterrupted flow of consciousness towards an object," and Absorption (*samadhi*) "is the uninterrupted merging of consciousness into an object where self-awareness is completely erased."[24] The threefold experience of meditation is sometimes referred to as one-pointed concentration (*samyama*). To illustrate the threefold process of *samyama*, I sometimes use the example of the one-pointed or contemplative exercise of the stations of the cross in which one moves, over the span of about an hour or two, through twelve stations directing the mind in concentration to each station's single subject. The process of disciplining one's attention through the icons moves one from being distracted by everything and anything (this serves to illustrate that concentration, *dharana*, is spontaneous as one's consciousness moves from object to object, noticing what is going on) to meditation (*dhyana*), the second stage, in which one can still the mind enough to focus on one idea. In the third stage, absorption (*samadhi*) comes when one recognizes one's true self. The goal of the exercise of the stations of the cross is to recognize Christ as the true self by becoming immersed in each icon's symbolic mode of presentation. One can also use the example of the creative process as leading to the moment of absorption. Artists throughout history have indicated that in the process of creating art objects the artist becomes immersed in the process.

When Purusa identifies with the psychophysical self rather than its own self-illuminated being, objects in the world take on an appearance of otherness that obscures seeing things as they are—that is, contingent. One-pointed concentration allows Purusa to shift attention away from the otherness of objects and what these objects can do for us. When self-interest dissolves in the final stage of concentration, the object stands forth in its true form and we know it for what it is. We know that we are *not that, not that*. As Patanjali points out in sutras 3.9–3.12, with each stage of concentration there is a corresponding transformation of consciousness. In the restraint transformation effected by concentration, the state of stillness mediates each instant of "outgoing and incoming impressions." Contemplative transformation occurs when "awareness moves from all-pointed to one-pointed consciousness." Absorption transformation "is that change where consciousness moves from one-pointed to no-pointed concentration."[25] No-pointed concentration is the state in which Purusa no longer identifies with Prakriti. Thus, the goal of involution is Purusa's liberation from identification with Prakriti.

Students often wonder about whether the inclusiveness that tends to characterize Indian thought is extended beyond the human realm. Going through the chart provided also can serve to address this question. Samkhya and Yoga, like most of the Indian philosophical traditions, are not necessarily anthropocentric; so, one is led to suppose that the karmic evolution of the psychophysical self generated by the *gunas* in the beginningless process of the winding and the unwinding of *sanskaras* is taking place across the spectrum of life-forms; however, with the human life form the development of the psychophysical self has reached its apex—that is, no other life form enjoys Prakriti and suffers more in this enjoyment than the human. It is also by virtue of being born into the human form, that one may practice yoga and begin the process of disentanglement from Prakriti.[26] It is only the human being who can experience the process of involution and attain the greatest good or liberation.

While there are several places where minor divergences between Samkhya metaphysics and Yoga can be looked into, the biggest difference between these two perspectives is indicated by the box "Yoga vs. Samkhya" that points at "Isvara (Supreme Purusa)." While Samkhya maintains that there are only the numerous transcendental selves, with no one Purusa serving a unique function in reality, Yoga suggests that there is a Supreme Purusa who has a particular function in controlling the universe in general and human society in particular. We can read this line of thought in chapter 4 of the *Gītā*, where Krishna tells Arjuna that if he did not act, whole worlds would fall apart. The *Yoga Sutras* also take up this existence of Isvara in sutras 1.23–1.28, in which Patanjali outlines the various ways to achieve stillness. Yoga's argument for an avatar or Supreme Purusa can be contrasted with Sri Vacaspati Misra's commentary on sutra 57 of Krishna's *Samkhya Karika*. In it Misra argues against the objection, raised at the end of the previous sutra, that there must exist an omniscient being who has control over Prakriti and that this sentient being is Isvara.

An important point of divergence between Indian thought and Western philosophy concerns the question "Who is doing the philosophizing?" When Edmund Husserl wrote his *Cartesian Meditations,* he cited the significant difference between the ancient and medieval worlds, on the one hand, and the modern world, on the other, as largely a difference between a naïve objectivism and a transcendental subjectivism.[27] Descartes, Husserl believes, inaugurated a new turn in European philosophy in which subjectivity was to be taken seriously. Husserl was right in at least one respect: Descartes did shift the focus away from the objective world and toward the subject, and his turning did begin a series of philosophers—Hume, Kant, Husserl, Heidegger, and Foucault, to name a few—on the path to a radical (re)appraisal of subjectivity. The topic of subjectivity can be an excellent way to begin exploring the ways in which Western philosophy has both succeeded and failed to take subjectivity seriously and what, if anything, Indian thought can add to the dialogue on subjectivity. One place to begin is with Descartes' identification of the self as the cogito, a thinking thing. From the Samkhya and Yoga points of view, Descartes' self is the false self and not the true self. The suffering that humans experience is due primarily to the identification of who we truly are (Purusa) with the psychophysical operations of cognition (Prakriti). Other areas of comparison might include post-Enlightenment theories of mind-body interaction, as well as contemporary research in parapsychology, which often appeals even to the most reticent student.

Samkhya Ontology and Yoga Practice

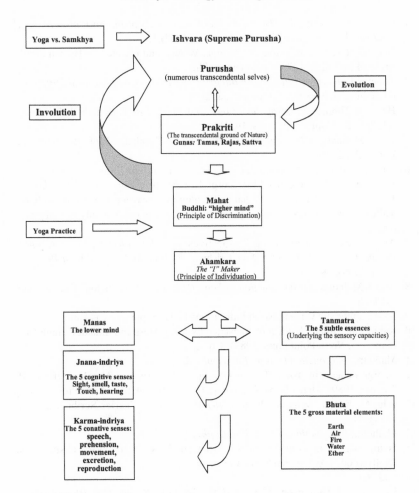

Notes

1. Charles A. Moore, ed., *The Indian Mind: Essentials of Indian Philosophy and Culture* (Honolulu: East-West Center Press, 1967),1.
2. Elda Hartley, dir., *India and the Infinite*. Written and narrated by Huston Smith. Mystic Fire Video, 1974. Documentary film.
3. Thomas P. Kasulis, *Intimacy or Integrity? Philosophy and Cultural Difference* (Honolulu: University of Hawaii Press, 2002).
4. Heinrich Zimmer, *Philosophies of India*, edited by Joseph Campbell (Princeton, NJ: Princeton University Press, 1951).
5. J. N. Mohanty, *Classical Indian Philosophy* (Lanham, MD: Rowman and Littlefield, 2000).
6. This is a controversial point made by Mircea Eliade in *Yoga: Immortality and Freedom* (1969) and echoed by George Feuerstein in *Yoga: The Technology of Ecstasy* (1989). Their point is that archaeological excavations in the Indus River Valley show evidence of yogic practices; hence, yoga is probably pre-Aryan in origin.
7. Arvind Sharma, "Competing Perspectives on *Indian Philosophy—A Counter Perspective*, nn. 8, 11, 14 by Daya Krishna," *Philosophy East and West* 49, no. 2 (April 1999): 194–206.
8. Ashok Malhotra, *An Introduction to Yoga Philosophy* (Burlington, VT: Ashgate, 2001), 6.
9. *Sahki*: aphoristic verse in North India as a vehicle for popular wisdom.
10. Kabir, *The "Bijack" of Kabir*, translated by Linda Hess and Shukdev Singh (San Francisco: North Point Press, 1983), 101–2.
11. Malhotra, *Introduction to Yoga Philosophy*, 25.
12. George Feuerstein, *Yoga: The Technology of Ecstasy* (Los Angeles: Jefferey P. Tarcher, 1989); Meher Baba, *Discourses* (Myrtle Beach, SC: Sheria Press, 1987).
13. John M. Koller, *Oriental Philosophies* (New York: Charles Scribner's Sons, 1985), 41.
14. Malhotra, *Introduction to Yoga Philosophy*, 7.
15. Isvara, Krishna, *Samkhya Karika*, translated by Swami Virupakshananda. (Hollywood, CA: Vedanta Press, 1995), 59.
16. Ibid., 64.
17. Dr. Richard Thompson, *Simulated Worlds* (San Diego, CA: Bhaktivedanta Institute).
18. George Feuerstein, *The Shambhala Encyclopedia of Yoga* (Boston: Shambhala, 1997).
19. Meher Beba, *Discourses*, 32.
20. Swami Prabhavananda, in *How to Know God: The Yoga Sutras of Patanjali*, translated with commentary by Swami Prabhavananda and Christopher Isherwood (Hollywood, CA: Vedanta Press, 1981), 16.
21. Sri Vacarpati Misra, in Krishna, *Samkhya Karika*, 11, my translation.
22. Mohanty, *Classical Indian Philosophy*, 75, my translation.
23. This form of Kriya Yoga is to be distinguished from its association with the later development of Kundalini Yoga, although an analysis of Samkhya physiology can be useful in understanding Samkhya's conception of matter.
24. Malhotra, *Introduction to Yoga Philosophy*, 42.

25. Ibid., 43.
26. It is not only Samkhya and Yoga that hold this position. It can be argued that other *darsanas* such as Vedanta and Buddhism also subscribe to this viewpoint.
27. Edmund Husserl, *Cartesian Meditations* (The Hague: Martinus Nijhoff, 1973), 4.

Suggested Readings

Ajaya, Swami. *Yoga Psychology*. Honesdale, PA: Himalaya Institute, 1989.

Aranya, Swami Hariharamanda. *Yoga Philosophy of Patanjali*. Albany: State University of New York Press, 1983.

Malhotra, Ashok Kumar. *Transcreation of the "Bhagavad Gītā."* Upper Saddle River, NJ: Prentice Hall, 1999.

Phillips, Stephen H. "Indian Philosophies." In *From Africa to Zen*, edited by Robert C. Solomon and Kathleen M. Higgins. New York: Rowman & Littlefield Publishers Inc., 1993, 221–265.

Puligandla, R. *Fundamentals of Indian Philosophy*. Nashville, TN: Abingdon Press, 1975.

Vivekenanda. *Bhakti-Yoga*. Calcutta: Advaita Ashrama, 1974.

Varenne, Jean. *Yoga and the Hindu Tradition*. Chicago: University of Chicago Press, 1976.

CHINA

Ronnie Littlejohn

Too Twisted to Fit a Carpenter's Square: Using and Teaching the *Daodejing*

> *An ancient gnarled tree:*
> *Too fibrous for a logger's saw,*
> *Too twisted to fit a carpenter's square,*
> *Outlasts the whole forest.*[1]

Loggers delight in straight, well-grained, strong, and fragrant wood. The raw naturalness of the twisted tree is the secret of its survival. The logger admires it but does not try to turn it into a desk, fine paneling, or a rafter for a home. So, it endures in all of its uncarved reality. Likewise, it is the gnarly fiber of the cobbled aphorisms of the *Daodejing* 道德經 (*DDJ*) that has enabled it to remain one of the most significant philosophical classics of humanity.

It is not my purpose to make a comprehensive argument in favor of teaching classical Chinese texts in general, or even the *DDJ* in particular.[2] The use of the resources of classical Chinese thought in the teaching of the humanities and social sciences may be motivated by many forces. Sometimes these works are used because professors are dissatisfied with the mainstream intellectual movements of the West and they believe that Chinese thought has a contribution to make in setting right some dead-ends and mistakes made by Western thinkers. In another sense, exploring these sources is an example of making use of the long-enduring and widely studied texts such as the *DDJ*. As a conversational partner in the project of gaining clarity about the most important questions humans ask, the *DDJ* has much to offer. In this essay I make suggestions about how the nonspecialist may teach some of the text's key concepts and themes.

Teaching the *DDJ*

In what follows I recommend two different models to use in teaching this central text.

Model One: Use of a Lexicon of Key Concepts

One approach to teaching the *DDJ* is to isolate some of its most fundamental concepts and use them to teach the content of the text. An advantage of this approach is that it minimizes the interpretive impact of questions about the composite nature of the chapters by bringing together passages containing the key concepts of the *DDJ* without necessarily connecting them with the rest of the chapters in which the passages are nested. A disadvantage of this approach is that the basic concepts of the *DDJ* are frequently interconnected. Very often the meaning of a concept such as "virtue" (*de*) depends on its relationship to "way" (*dao*) or "effortless action" (*wuwei* 無為). So, teaching concepts separately will always be somewhat deficient unless attention is given to the interrelationship of the ideas.

Dao 道 Chapters 1, 4, 8, 9, 14, 16, 18, 21, 23, 24, 25, 30, 31, 32, 34, 35, 37, 38, 40, 41, 42, 46, 47, 48, 51, 53, 54, 55, 59, 60, 62, 65, 67, 77, 79, 81

The term *dao* is one of the most crucial concepts in the *DDJ*. The word means "a road," and is often translated as "the Way." This is because sometimes *dao* is used as a noun ("the *dao*") and other times as a verb ("*dao*ing"). *Dao* can refer to the way something is done— for example, the way (*dao*) a butcher cuts or an artisan makes a bell stand.[3] But of more compelling interest to most teachers is its use for the process of reality itself (chap. 41). *Dao* is the movement of the forces most often simply called *yin* 陰 and *yang* 陽 and the combining and transforming of the five phases of which all things are made (*wuxing* 五行).

Dao cannot be understood by being put into words (chaps. 1, 35). It is the source of all things, but it is not a proper name of an object or thing (chaps. 25, 32, 34, 42). The text says *dao* is nameless (chaps. 1, 32, 37, 41). "There is a thing confusedly formed, born before heaven and earth. Silent and void, it stands alone and does not change, goes round and does not weary. It is capable of being the mother of the world. I know not its name. So I style it 'the way'" (chap. 25).[4]

If one moves in harmony with *dao* "he will 'virtue'" (*de*), and his virtue will be genuine and long-lasting (chap. 54). While the nature of *dao* is elusive in itself, virtue (*de*) comes from it (chap. 21). *Dao* moves persons to find the same kinds of things to be repulsive (chap. 24). *Dao* is always on the side of the good (chap. 79). Its way is to benefit and not to harm (chap. 81). What causes this natural embedding of good and benefit in the *dao* is vague (chap. 35). The text says *dao* does nothing by intention or purpose (chap. 37). Yet, not even the sages know why *dao* always does good, why it "virtues" (*de*) as it does (chap. 76). In this connection, the *DDJ* likens the world to a sacred vessel that is filled with spiritual force *shen qi* 神器 (chap. 29). Indeed, in the *DDJ*, *dao* is to reality as the family altar for venerating the ancestors and gods is to the house (the *ao* 奧 of the house, chap. 62). It is only when the Great Way (*da dao* 大道) is abandoned that the human discriminations and distinctions that cause strife emerge (chaps. 18, 38).

De 德 Chapters 10, 21, 23, 28, 38, 41, 49, 51, 54, 55, 59, 60, 63, 65, 68, 79

There are some excellent recent essays on the meaning of virtue (*de*) in Chinese thought.[5] In classical Chinese texts *de* is used as "excellence," "virtue," "power," or "force." In the *DDJ* one who acts with no expectation of reward and who leads without lording it over others has *de* (chaps. 10, 51). Likewise, a person of great *de* follows *dao*, and indeed his *de* comes from following *dao* (chap. 21). If we cultivate *dao,* we will have *de* (chap. 54). Having consistent *de* results from being receptive and open to *dao* (chap. 28). *De* does not come as a result of striving, but from "effortless action" (*wuwei*) (chap. 38). Being good to those who are not good is *de* (chap. 49). *De* causes no injury (chap. 60). And we are admonished to repay resentment with *de* (chap. 63).[6] Not contending with others is *de* (68). "If you deeply accumulate virtue (*de*), nothing can stand in your way" (chap. 59). Persons cannot be forced to be good; the only way to influence them is by one's *de* (chap. 79).

Wuwei 無為 Chapters 2, 3, 10, 19, 20, 22, 24, 41, 43, 47, 48, 57, 63, 64, 73, 75, 78

Wuwei is one of what are called the *wu* forms in the *DDJ* (*wuwei* 無為; *wuzhi* 無知; and *wuyu* 無欲). These characters (無為) were rendered by the previous generation of translators as "inaction." Consequently, many interpreters understood *wuwei* to mean that the *DDJ* was recommending quiescence and inactivity as the way to practice the *dao*. It is now generally agreed that this traditional rendering of *wuwei* as "inaction" or "no action" can be better translated if we pay more attention to the entire system of Daoist thought. The *DDJ* says clearly that persons should act (chap. 63). So, Daoism is not a philosophy of "doing nothing."

Scholars now translate *wuwei* as "act naturally," "effortless action," "spontaneous action," or "nonwillful action."[7] *Wuwei* is the sort of conduct one observes when moving with the *dao* in a natural way, without effort. Sometimes the *DDJ* says persons *should wuwei*, using the concept in a normative manner. What is important is that although the agent does not engage in extended deliberation or analysis, the conduct nonetheless accords with the situation at hand with an efficacy that can only be attributed to the *dao*. Not even the sages know why *dao* works with this extraordinary efficacy (*de*) (chap. 73).[8]

The *DDJ* does not say that this efficacy fails to accord with the virtues and moral demands set up by the Confucians and others. This is not the point of its criticism of moral and aesthetic distinctions. What it does say is that following the demands and rules set up by convention as ends in themselves leads only to frustration and misery, whereas *wuwei* conduct will result in one's "gaining the world" (chaps. 10, 19, 48, 57).[9]

When one's conduct is *wuwei*, the individual is in harmony with the *dao*, and this creates virtue (*de*) (chap. 3). *Wuwei* is not a type of conduct one does instinctively, nor is it entirely unconscious. Neither must *wuwei* be completely free from deliberation or choice; instead, it is the choice that comes with ease and naturalness.[10]

Model Two: Use of a Major Theme Woven throughout the Text

Another approach to use in teaching the *DDJ* is to trace the way some of its major themes are developed in various chapters.

Emptiness Chapters 5, 6, 11, 15, 20, 28, 35, 40, 45, 48, 61, 63

Consider the theme of emptiness and how it is developed in the *DDJ*. At first, this theme sounds mysterious and vague. But emptiness is represented as full of power in many places in the text. "Is not the space between Heaven and Earth like a bellows? Empty yet inexhaustible!" (chap. 5). In other examples, it is *what is not there* in a wheel that makes it useful, and *what is removed* that makes something a cup, pitcher, or bowl. It is only by *relying on emptiness* that a door or window is what it is (chap. 11). "The world and all its creatures arise from what is there; what is there arises from what is not there" (chap. 40). Since human discriminations and distinctions fill the heart-mind (*xin* 心), we cannot act naturally, moving with the *dao*. Those who seek the *dao* do not desire fullness; they want to make themselves empty and natural (chap. 15). Being empty is a way of talking about getting rid of desires and preconceptions, and doing this is a precondition for oneness with *dao*. Emptiness means one is in a natural state, like uncarved wood.

Emptiness also is linked closely with the counsel that we should be a valley for all the world. A valley is a good analogy for emptiness, because it is the void between mountains. "If you are a valley for all the world, constant virtue will always be sufficient, and you can return to being unhewn wood (*pu* 朴)" (chap. 28).

Being empty indicates one's receptivity. This explains the association of emptiness with the feminine. In sexual relations, the female organ receives. To the would-be follower of the *dao*, the *DDJ* asks: "When the portal of Heaven opens and closes, can you play the part of the feminine?" (chap. 10). Chapter 6 makes an explicit analogical connection between emptiness, the valley, and the female:

> The spirit of the valley never dies;
> This is called the mysterious female (*xuan pin* 玄牝).
> The gateway of the mysterious female
> Is called the root of heaven and earth.
> Dimly visible, it seems as if it were there,
> Yet use will never drain it.

In Daoism, the ideal person is the *zhenren* (真人) or "real person," and this person is called the female of the world (chap. 61). The text says, "Know the male but preserve the female, and be a canyon for all the world" (chap. 28).

Correlativity Chapters 1, 2, 20, 22, 29, 30, 44, 48, 52, 55, 56, 63, 71, 77, 80, 81

"The myriad creatures shoulder *yin* and embrace *yang*; and by blending these inner energies (*qi* 氣) they attain harmony" (chap. 42). This statement is the only explicit mention of yin and yang in the *DDJ*,[11] but the theme of correlation is rather prominent in the text. Ames and Hall think of correlation as the mutuality of opposites, where the present condition of anything entails its opposite. Young is *young-becoming-old*; dark is *dark-becoming-light*; soft is *soft-becoming-hard*.

Correlativity in the *DDJ* often functions as a criticism of human distinctions and judgments. To have and to lack generate each other. Difficult and easy give form to each other. The noble and the lowly give content to each other (chap. 2). Sometimes one leads, and sometimes one follows. Sometimes one is strong and sometimes weak (chap. 29). Not every gain is a gain, and not all losses are losses (chap. 44).

An implication of the correlative thought of the *DDJ* is that which looks like evil, and may be actually experienced at the time as a misery or injury, should nevertheless not be labeled this way, as we would conventionally learn to do in making a discrimination. The text is not contending that an injury is not an injury, or that injury is an illusion and unreal, but only that this is not the final word, since even injury is already moving toward health while still an injury. This is how the *dao* blunts the sharp edges of life, untangles life's knotted problems, and softens the glare of stark experiences (chap. 56). It is also why when we think that life's occurrences are unfair (a human discrimination), we should remember that heaven's net (*tian wang* 天網) misses nothing, and leaves nothing undone (chap. 73). The *DDJ* calls this a deep enigma: "Within this enigma is yet a deeper enigma (*xuan zhi you xuan* 玄之又玄). The gate of all mysteries!" (chap. 1).

> Those who are crooked will be perfected.
> Those who are bent will be straight.
> Those who are empty will be full.
> Those who are worn will be renewed.
> Those who have little will gain.
> Those who have plenty will be confounded.
> (chap. 22)

Embracing correlativity is "practicing the constant" (*xi chang* 習常), and this is enlightenment in the Daoist sense.[12]

Sage Chapters 2, 3, 5, 7, 10, 12, 15, 19, 22, 26, 28, 29, 47, 49, 60, 63, 64, 66, 67 (first person), 70, 71, 72, 73, 75, 77, 78, 79, 81; autobiographical 16, 20, 25, 37, 69, 70

What is the image of the ideal person, the sage (*shengren* 聖人), the real person (*zhenren*) in the *DDJ*? The text tells us that sages practice emptiness (chap. 11). They preserve the female (*yin*), meaning that they know how to be receptive toward the *de* of *dao* and are not unbalanced favoring assertion and action (*yang*) (chap. 28). They shoulder yin and embrace yang, blend internal energies (*qi*), and thereby attain harmony (*he* 和) (chap. 42). They do not strive, tamper, or seek control (chap. 64). They do not endeavor to help life along (chap. 55), or use their heart-minds (*xin*) to "solve" or "figure out" life's apparent knots and entanglements (chap. 56). They live naturally and free themselves from desires given by men (chap. 37). They settle themselves down and know how to be content (chap. 46). We are also warned that those who try to do something with the world will fail, and they will actually ruin it (chap. 29). Instead of forcing their will on life, sages are pliable and supple, not rigid and resistive (chaps. 76, 78).

The *DDJ* makes use of some famous similes to describe the sage. Sages are *like newborn infants* (chaps. 10, 15, 20, 28, 49, 52, 55), who move naturally, without planning and reliance on the structures given to them by others. They are *like water* (chaps. 8, 32, 34, 35, 36, 43, 61, 62, 65, 66, 78), finding their own place, overcoming the hard and strong by suppleness (chap. 36). Sages clean their heart-mind's vision and purify their thoughts (chap. 10), so they can manifest plainness, and become *like uncarved wood* (*pu*) (chaps. 15, 19, 28, 32, 37, 57).

The characteristics of sages are an appealing subject to students. Sages act with no expectation of reward (chaps. 2, 51). They put themselves last and yet come first (chap. 7). They never make displays of themselves (chaps. 22, 72). They do not brag or boast (chaps. 22, 24), nor do they linger to receive praise after their work is done (chap. 77) because they leave no trace (chap. 27). Sages embody *dao* in practice, and by so doing have longevity (chap. 16), and they create peace (chap. 32). Heaven (*tian* 天) protects sages, and they become invincible (chap. 67).[13] Sages "practice the constant" and do not understand life's events using conventional discriminations.

The *DDJ* and Western Philosophy

Having looked carefully at some of the major concepts and themes of the *DDJ,* we are now ready to ask how this text might be appropriated for use in courses that have focused exclusively on Western traditions.

One approach is to use the *DDJ* to clarify questions in moral discussions. Some scholars think the *DDJ* dissolves all moral distinctions, setting them aside in a kind of moral nihilism or radical ethical relativism. However, while the text cautions repeatedly against following human moral discriminations, it also teaches that oneness with *dao* leads one to virtue (*de*). When we follow *dao*, we act in a way describable in moral concepts. While later Daoist traditions make these moral norms explicit,[14] it is true that the *DDJ* does not say humans should be activists or that we can save nature and humanity.[15]

We may consider another application of the *DDJ* by asking whether the text has a coherent epistemology, and if so, how it relates to versions of rationalism or empiricism with which we are familiar in Western philosophy and social science. The *DDJ* clearly warns against an overreliance on reason to achieve knowledge. This warning has led scholars to argue about whether the *DDJ* takes an antirationalist or irrationalist position, and how its concept of *wuwei* enters into conversation with Western epistemologies. Ames and Hall characterize its teachings as an "epistemology of feeling."[16] Chad Hansen believes we cannot understand the epistemology of the *DDJ* until we first come to grips with its radical "anti-language" dispositions.[17] And the work of Karen Carr and P. J. Ivanhoe explores the epistemologies of Daoism.[18]

Some *DDJ* themes seem to prevent certain Western intellectual problems and questions from arising, or at least require significant revisions of the way problems are framed. Consider one such problem already mentioned in our discussion of correlativity. While the traditional problem of evil is very much rooted in the particular forms of theism common to Western philosophy, the *DDJ* seems nonetheless to support another and distinctly different approach that is based on its understanding of correlativity. The problem of evil in the way we typically find it formulated in the West is not addressed. Reasons for this absence are far more complex than the simple fact that the *DDJ* has no concept of an all good, omniscient, and omnipotent God. More to the point is the fact that its correlative worldview puts aside the question of evil by dissolving it.

The correlative movements of *dao* undermine the use of the human distinctions of good and evil, success and tragedy, from the outset.[19]

Conclusion

In the system of symbolism expressed in the medieval coat of arms, the symbol of a carpenter's square is awarded to a person who is known for conforming his actions to the laws of right and equity—the square is an ancient instrument for measuring and marking straight lines and angles. Yet, like the uncarved wood that it so frequently valorizes, the *Daodejing* is itself a twisted and gnarled composite work. Through the centuries, its uses and applications have followed many turns and variations. We should be wary, therefore, of attempts to put too heavy hands onto the text and distort its messages in the interest of making it fit into a well-squared package of meanings.

Notes

1. Ming-dao Deng, *365 Tao Daily Meditations* (San Francisco: Harper Books, 1992), 25.
2. Bryan Van Norden considers the place of comparative philosophical study in his essay, "What Should Western Philosophy Learn from Chinese Philosophy?" in Philip J. Ivanhoe, *The "Daodejing" of Laozi* (New York, Seven Bridges Press, 2002), 224–50. See also Henry Rosemont, Jr., "Beyond Post-Modernism," in Ivanhoe, *"Daodejing" of Laozi*, 155–73. This is a clear and well-argued objection to the claim that cultural dependency means incommensurability.
3. Many readers will recognize that I am referring to the butcher Ding and the bell stand maker Qing from the *Zhuangzi*.
4. D. C. Lau, trans., *Tao Te Ching* (Baltimore: Penguin Books, 1963), chap. 25.
5. Philip J. Ivanhoe, "The Concept of *de* ('Virtue') in the Laozi," *Religious and Philosophical Aspects of the "Laozi,"* edited by Mark Csikszentmihalyi and Philip J. Ivanhoe (Albany: State University of New York Press, 1999), 239–55. Roger T. Ames, "Putting the *Te* Back into Taoism," in *Nature in Asian Traditions of Thought*, edited by J. Baird Callicott and Roger T. Ames (Albany: State University of New York Press, 1989), 113–44. David Nivison, "'Virtue' in Bone and Bronze," in *The Ways of Confucianism: Investigations in Chinese Philosophy* (Chicago: Open Court, 1996), 17–30.
6. Even so, we should not conclude that *de* here means that we should repay resentment by overlooking evil or showing some sort of sacrificial love. Later Daoist morality texts have a clear sense of justice and righteous indignation. So, to repay resentment with *de* may mean to recompense it with justice and fairness.

7. Edward Slingerland thinks that *wuwei* does not have to do with observable conduct or movement, but with the mental state of the agent. Edward Slingerland, *Effortless Action:* Wu wei *as Conceptual Metaphor and Spiritual Ideal in Early China* (New York: Oxford University Press, 2003), 7.

8. Slingerland thinks that this effect comes with an "almost supernatural efficacy." So, Slingerland calls *wuwei* a "religious ideal" according to which the individual realizes his place in the cosmos (ibid., 8).

9. The *DDJ* objects to an ethic imposed upon people from outside, not from that born out of unmediated *de* arising from oneness with *dao*.

10. Some other concepts that play prominent roles in the *DDJ* are: *he* 和 (chaps. 2, 4, 18, 35, 42, 49, 54, 55, 56, 77, 79); *qi* 氣 (chaps. 10, 12, 21, 25, 42, 43, 51, 52, 55, 59); *tian* 天 (chaps. 5, 7, 9, 16, 23, 25, 47, 59, 67, 73, 74, 77, 78, 81); *the One* (chaps. 10, 14, 22, 39, 42, 45, 46, 80); and *ziran* 自然 (chaps. 17, 23, 25, 51, 64).

11. Lau uses this fact as the main support for his argument against interpreters who find an affinity between the *DDJ* and the *Yijing*. He thinks that the passage in chapter 42 represents a "school" that is widely divergent from the main body of *DDJ* and thus may be set aside. Much of what Lau says depends on his view that the theory of change in the *Yijing* is cyclic. See Lau, *Tao Te Ching,* xli–xlii; and Lau, "The Treatment of Opposites in Lao Tzu," *Bulletin of the School of Oriental and African Studies* 21 (1958): 344–60. While Lau speaks of change as cyclical, in the *DDJ* this does not mean that cosmic processes repeat themselves or are reversible. See Roger T. Ames and David Hall, *Daodejing: "Making This Life Significant": A Philosophical Translation* (New York: Ballantine Books, 2003), 28.

12. A very useful comparison can be made by consulting the "Discussion on Making All Things Equal" chapter of the *Zhuangzi*.

13. Some other themes in the *DDJ* are: softness (suppleness) and weakness (chaps. 14, 36, 40, 43, 52, 55, 64, 66, 67, 68, 72, 73, 76, 78); rulership (chaps. 17, 19, 25, 26, 29, 30, 31, 32, 35, 37, 39, 45, 48, 49, 53, 54, 57, 58, 59, 60, 61, 62, 65, 66, 67, 68, 69, 72, 74, 75, 80); criticism of Confucianism (chaps. 18, 19, 20, 38, 48, 56, 70, 71, 81).

14. Erin Cline and Ronnie Littlejohn, "Taishan' s 泰山 Tradition: The Quantification and Prioritization of Moral Wrongs in a Contemporary Daoist Religion," *Dao: A Journal of Comparative Philosophy* 2 (2002): 117–40. Ronnie Littlejohn, "Transmission of the Chinese Moral Culture: Morality and Ledger Books in the World of Moral Self-Regulation," *Southeast Review of Asian Studies* 21 (1999): 15–31.

15. *Dao* is the most powerful force and should be followed, not interfered with. As such, Russell Kirkland discourages ethical activism. Russel Kirkland, "Responsible Non-Action" in a Natural World," in *Daoism and Ecology*, edited by N. J. Girardot, James Miller and Liu Xioagan (Cambridge, MA: Harvard University Press, 2001), 293. Holmes Welch thinks that this is why the *DDJ*'s ethic is too radical to apply to modern social and political problems. Holmes Welch, *Taoism: Parting of the Way* (Boston: Beacon Press, 1965), 164–78. For other interpretations, see Terry Kleeman, "Taoist Ethics," in *A Bibliographic Guide to the Comparative Study of Ethics*, edited by John Carman and Mark Juegensmayer (Cambridge: Cambridge University Press, 1991).

16. Ames and Hall, *Daodejing*, 108–9. A work of interest on Daoist epistemology is Cheng Chung-ying, "The Nature and Function of Skepticism in Chinese Philosophy," *Philosophy East and West* 27 no. 2 (1977) 137–54. Another intriguing

reading of *DDJ* epistemology based on its ontology is Tateno Masami, "A Philosophical Analysis of the *Laozi* from an Ontological Perspective," in *Religious and Philosophical Aspects of the "Laozi,"* edited by Mark Csikszentmihalyi and Philip J. Ivanhoe (Albany: State University of New York Press, 1999).

17. Chad Hansen, *A Daoist Theory of Chinese Thought* (New York: Oxford University Press, 1992), 211.

18. The work is principally on the *Zhuangzi*, but there are many applications of the findings of Carr and Ivanhoe to the *DDJ* as well. See Karen Carr and P. J. Ivanhoe, *The Sense of Antirationalism: The Religious Thought of Zhuangzi and Kierkegaard* (New York: Seven Bridges Press, 2000).

19. Ames and Hall think there is an implicit theory of evil in the worldview of the *DDJ* (Ames and Hall, *Daodejing*, 119–20).

Selected Readings on the *Daodejing*

Translations

A chronological list of the major English translations of the *DDJ* up to 1993 is in Livia Kohn and Michael LaFargue, *Lao-Tze and the "Tao-te-ching"* (Albany: State University of New York Press, 1998), 299–301.

Addiss, Stephen, and Stanley Lombardo. *Lao-Tzu, Tao Te Ching.* Indianapolis: Hackett Publishing Co., 1993.

Ames, Roger, and David Hall. *Daodejing: "Making This Life Significant," A Philosophical Translation.* New York: Ballantine Books, 2003.

Chan, Alan. *Two Visions of the Way.* Albany: State University of New York Press, 1991.

Chan, Wing-tsit. *The Way of Lao Tzu (Tao te ching).* Chicago: University of Chicago Press, 1963.

Henricks, Robert. *Lao-Tzu: Te-Tao Ching.* New York: Ballantine Books, 1989.

Ivanhoe, Philip J. *The "Daodejing" of Laozi.* New York: Seven Bridges Press, 2002.

LaFargue, Michael. *The Tao of the Tao-te-ching.* Albany: State University of New York Press, 1992.

Lau, D. C. *Chinese Classics: Tao Te Ching.* Hong Kong: Hong Kong University Press, 1982.

———, trans. *Tao Te Ching.* Baltimore: Penguin Books, 1963.

Legge, James, trans. *Tao Te Ching.* New York: Dover Publications, 1997.

Lynn, Richard John. *The Classic of the Way and Virtue: A New Translation of the "Tao-Te Ching" of Laozi as Interpreted by Wang Bi.* New York: Columbia University Press, 1999.

Mair, Victor. *Tao Te Ching: The Classic Book of Integrity and the Way.* New York: Bantam Press, 1990.

Mitchell, Stephen. *Tao Te Ching.* New York: Harper Collins, 1988.

Waley, Arthur. *The Way and Its Power: A Study of the "Tao Te Ching" and Its Place in Chinese Thought.* New York: Grove Weidenfeld, 1958.

Some Other Works

Allen, Sarah, and Crispin Williams. *The Guodian Laozi: Proceedings of the International Conference, Dartmouth College, May 1998*, Early China Special Monograph Series, no. 5. Berkeley, CA: University of California Institute of East Asia Studies, 1999.

Bebell, Damian, and Shannon Fera. "Comparison and Analysis of Selected English Interpretations of the "Tao Te Ching." *Asian Philosophy* 10, no. 2 (2000): 133–47.

Clarke, J. J. *The Tao of the West: Western Transformations of Taoist Thought.* London: Routledge, 2000.

Csikszentmihalyi, Mark, and Philip J. Ivanhoe. *Religious and Philosophical Aspects of the "Laozi."* Albany: State University of New York, 1999. (A collection of nine essays on the *DDJ*.)

Graham, Angus. *Disputers of the Tao: Philosophical Argument in Ancient China.* LaSalle, IL: Open Court, 1989.

Hansen, Chad. *A Daoist Theory of Chinese Thought.* New York: Oxford University Press, 1992.

Henricks, Robert. 1992. "On the Chapter Divisions in the 'Lao-tzu.'" *Bulletin of the School of Oriental and African Studies* 45, no. 3 (1992): 501–24.

Kaltenmark, Max. *Lao Tzu and Taoism.* Translated by Roger Greaves. Stanford, CA: Stanford University Press, 1969.

Kirkland, Russell. "'Responsible Non-Action' in a Natural World." In *Daoism and Ecology: Ways within a Cosmic Landscape*, edited by N. J. Girardot, James Miller, and Liu Xiaogan, 283-305. Cambridge, MA: Harvard University Press, 2001.

———. "Varieties of Taoism in Ancient China: A Preliminary Comparison of Themes in the *Nei Yeh* and Other Taoist Classics." *Taoist Resources* 7, no. 2 (1997): 73–86.

Kohn, Livia, and Michael LaFargue. *Lao-tzu and the "Tao-te-ching."* Albany: State University of New York Press, 1998.

LaFargue, Michael. *Tao and Method: A Reasoned Approach to the "Tao Te Ching."* Albany: State University of New York Press, 1994.

Lai, Karyn. "The 'Daodejing': Resources for Contemporary Feminist Thinking." *Journal of Chinese Philosophy* 27 no. 2. (2000): 131–53.

Littlejohn, Ronnie. "The *Daodejing* as a Ritual Text: Implications for Philosophical Interpretation." Paper presented at "Daoism and the Contemporary World: An International Conference on Daoist Studies" at Boston University, June 5–7, 2003.

Masami, Tateno. "A Philosophical Analysis of the *Laozi* from an Ontological Perspective." In *Religious and Philosophical Aspects of the "Laozi,"* edited by Mark Csikszentmihalyi and Philip J. Ivanhoe Albany: State University of New York, 1999.

Mou, Bo. "Moral Rules and Moral Experience: A Comparative Analysis of Dewey and Laozi on Morality." *Asian Philosophy* 11, no. 3. (2001): 161–78.

Owens, Wayne. "Tao and Difference: The Existential Implications." *Journal of Chinese Philosophy* 20, no. 3 (1993): 261–77.

Roberts, Moss. "The Metaphysical Polemics of the *Tao Te Ching*: An Attempt to Integrate the Ethics and Metaphysics of Lao Tzu." *Journal of the American Oriental Society* 95, no. 1 (1975): 36–42.

Robinet, Isabelle. *Taoism: Growth of a Religion.* Stanford, CA: Stanford University Press, 1997.

Roth, Harold. *Original Tao: Inward Training (*Nei Yeh*) and the Foundations of Taoist Mysticism*. New York: Columbia University Press, 1999.

Shuhai Wenyuan. http://kongzi.arthum.hawaii.edu:8080/index.html.

Slingerland, Edward. *Effortless Action:* Wu wei *as Conceptual Metaphor and Spiritual Ideal in Early China*. New York: Oxford University Press, 2003.

Wang, Qingjie. "On Lao Zi's Concept of 'Zi Ran.'" *Journal of Chinese Philosophy* 24, no. 3 (1997): 291–321.

Watson, Burton. *Chuang Tzu*. New York: Columbia University Press, 1968.

Welch, Holmes. *Taoism: Parting of the Way*. Boston: Beacon Press, 1965.

Robin R. Wang

Performing the Meanings of Dao: A Possible Pedagogical Strategy for Teaching Chinese Philosophy

In the opening paragraph of the *Daodejing*, the classical text of Daoism, Laozi claims: "The Dao that can be spoken is not the true Dao, the name that can be named is not the true name." This saying raises a profound problem, not only regarding the nature of language and how, if at all, it conveys meaning and truth, but also regarding the appropriateness of conventional conceptually oriented pedagogies for learning classical Chinese philosophical texts. As perhaps some *Daodejing*'s interpreters have assumed, Laozi's saying entails a reverential silence that remains skeptical that any insight can be gained from discursive analysis. If such an assumption were to be accepted, it necessarily would render any attempt to teach and learn the meanings of the *Daodejing* in a conventional philosophy classroom as highly questionable as it would be unauthentic and inappropriate. Students might get the all-too-common idea that *Laozi* is teaching us to go with the proverbial flow in which there are no wrong answers, and all insights, no matter how trivial or tangential, are equally valid.

The problems raised by the opening of the *Daodejing*, however, are not exclusive to trying to think authentically about the Dao. As recent translators of Chinese philosophical texts have noted, similar difficulties are to be encountered across the entire spectrum of the philosophical vocabulary of the Chinese classics.[1] While previous generations of translators in one way or another have attempted to make the classics seem more familiar by narrowing the differences between their meanings and those sanctioned by the Western canon of philosophical writings, contemporary scholars are seeking to restore a respect for the otherness of the Chinese philosophical tradition. But at what point—good intentions to the contrary notwithstanding—does respect for otherness force teachers and students of Chinese philosophy to lapse into the same kind of silence that once was reserved only for allegedly "mystical" writings? If Chinese classical texts like the *Daodejing* cannot be studied and rigorously analyzed, then how can we or should we include them in an academic curriculum?

It is the purpose of this essay to elaborate a possible model of an appropriate pedagogical strategy for interpreting the Chinese classics. It requires teachers and learners to set aside conventional and superficial approaches to studying and analyzing texts, in favor of an exploration of meanings that is open-ended, multivalent, and ambiguous. Such an exploration invites readers to pay as much attention to context as to text, and to what is not said as well as to what is said. This pedagogy will challenge the limitations of linear readings and parsings of classical texts in the classroom, and will enhance students' ability to develop a philosophical conception of the ancient "Dao language" (*daoyan*) in which the text's full range of meanings may be understood and appreciated.

The theoretical challenge afforded by the understanding of "Dao language" is usefully explored in an exchange between Zhang Xianlong and Merold Westphal comparing the philosophy of language elaborated in the later Heidegger with the writings of the *Laozi* and *Zhuangzi*. Zhang and Westphal agree that "Lao-Zhuang" thought, including in its evocation of "nonbeing," represents "a challenge, even a threat, to the ultimacy of ordinary discourse."[2] But they demonstrate convincingly that the appropriate response to that challenge is not a withdrawal into the silence afforded by either "skeptical relativism" or "mysticism" but rather a careful reconstruction of the performative or constitutive nature of the text itself.[3] Implicit in their theoretical reflections on what Lao-Zhuang thought may contribute to the philosophy of language is a pedagogical strategy that can actually enhance the teaching and learning of Chinese philosophical texts.

The path of understanding opened through the Dao that cannot be spoken suggests that teaching and learning Dao language can only be approached as a progressive initiation into the "great language" (*dayan*) that transcends, yet is immanent in, ordinary language. According to

Zhang and Westphal, Lao-Zhuang thought teaches a method for achieving this initiation. Based on Zhang's reading of the opening chapter of the *Daodejing*, the method can be formulated very succinctly as "great X not x."[4] While the "true Dao" (great *X*) "is not the *dao* that can be spoken" (not *x*), the *dao* that is spoken still may point us in the direction of true Dao. Similarly with *ming* (name), "the name that can be named is not the true name." In short, a genuinely philosophical approach to the Chinese classics must respect the ways in which ordinary language and conventional discourse are decentered, in order to achieve, as Zhang suggests "a non-representational, unconceptualizable view of language that is embodied in the great *dao* and the great language (*dayan*)."[5]

There are two components involved in the construction of this innovative approach. The first is its philosophical justification. Why is this pedagogy critical, if not imperative, to learning about Chinese classical texts, particularly Daoist works? As Roger Ames has observed correctly, the *Daodejing*, like many Chinese classics, invites its readers to an "inescapable process" in which "students through many readings of the text acquire their own unique understanding of its insights informed by their own life experience. . . ."[6] Each student will get out of it what he or she is willing or able to put into it. But for students in this particular culture, this process is shaped not only by the development of the academic study of Daoist philosophy, but also by over three hundred years of Western popular culture, which has appropriated these texts for its own purposes. *Dao* (*Tao*) is a term that evokes all sorts of images, from scientific discussions like that featured in the *Tao of Physics* to those generated in Hollywood movies like the *Tao of Steve*, from sage advice on how to live masquerading as a children's tale, as in the *Tao of Pooh*, to instructions in various arts seeking to deepen their own profundity, as in the *Tao of Photography*. Each of these has penetrated popular Western consciousness.

Our students thus come to the reading of Daoist texts with assumptions about Daoism that inevitably shape their initial appropriation of the texts. The teacher seeking to lead such students to a philosophical comprehension of Daoism is faced with a twofold challenge. He or she must guide them not only in learning, but also in unlearning what they assume they already know of Daoism. Otherwise, they will never even glimpse the possibility of *daoyan* as *dayan* insofar as their initial preconceptions rarely, if ever, transcend conventional truisms embedded in ordinary language. Thus, the contextual preconceptions that students bring to studying Daoism in the classroom, while rightly regarded as indispensable to the "inescapable process" described by Ames, may be as much a hindrance as a help in an appreciation of the text. In either case, there is no way to address students' assumptions without integrating pedagogies into the classroom that will allow them to explore critically the cultural context(s) of their own reflections. As Ames has suggested, "Knowledge is always proximate as the condition of an experience rather than of an isolated experiencer."[7] To become reflective in this way, of course, is one of the central tasks of all study in philosophy; but here it must be focused in a particular way to address the concrete problem our students face in interpreting classical Chinese philosophical texts. Thus, the familiar problem of preunderstanding, so well elaborated in the hermeneutical philosophy of Hans-Georg Gadamer's *Wahrheit und Methode*, requires that we become intentionally creative pedagogically.

The second component is the specific challenge of grasping the nature of Chinese classical texts. What genre conventions ought to be observed in seeking to appreciate Daoist works? Are the *Daodejing, Zhuangzi*, and the *Sunzi bingfa* (*The Art of War*) to be read, respectively, as philosophical works, collections of literature, or as military treatises? If so, how can they be studied for their contribution to a comprehensive understanding of Daoist philosophy? Victor Mair strongly argues, "To ignore the poetics of the *Chuang Tzu* [*Zhuangzi*] by treating it simply as a piece of philosophical prose would do it a grave injustice. . . . This is not some dry moralistic treatise, nor is it a demanding, philosophical disquisition. Rather, the sublime wisdom of the *Chuang Tzu* is imparted to us by poking holes in our conventional knowledge."[8] His claim may strike some as raising a prima facie objection to teaching the *Zhuangzi* as philosophy. If the text is no "demanding, philosophical disquisition," then are we not best advised to forgo any attempt at rigorous philosophical analysis? The answer, obviously, depends on what is recognized as philosophical analysis. Once again, following Zhang's and Westphal's suggestion that Dao language seeks to reveal the great language beyond ordinary language, we may usefully analyze the *Zhuangzi* as philosophy to the extent that we are prepared to discover and explore the distinctive ways in which the text's very unconventionality validates its own claim as *daoyan*. In this way, true to the text's own intentionality, appreciation of the *Zhuangzi* may assist students to participate in the deeper inquiry about the nature of philosophy and especially what it means to be doing philosophy. Otherwise, they will be left with the dilemma afforded by conventional assumptions about philosophical analysis: on the one hand, philosophy is restricted to a range of methods of argumentation, responsive mostly to the cognitive style canonized by the history of modern Western science; on the other hand, texts such as the *Zhuangzi*, rather than acknowledged as among the most valuable philosophical texts, are ignored or patronizingly relegated to so-called humanistic or interdisciplinary studies. Failure to confront this dilemma squarely, by pointing out its arbitrarily reductive assumptions, eventually will subvert any attempt to integrate not just Daoism, but also the Chinese intellectual tradition, into the study of philosophy.

The discussion of a philosophical justification for the pedagogy to teach Chinese philosophical texts leads to a practical question: How can it be done? In its third chapter, devoted to offensive strategy, the Chinese classical treatise on strategy and tactics *Sunzi bingfa* summarizes its advice to military commanders in a way that may also guide us to an appropriate pedagogy: "If you know both your opponents and yourself, you will fight a hundred battles and win a hundred battles; if you are ignorant of your opponents but only know yourself, your chances of winning and losing are equal; if you know neither your opponents nor yourself, you will certainly be defeated in every battle."[9] The hope that the *Sunzi bingfa*'s ancient wisdom will lead to success has stimulated many serious treatments of this work. Its precepts have been pondered and attempted in practice in a variety of contexts ranging from military academies to Fortune 500 business corporations, by both management trainees and athletes seeking to discipline their minds as well as their bodies for competition. Could the principles enunciated by the *Sunzi bingfa* two thousand years ago in such an utterly different cultural environment be of value and relevance in the twenty-first century classroom? Could the strategy developed in the *Sunzi bingfa* make a contribution to our search for a better way to teach Chinese philosophy? While it may be very unconventional to see the classroom as a battlefield (sometimes this may be the case), the dynamics and complexities of today's classroom require us to reflect about the strategies and tactics involved in an appropriately pedagogical design.

Teaching and learning create a space between teacher and learners that can be compared to a battlefield. But our opponents, if we are teachers, are not the students; nor are they teachers, if we are truly students. The opponent in the classroom is the subject matter to be understood and mastered. Teachers thus may usefully be compared with the military commanders addressed by Sunzi, and students may be regarded as the troops. Within the space created by their relationships of mutual dependence, the teacher must enable students to fulfill their own roles in achieving a common objective: the development, in this case, of a genuine philosophical discernment of the text.

The space in which teacher-students must fulfill their common mission is not simply the physical arrangement of the classroom, but also the boundaries of the subject matter, the emotional tone of the teacher-student relationships, and the degree of readiness by which they are prepared to collaborate in a successful process of philosophical reflection. Within this situation, viewed from the perspective of the teacher, there are three possible conditions:

1. You don't know yourself and don't know your students. This can only spell disaster.
2. You know yourself, yet don't know your students. Thus, you have only a fifty-fifty chance of having a good class.
3. You both know yourself and know your students. This is clearly the best condition, and it defines the hoped-for pedagogical outcome.

As the teachings of Sunzi clearly indicate, the greatest challenge for the teacher, like that of the military commander, is knowing oneself. This also is the point, if Socrates is to be believed, of taking up the study of philosophy in the first place. Teaching as a vocation is one of the most difficult and important of human endeavors. What is the role of the teacher in classroom? To what is teaching to be compared? Are we gardeners? Captains in a spaceship or tour guides on an intellectual bus trip? Knowing our role in the classroom is of the utmost importance. Conventionally, there are three possible ways to realize the role of the teacher: The teacher as expert, the teacher as formal authority, and the teacher as facilitator. With the first way, the teacher possesses knowledge and expertise that students need. We strive to maintain our status as experts among students by displaying detailed knowledge and by challenging students to enhance their competence. The role of an expert is concerned with transmitting information and ensuring that students are well prepared. With the second way, the teacher has a status recognized by students because of his or her delegated role as an authority. We establish learning goals, expectations, and rules of conduct for students. The role of formal authority is concerned with the correct, acceptable, and standard ways to do things and with providing students with the structure they need in order to learn. With the third way, the emphasis shifts to the personal nature of teacher-student interactions. We guide and direct students by asking questions, exploring options, suggesting alternatives, and encouraging them to develop criteria to make informed choices. The overall goal is to help students acquire the capacity for independent action and responsibility. The facilitator will work with students in a consultative fashion and will try to provide as much support and encouragement as possible.

While all of these teaching styles/roles have their own advantages and disadvantages, that of the facilitator might succeed the best for teaching non-Western—and especially Chinese—philosophy. This role generates the necessary space for teaching and learning by inviting students to participate in a dialogue in which they collaborate with the teacher to gain a better, deeper understanding of the subject matter. This collaborative approach is not only mutually beneficial, but also consistent with the nature of the common objective of a genuinely philosophical understanding—in this case, of *daoyan*—an open-ended quest in which the teacher's leadership is based on his or her own struggle for self-knowledge, and not primarily on either mere expertise or institutional authority. The facilitator's role is especially fitting in the study of Chinese philosophy where genuine discernment is inconceivable apart from the cultivation of a human heart as well as of a rigorous mind.

The *Sunzi bingfa* allows us to realize the importance of knowing ourselves as teachers, but also directs our attention to how indispensable it is to know our students. But how is it possible for us to know our students? In my own case, the challenge is especially formidable, since my own life experience has been very different from theirs. Thus, I have employed different strategies to get a glimpse of students' basic knowledge, perspectives, and overall abilities.

One strategy is homework assignments. Prior to each classroom meeting, I assign students two questions about the readings. This gives me a reality check on their comprehension of the subject matter, our common "opponent," to recall Sunzi's teaching once more. Thus, I know how much students take in the readings and how much they do not, or whether they have missed something. It also gives students a first exposure to the material so we can use class time more effectively. Instead of introducing the content in a conventional lecture format, we can get into major issues at the beginning.

Another strategy is student presentation. Each student in my Chinese philosophy class has to do one presentation for the course. Classes normally start with a student's presentation. The presenters for the class are asked to deal with three general questions:

1. What are the main arguments of the reading?
2. What is the most interesting point of the reading?
3. What questions or issues does this reading raise that merit further discussion and evaluation? What questions should we ask in order to advance our understanding of the text and the issues?

Each presenter has to pose two questions and then lead the class discussion. This usually takes fifteen minutes of class time, though sometimes it can go on for thirty. The students' presentations and discussion give teachers a good sense of their level of comprehension and provide important background and context for the lecture.

This pedagogical design allows the teacher to address whatever thought pattern may be emerging from class discussion. Deliberately opening the space for teaching and learning in this way can often be risky. One does not know where it may go, yet it could be more exciting, because teachers could discover something unforeseen about the text and their students. Such calculated risks, however, were well understood by Sunzi, whose teachings clearly emphasized the advantages of an appropriate flexibility that flows from genuine knowledge, not only of oneself, but also of one's students and the specific challenges of mastering texts. Such flexibility is far less likely to confuse actual progress in learning *daoyan* with routine measures of success in extracting and analyzing concepts. The teacher's success in enabling such flexibility in herself and her students is perhaps the most effective performance of the *dayan* to be discovered in the Daoist texts themselves.

Here is a modest example, illustrating how my students often exceed their own expectations by following the path of open-ended understanding. It concerns an attempt to teach Xunzi's view of the role of ritual in the cultivation of human nature. According to Xunzi, human nature is bad (*xinge*). The transformation of a human being into a moral being relies on ritual practice. However, ritual is a remote concept for many students, because in their world rituals are viewed as restrictions, as obstacles to personal freedom. But rituals, in Xunzi's view, are not intended to eliminate or diminish human desire; they are to cultivate, train, and refine our desires. Rituals place limits on how much and in what ways one may seek the fulfillment of one's own desires. One of my students gave the following example in his presentation to illustrate his own appreciation of Xunzi's view. He observed that often a young man has the desire to get some attention or win admiration from the woman he likes. But he is often at a loss, since by nature he is a somewhat unrefined person. Nevertheless, he will try very hard to follow certain rituals—be proper and act like a gentleman—even if he does not normally do so. After a few successes obeying the rituals, he continues to perform them. Eventually, he becomes so used to acting in this proper way that it turns out to be a part of his own disposition. The student giving this example used his own experience to overcome his aversion to rituals, and thus established a better way to value Xunzi's view. I could never have come up with this sort of example.

To be sure, such effective outcomes are not automatic. There is a Chinese saying worth recalling here: "Teaching with a target is just like suiting the medicine to the illness and making the clothes fit the body." The pedagogical examples I have just given can also produce problems that require "teaching with a target." The problem I run into is the unevenness of the quality of student presentations. Sometimes they are excellent, but at other times students show little intellectual curiosity and learn only what is required. Their presentations not only are poorly organized but also fail to stimulate any thinking for the discussion. In such cases, students seem to be trying to shift the classroom away from the approach I have described and back to the conventional learning styles involved in the acquisition of mere information and expertise. If they succeed in derailing the facilitator's approach, they usually end up failing even in their own minimalist objectives for learning. In these situations, the teacher, like Sunzi's successful military commander, has to become skilled at how effectively to monitor his or her troops. I respond to such challenges by giving specific guidelines, set boundaries, and make the extra effort to redirect the students' attention, until once again they are prepared to work fruitfully with something more demanding and open-ended.

I would like to conclude these reflections with a story told by a Buddhist monk named Shi Sengyou of the Liang dynasty (502–57 CE). Once when the musician Gongming Yi was playing a lute, he saw a cow munching grass nearby. He thought that maybe he could play some music for the cow. He began to play an exquisite melody, but the cow took no notice of him and continued to munch grass. "How can I expect a cow to understand this kind of profound music?" he wondered. Gongming Yi came to a realization. He began to play another melody that imitated the buzzing of the mosquitoes and the cry of a calf. The cow wagged its tail, pricked its ears, and began to listen attentively. This story later became the basis for a proverb familiar to generations of Chinese teachers: when teaching one should avoid the situation of *Dui niu tan qing* ("Playing the lute to the cow") or, as it might be rendered in English equivalent, "casting pearls before swine." Of course, this story does not imply that we have to sacrifice our academic standards for students' interests. In fact, a teacher should be like a musician and play the melody according to the ability of the audience. There are some inner forces that disconnect us from our students and our subject matter, and there are certain inner practices that can overcome these forces, so that teachers and students work together in a successful process of mastering the subject matter. In teaching the classics of Chinese philosophy, the one key is to acquire a pedagogy that is consistent as performance with the way of understanding opened up by the texts. The reflections about this pedagogy are the results of one ongoing experiment in seeking to achieve the harmony between pedagogical theory and the practice of learning together the meanings of Dao.

Notes

1. See Roger T. Ames and David L. Hall, *Focusing the Familiar: A Translation and Philosophical Interpretation of the "Zhongyong"* (Honolulu: University of Hawaii Press, 2001); and Roger T. Ames and David L. Hall, *Daodejing: A Philosophical Translation* (New York: Ballantine Books, 2003). The glossaries developed in these translations try to rescue the Chinese philosophical vocabulary from all-too-easy comparisons with certain benchmarks in the history of Western philosophy.
2. Robin R. Wang, ed., *Chinese Philosophy in an Era of Globalization* (Albany: State University of New York Press, 2004), 22.
3. Speaking on behalf of Zhang as well as his own views, Westphal offers the following observation: "Beyond the skeptical relativism which uses language to establish its own superiority to language that it judges to be inadequate, and on this side of the intuitionism and mysticism which give up on language without giving up on the Ultimate, the *dao* speaks. In spite of the relativism and the mysticism which, in giving up on human language, render the Ultimate mute, the *dao* speaks. That is the central point, which Zhang seeks to reinforce with his second theme. Both Heidegger and Lao-Zhuang give a prominence to non-being in their thinking that is atypical of the contexts in which they have emerged. But they do not, Zhang insists, give priority to non-being; they are not ontological nihilists. Their view is better described as the 'mutual evocation' of being and non-being. Like Hegel, they find being and non-being unthinkable apart from each other. To be sure, their talk of non-being is a challenge, even a threat, to the ultimacy of ordinary discourse. But it does not signify a first principle, nor is non-being some kind of substance. Rather, they use the language of non-being, in its reciprocity with the language of being, for two purposes: first, to undermine conceptual-representational thought, which takes being to be a first principle and, in some form or other, a substance; and second, in this way to clear the way for something better, 'to manifest an original, pure region of language or *dao*-language' so that 'we will be able to hear the surging call of this region itself.'" "Speech from Beyond the Reach of Language: A Response to Zhang Xianglong" by Merold Westphal in Wang, *Chinese Philosophy*, 222.
4. Here is Zhang's complete explanation of the formula: "There are many examples in the *Zhuangzi* of *dao* being used in the sense of '*dao*-language.' For instance, in the chapter 'The Sorting which Evens Things Out,' we find: 'The greatest *dao* does not commend, / the greatest discrimination is unspoken, / the greatest benevolence is non-benevolent, / . . . Who knows an unspoken discrimination, an untold *dao*? It is this, if any is able to know it, which is called the Treasury of Heaven.' This is a method often used in ancient Chinese texts, and particularly in the *Laozi* and *Zhuangzi*, to express subtle meanings: give a series of parallel sentences, each one containing the structure 'great X not x' or something very like it. The X refers to the meaning that transcends dualisms and cannot be expressed using conceptual language; the x refers to the meaning that is still trapped in dualistic, conceptual language. 'X' and 'x' are sometimes the same word, as in 'great benevolence is non-benevolent' and 'highest virtue is not virtuous'; other times different but similar words are used such as 'discrimination' and 'speak' or '*dao*' and 'commend.' Therefore, saying 'The greatest *dao* does not commend' makes clear that

in Zhuangzi's mind, '*dao*' and 'commend' are close in meaning, and have connotations of 'say' or 'speak.'" Relying on this meaning, Zhuangzi uses 'the greatest *dao* does not commend' or 'the greatest *dao* does not *dao*" to deny that the great *dao* can be expressed as an object of conceptual language ('commend,' 'small way,' 'small name'), and to disclose the primordial and spoken nature of *dao* itself" Zhang Xianglong, "Heidegger's View of Language and Lao-Zhuang's view of Dao-Language" in Wang, *Chinese Philosophy,* 208).

5. Ibid., 204.
6. Ames and Hall, *Daodejing,* 8.
7. Roger T. Ames, *Wandering at Ease in the "Zuangzi"* (Albany: State University of New York Press, 1998), 73.
8. Victor H. Mair, *Wandering on the Way: Early Taoist Tales and Parables of Chuang Tzu* (Honolulu: University of Hawaii Press, 1954), xii, xiv.
9. My translation. See *Sun-Tzu: The Art of Warfare,* translated, with an introduction and commentary by Roger Ames (New York: Ballantine Books, 1993), 113.

Suggested Readings

Ames, Roger T. and David L. Hall. *Daodejing: "Making This Life Significant," A Philosophical Translation.* New York: Ballantine Books, 2003.
———. *Wandering at Ease in the "Zhuangzi."* Albany: State University of New York Press, 1998.
Ames, Roger T., trans. *Sun-Tzu: The Art of Warfare.* New York: Ballantine Books, 1993.
Allinson, Robert. *Understanding the Chinese Mind: The Philosophical Roots.* Oxford University Press, 1993.
Mair, Victor H. *Wandering on the Way: Early Taoist Tales and Parables of Chuang Tzu.* Honolulu: University of Hawaii Press, 1994.
Wang, Robin R., ed. *Chinese Philosophy in an Era of Globalization.* Albany: State University of New York Press, 2004.

Xinyan Jiang

Mengzi:
Human Nature Is Good

Mengzi (371?–289? BCE) is one of the best-known Confucian philosophers, and second only to Kongzi. In China he is called "*yasheng*" (Number Two Sage). In one sense, his philosophical influence on the later development of Confucianism even has been greater than that of Kongzi himself. The *Book of Mengzi* provides much more systematic elaborations of Confucianism and puts forward some novel ideas that were widely accepted later on and served as the foundation of Neo-Confucianism. Mengzi's most famous idea is that human nature is originally good. Understanding his view of human nature is the key to the comprehension of his whole philosophy. It is on the basis of his theory of human nature that Mengzi justifies the virtuous life and argues for the kingly way or benevolent government.

To help beginning students to learn and newcomers from the faculty ranks to teach Mengzi's text, in this essay I would like to offer a step-by-step guide to Mengzi's theory of human nature with references to relevant passages in the *Book of Mengzi*. The essay consists of the following subsections: (1) What does Mengzi mean by "human nature?" (2) In what sense does Mengzi believe that human nature is good? (3) Why are there bad human beings in society according to Mengzi? In the process of answering these questions, various interpretations of Mengzi's texts are discussed.

What does Mengzi mean by "human nature?"

In Mengzi's text there is not a single passage that clearly states what Mengzi means by "human nature," but we can see what he refers to by "human nature" by analyzing various relevant passages in context. A well-accepted view among scholars in Chinese philosophy on this matter is that in Mengzi's text "human nature" refers to the special nature of human beings that differentiates human beings from other animals.[1] In human beings, there are some elements humans share with other animals, such as desires for food, shelter, and sex. For Mengzi, these elements should not be considered part of the nature of human beings. Human nature is not what human beings happen to be born with, but only that which makes them different from other beings. Mengzi makes this point when he argues against Gaozi (告子), a contemporary of Mengzi who is well known for arguing that human nature is what human beings are born with and that human nature is morally neutral. The following is a debate between Gaozi and Mengzi: "Gaozi said: 'What is inborn is called nature.' Mengzi said, 'When you say that what is inborn is called nature, is that like saying that white is white?' 'Yes.' 'Then is the whiteness of the white feather the same as the whiteness of snow? Or, again, is the whiteness of snow the same as the whiteness of white jade?' 'Yes.' 'Then is the nature of a dog the same as the nature of an ox, and is the nature of an ox the same as the nature of a man?'" (*Mengzi* 6A3).[2]

What Mengzi is showing is that each species has its own special nature and that it is absurd to regard the common features of different species as their nature. Apparently, Gaozi could have maintained that precisely because what is inborn is called nature, he does not have to commit himself to the seeming absurdity that the nature of an ox is the same as the nature of human beings, since what is inborn in an ox is not the same as what is inborn in human beings. But, given Gaozi's naturalist position, which defines what is inborn in terms of basic instinctual demands, Gaozi hardly can distinguish human nature from animal nature in general.[3] Gaozi said: "By nature, we desire food and sex" (*Mengzi* 6A4, trans. Chan 52). If the desire for food and sex is what he calls "human nature," he indeed has to say that a dog, an ox, and a human being have the same nature. For Mengzi, as far as basic instinctual demands are concerned, human beings are very similar to animals. "Slight is the difference between man and brutes. The common man loses this distinguishing feature, while the gentleman retains it" (*Mengzi* 4B19).[4] So, according to Tu Wei-ming, "in Mengzi's opinion, the proposition that human nature is what we, as human beings, are born with cannot fully account for the something that is inherent in each of us as the defining characteristic of our being human. The proposition is too general to appreciate the unique human quality that is not explainable in terms of the animal instincts that we seem to share with oxen and dogs."[5]

For Mengzi, human nature consists of the special feelings and abilities of human beings that are, in fact, common features of all human minds. In arguing that there are indeed common features shared by all human minds, Mengzi says that things of the same kind are all alike. For example, all human feet are similar, and this is why all shoes are alike. When someone makes a shoe for a foot he has not seen, he will not produce a basket. Although there are differences between different people's feet, all human feet have something in common. Such a common feature makes human feet not something else. The same is true of human mouths, ears, and eyes. Therefore, "there is a common taste for flavor in our mouths, a common sense for sound in our ears, and a common sense for beauty in our eyes" (*Mengzi* 6A7, trans. Chan 56). Similarly, human minds must also share something in common. What is common to all human minds is the sense of principle and righteousness (*li yi* 理義). Principle and righteousness please our minds just as meat pleases our palates (*Mengzi* 6A7).

Clearly, Mengzi believes that all human beings share something that is lacking in animals and any other beings. Such unique human qualities constitute what he refers to as "human nature."

In What Sense Does Mengzi Believe that Human Nature Is Good?

Although Mengzi believes that unique human qualities are good, he does not think that people may be perfectly virtuous without moral cultivation. By "human nature is good" Mengzi does not mean that every person is born moral and that every person is naturally virtuous. What he means is that in human beings there are some dispositions that incline human beings toward behaving and feeling in moral ways. According to Mengzi, the human being is disposed to goodness just as water is disposed to flow downward. Again, this point of Mengzi is seen clearly in his argument against Gaozi:

Gaozi said, "Man's nature is like whirling water. If a breach in the pool is made to the east it will flow to the east. If a breach is made to the west it will flow to the west. Man's nature is indifferent to good and evil, just as water is indifferent to east and west." Mengzi said, "Water, indeed, is indifferent to the east and west, but is it indifferent to high and low? Man's nature is naturally good just as water naturally flows downward. There is no man without this good nature; neither is there water that does not flow downward. Now you can strike water and cause it to splash upward over your forehead, and by damming and leading it, you can force it uphill. Is this the nature of water? It is the forced circumstance that makes it do so. Man can be made to do evil, for his nature can be treated in the same way." (*Mengzi* 6A2, trans. Chan 52)

By talking about water, Gaozi is trying to show that there is no essential disposition to good or evil in human beings, and it is equally natural for people to be good or evil. For Mengzi, even water has a disposition toward a particular direction—that is, being disposed to flow downward, not upward. By his water analogy, Mengzi argues that human beings do have dispositions and that human nature is not neutral. According to Mengzi, human beings not only have dispositions in a certain direction but also are disposed toward goodness or virtues. Each human being can be virtuous if his or her dispositions toward virtues are nurtured and developed. Virtues are developed from these dispositions, just as a tree grows from the seed, or a flower from the bud. Human beings have the seeds of virtues inside, and if the environment is right and these seeds of virtues develop, they will become virtuous people: "If you let people follow their feelings (original nature), they will be able to do good. This is what is meant by saying that human nature is good. If man does evil, it is not the fault of his natural endowment" (*Mengzi* 6A6, trans. Chan 54). By now we can see clearly that Mengzi's claim that human nature is good is about the goodness of human dispositions and not the perfection of innate virtue. Given such an understanding of Mengzi's belief in the original goodness of human nature, we are ready to comprehend his theory of the Four Beginnings.

Benevolence or humanity (*ren* 仁),[6] righteousness (*yi* 義), propriety (*li* 禮), and wisdom (*zhi* 智) are the four main Confucian virtues. According to Mengzi, human dispositions that progress toward virtues are grounded in four kinds of feelings or senses that are the starting points for the above four virtues, which Mengzi calls the "Four Beginnings." The Four Beginnings are: the feeling of commiseration, which is the beginning of benevolence; the feeling of shame and dislike, which is the beginning of righteousness; the feeling of deference and compliance, which is the beginning of propriety; and the feeling of right and wrong, which is the beginning of wisdom. These four beginnings are found in all human beings (*Mengzi* 2A6 and 6A6).

As far as the feeling of commiseration is concerned, it has been well explained by Mengzi in this passage: "When I say that all men have the mind which cannot bear to see the suffering of others, my meaning may be illustrated thus: Now, when men suddenly see a child about to fall into a well, they all have a feeling of alarm and distress, not to gain friendship with the child's parents, nor to seek the praise of their neighbors and friends, nor because they dislike the reputation [of lack of humanity if they did not rescue the child]" (*Mengzi* 2A6, trans. Chan 65). Mengzi emphasizes not only that we feel distressed when we see a child about to fall into a well, but also that our distress is not the result of our deliberation but of something spontaneous.[7] Therefore, we must have the feeling of commiseration within us. Such a feeling is not benevolence, yet it makes benevolence possible. When one cannot bear to see the suffering of others, one might not necessarily take any action to relieve the suffering of others, but one at least will have the desire to do so. The feeling of commiseration is a necessary, although not sufficient, condition for benevolence. A truly benevolent person must have such a feeling, although it is not the case that each person who has such a feeling is necessarily benevolent. Such a feeling is a starting point of benevolence; without it, benevolence is impossible.

The feeling of shame and dislike is a shared human sentiment or emotion that is connected with righteousness. Righteousness is living up to ethical standards and never doing what is not right. How could the feeling of shame and dislike be the beginning of righteousness? For Mengzi, by nature, human beings dislike what is not right and feel ashamed of wrongdoing by themselves or by those who are related intimately to them. Obviously, disliking what is wrong makes people feel ashamed if they or those who are close to them do what is wrong—that is, what they hate. The feeling of shame is painful; it not only makes people feel bad after they, or those to whom they are emotionally close, have done something very shameful, but also prevents people from doing what they regard as shameful in the future. Since dislike and shame are connected with doing wrong, to avoid what is shameful and what is disgusting is to avoid doing what is wrong. Therefore, the feeling of shame and dislike can prevent people from doing what is wrong (*pu yi*). The feeling of shame and dislike can be so powerful that it may prevent one from doing or accepting what is wrong, even at the cost of one's life. To illustrate this point, Mengzi says the following:

> I like life and I also like righteousness. If I cannot have both of them, I shall give up life and choose righteousness. . . . There are cases when a man does not take the course even if by taking it he can preserve his life, and he does not do anything even if by doing it he can avoid danger. Therefore there is something men love more than life and there is something men hate more than death. It is not only the worthies alone who have this moral sense. All men have it, but only the worthies have been able to preserve it. Suppose here are a small basket of rice and a platter of soup. With them one will survive and without them one will die. If you offer them in a loud and angry voice, even an ordinary passer-by will not accept them, or if you first tread them and then offer them, even a beggar will not stoop to take them. (*Mengzi* 6A10, trans. Chan 57–58)

According to Mengzi, all human beings have a feeling of shame and dislike. Their love for what is right and hatred for what is wrong make their righteousness possible. Therefore, the feeling of shame and dislike is the beginning of righteousness.

Among the four beginnings, or four feelings, the feeling of deference and compliance is the one Mengzi explains the least. Perhaps this absence is explained by its obvious connection with propriety. Propriety requires proper conduct, attitude, and emotion toward others as well as toward oneself. Such a virtue has to start with some kind of feeling of respect. The feeling of deference and compliance is such a feeling.

Then, what is the feeling of right and wrong? According to Mengzi, by intuition human beings can feel that certain things are right and certain things wrong. One's feeling of right and wrong may not always be correct—one may feel a certain thing is right when it is actually wrong, but the feeling is the starting point to make correct distinctions between right and wrong. When one has attained moral knowledge and is able to distinguish correctly between right and wrong under any circumstance, one has the virtue of wisdom. One's moral cultivation and education are necessary for one to eventually attain moral knowledge, but such a process may start from a place where the distinction between right and wrong has been made only approximately. Clearly, the feeling of right and wrong is not wisdom itself, but it is indeed the beginning of wisdom. One's feeling of right and wrong sets up a moral standard for one's life and provides reasons for one to desire what is right and hate what is wrong. The feeling of right and wrong not only helps one distinguish right from wrong, but also makes one feel that the right ought to be done and the wrong ought not to be done. So, the feeling of right and wrong has both cognitive and emotional sides.[8]

As far as the feeling of right and wrong is concerned, Mengzi does not argue much for it, but his followers subsequently do. For example, Wang Yang-ming (1472–1528), a Neo-Confucian, argues that each person has innate or intuitive knowledge of what is right and what is wrong and that to be moral is essentially to make fully manifest such innate knowledge. There is a story showing how plausible this idea may be. It was said that a follower of Wang once caught a thief in his house at night, whereupon he gave him a lecture about intuitive moral knowledge. The thief laughed and asked: "Tell me, please, where is my intuitive knowledge?" At that time the weather was hot, so the thief's captor invited him first to take off his jacket, then his shirt, and then continued: "It is still too hot. Why not take off your trousers too?" At this moment, the thief hesitated and replied: "That does not seem to be quite right." Thereupon his captor shouted at him: "There is your intuitive knowledge!"[9] Common sense suggests many people do not have a sense of right and wrong, but this story shows that this may not be true. Although different people may have different criteria of what is right and what is wrong, they may all have a sense of right and wrong and therefore believe that there are certain things that they should do and certain things that they should not do.

To summarize, this section shows that Mengzi believes that human nature is good in the sense that human beings are disposed to be morally good. What makes human beings so disposed are four feelings: commiseration, shame and dislike, deference and compliance, and right and wrong. These feelings are called the Four Beginnings. We may think of them as seeds of virtues inside all human beings. If people let those seeds of virtues grow by appropriate cultivation, they will become virtuous.

Why Are There Bad Human Beings in Society According to Mengzi?

Mengzi admits that there are people in society who do not have compassion for others and who do evil things without feeling they are wrong. How can he explain this phenomenon if he insists that each human being originally has the Four Beginnings? In dealing with this problem, Mengzi argues that the reason why some people in society do wrong is not that they lack the original Four Beginnings in their nature, but they have lost their nature because of both external and internal causes.

First, external reasons may cause loss of the goodness of human nature. The most important external force for this is the environment in which one grows up and lives. Although human nature is disposed to morality, a person can be made bad by an external force, just as water can be forced to go uphill (Mengzi 6A:2). Although human nature is the same in everyone, some may behave differently under different environmental circumstances. To make this point, Mengzi uses several analogies.

One analogy Mengzi uses concerns barley. When the same kind of barley seed is sown and there is any unevenness in harvest yield, "it is because the soil varies in richness and there is no uniformity in the fall of rain and dew and the amount of human effort devoted to tending it" (*Mengzi* 6A7, trans. Lau 164). As the barley seeds all have the same potential to grow, human beings have the same nature, but their potential might be developed in different degrees under different circumstances: "In good years the young men are mostly lazy, while in bad years they are mostly violent. Heaven has not sent down men whose endowment differs so greatly. The difference is due to what ensnares their hearts" (*Mengzi* 6A7, trans. Lau 164). Such a difference in behavior clearly is not caused by the difference in human nature but by differences in the environment. The same point is illustrated by the metaphor of Niu Mountain:

> The trees of Niu Mountain were once beautiful. But can the mountain be regarded any longer as beautiful since, being on the border of a big state, the trees have been hewed down with axes and hatchets? Still, with the rest given them by the days and nights, and nourishment provided them by the rains and the dew, they were not without buds and sprouts springing forth. But then the cattle and the sheep pastured upon them once and again. That is why the mountain looks so bald. When people see that it is so bald, they think that there was never any timber on the mountain. Is this the true nature of the mountain? Is there not [also] a heart of humanity and righteousness originally existing in man? The way in which he loses his originally good mind is like the way in which trees are hewed down with axes and hatchets. (*Mengzi* 6A8, trans. Chan 56)

This metaphor of Niu Mountain shows bad behavior does not indicate that people are not originally good, just as the mountain's being bald now does not prove that it is not the nature of the mountain to grow buds and sprouts. This metaphor suggests further that despite their original good nature people might become bad and remain bad as a result of external forces, just as the mountain became bald as the result of overwhelming external destruction and cannot restore its original beauty unless its environment is changed. The point is that just as certain external conditions are necessary for the mountain to maintain its original natural beauty, so the economic, social, and political environment is extremely important for preserving and developing good human nature: "Therefore with proper nourishment and care, everything grows, whereas without proper nourishment and care, everything decays" (*Mengzi* 6A8, trans. Chan 57).

Second, there is something within each human being that may contribute to the loss of the original goodness of human nature. According to Mengzi, the maintenance and growth of the goodness in one's nature requires one's constant effort, because there is also something in people that may drive them to immorality. Although for Mengzi human nature is good in the sense that unique human qualities incline us to be moral, part of the innate nature of human beings is shared with animals and may lead to evil. What we share with animals is certain natural desires and instincts for material and physical needs. These desires and instincts are not evil in themselves, but the pursuit of the satisfaction of them without regulation will make people part from morality. Therefore, to be virtuous, one needs to build up the nobler part of his or her nature and overcome the lower part. The reason why some people become moral but some do not given similar environments, is that they do not cultivate their inner selves to the same degree. So Mengzi believes: "Those who follow the greater qualities in their nature become great men and those who follow the smaller qualities in their nature become small men. . . . If we first build up the nobler part of our nature, then the inferior part cannot overcome it. It is simply this that makes a man great" (*Mengzi* 6A15, tran. Chan 59). Mengzi has shown clearly that human nature is originally good, but it can be lost if it is not nurtured. So, the fact that in society some people do not have moral inclinations does not falsify the claim that human nature is originally good. For Mengzi, all human beings, no matter whether they are sages or common people, have the same nature. Every human being has the potential to become a moral sage. So he says that every person can become a sage like Yao or Shun (*Mengzi* 6B2).

For Mengzi, moral development starts with the goodness of human nature, but it requires a long term of cultivation to complete the process. In the course of the process of growth of the innate goodness, one gains greater and greater moral strength. When one achieves a high level of moral perfection, one will obtain what Mengzi called *hao ran zhi qi* (浩然之氣 floodlike *qi* or energy). Although *qi* (氣 vital energy or force) was used widely in Chinese philosophy before Mengzi, *hao ran zhi qi* is a term invented by Mengzi.[10] According to Mengzi, the floodlike *qi* is not a kind of ordinary vital force. It unites the moral ideal with physical force. It is, to the highest degree, vast and unyielding. *Qi* is accompanied by righteousness and the Way, and is produced by the accumulation of righteous deeds but not by incidental acts of righteousness (*Mengzi* 2A2). As one's moral strength grows, one is able to perform more and more difficult moral actions. The person who has obtained floodlike *qi* displays great moral courage and is able to face great dangers with an unmovable mind for the sake of righteousness.[11] Eventually, one will be an ideally moral person: "When he achieves his ambition he shares these with the people; when he fails to do so he practices the Way alone. He cannot be led into excesses when wealthy and honoured, or deflected from his purpose when poor and obscure, nor can he be made to bow before superior force. This is what I would call a great man" (*Mengzi* 3B2, trans. Lau 10). The morally ideal person portrayed above has been the moral inspiration of Chinese intellectuals for more than two thousand years and still inspires, and continues to inspire, the Chinese, especially Chinese intellectuals, to take moral responsibility and maintain integrity under any circumstance.[12]

Given what has been presented in this section, we can see that Mengzi's optimistic view of human nature is consistent with his emphasis on moral self-cultivation, moral education, and social reform. The original goodness of human nature only serves as the beginning of moral development. One can be truly virtuous only if appropriate external and internal conditions for one's moral development are satisfied.

In the three sections above, I have outlined Mengzi's view on human nature.[13] I hope that such an outline will initiate beginners into Mengzi's philosophy and even incite some to pursue Mengzi studies in depth. There is already a huge body of literature on Mengzi, and in looking through it interested readers will find that Mengzi is one of the Chinese philosophers who offers much of what contemporary philosophers, especially moral philosophers, seek.

Notes

1. See Fung Yu-lan, *A Short History of Chinese Philosophy* (New York: Macmillan, 1948), 69.
2. Here I follow Wing-Tsit Chan's translation in *A Source Book in Chinese Philosophy* (Princeton, NJ: Princeton University Press, 1963), 52.
3. See Tu Wei-ming, *Humanity and Self-Cultivation: Essays on Confucian Thought* (Berkeley, CA: Asian Humanities Press, 1978), 60.
4. Here I follow D. C. Lau's translation in *Mencius* (New York: Penguin Books, 1970), 131.
5. Tu, *Humanity and Self-Cultivation*, 60–61.
6. There are various translations of *ren*. However, the interpretation of the word might be summarized as follows: in a broader sense, *ren* refers to the total of virtue or perfect virtue; and in a narrower sense, *ren* means love of others (see Fung, *Short History*, 42–43). In Mengzi's text, *ren* is more often used in the narrow sense. So, I translate *ren* as "benevolence" in most cases. For more detailed discussion on *ren* in Mengzi, see Kwong-loi Shun, *Mencius and Early Chinese Thought* (Stanford, CA: Stanford University Press, 1997), 49.
7. D. C. Lau highlights this point in "Theories of Human Nature in Mengzi and Xunzi," reprinted in *Virtue, Nature, and Moral Agency in the Xunzi*, edited by T. C. Kline III and Philip J. Ivanhoe (Indianapolis: Hackett Publishing Company, 2000), 196. Lau's paper, under the title "Theories of Human Nature in Mencius

and Shyuntzyy," originally appeared in the *Bulletin of the School of Oriental and African Studies* 15 (1953).

8. See Lau, 2000, 194.

9. Fung, *Short History*, 313.

10. Ibid., 78.

11. I have discussed in detail Mengzi's view on courage in "Mengzi on Human Nature and Courage," *Journal of Chinese Philosophy* 24 (1997): 265–89, reprinted in *Essays on the Moral Philosophy of Mengzi*, ed. Xiusheng Liu (Indianapolis: Hackett Publishing, 2002), 143–62.

12. For a more detailed discussion of Mengzi's view on responsibility, see my paper, entitled "Mencius' View on Moral Responsibility," in *The Examined Life— Chinese Perspectives*, ed. Xinyan Jiang (Binghamton, NY: Global Publications, SUNY Binghamton, 2002), 141–59.

13. My understanding of Mengzi's theory of human nature presented in this paper to a great degree has been inspired by Professor Kwong-loi's lecture on Mengzi given in a class on Chinese philosophy offered at the University of California-Berkeley in Spring 1993.

JAPAN

Brian Schroeder

The Dilemma of Dōgen

Our Dilemma

Zen evokes a wide range of connotations—paradoxical, nonsensical, irrational, mystical, religious, meditative, stoic, humorous, and even comical—but only occasionally is it initially associated with philosophy. This lack of association is somewhat understandable, given that philosophy generally refers to rational argumentation and various metaphysical and epistemological methods for attaining truth and knowledge. Indeed, in its popular conception, Zen seems to be almost the very antithesis of philosophy; it focuses rather on the attainment of "enlightenment," which is more often than not vaguely conceived as "becoming one with everything." In part, this conception is because of Zen's association with Buddhism, which is primarily construed as a religion. But it is also due to a rather limited understanding of what exactly philosophy is. Many famous Western thinkers, ranging from the pre-Socratics, Augustine, Spinoza, Kierkegaard, and Nietzsche, up to and including an array of phenomenological and postmodern theorists, are not even considered "real" philosophers by many in the profession. Much of the same prejudice, and to a considerably larger degree, has affected the overall reception of Eastern thinking in the Western world. But what constitutes real philosophy? For that matter, what constitutes genuine understanding or comprehension? And, for our purposes, how can one read traditional Zen texts with an eye to possibly teaching—or perhaps better put, communicating—those texts?

As good a place as any to begin is within one's own background. Understanding an Eastern perspective (or any perspective other than one's own) means partially being able to render it accessible in conceptual terms familiar to readers or listeners. A principal realization of late modern Western philosophy, beginning with Hegel, is that even the most abstract philosophy is historically and culturally grounded. The "philosophy" or "wise learning" (*tetsugaku*) of Zen is no different, even if its understanding of "rationality" is significantly different from the standard Western view. Zen, and indeed Buddhist thinking as a whole, always has acknowledged the historical context of its project, even if it ultimately has dismissed that history as illusory insofar as it is impermanent. This has led to the common erroneous conclusion that Buddhist philosophies are abstractly metaphysical and without any real point of contact with actuality. Zen is, of course, the product of the interaction between several distinct cultural, religious, and intellectual traditions—for example, Indian Buddhism and Yoga, Chinese Daoism, and Japanese ethics and aesthetics, as well as various other influences such as those of Korea and Vietnam. More recently, Zen has been profoundly and decidedly affected by its contact with the West, beginning with the interaction between several prominent Japanese and European philosophers in the 1920–30s, and later through the counterculture movements of the 1950s to the 1970s, leading up to the establishment of numerous Zen centers throughout the United States and Europe; it has also been marked significantly by the important and transforming inclusion of women masters and teachers. Simply stated, only if Zen (or any philosophy, for that matter) is seen as fundamentally hermeneutical, as taking shape through a diverse history of development, can it be adequately and effectively understood.

Zen certainly does incorporate a necessary and fundamental non-philosophical standpoint, but it also denotes a particular philosophical orientation, albeit one that is not immediately familiar and accessible to the typical Western thinker for whom reading and consequently teaching or communicating the philosophy of Zen can be either an exciting, illuminating experience or a great frustration. My own personal experience as a student, practitioner, and philosophy of Zen instructor over the course of twenty-five years has been both, and usually at the same time. Setting aside my numerous difficulties and sporadic "breakthroughs" or insights as a practitioner of the Zen way, as a reader and educator I have focused increasingly on engaging Zen and Buddhist philosophy through a comparative standpoint, being persuaded that this is the best and most direct approach to take, though it is not without its own pitfalls. In this essay, I take up the question of how one might approach the reading and teaching of a classic Zen text, Dōgen's

Shōbōgenzō, by contextualizing it in the immediate experience of the reader through a series of diverse comparative exercises.

The thinking of Eihei Dōgen (1200–1253), perhaps more than that of any other single figure, has shaped the philosophy of Zen. Yet this thirteenth-century master, the founder of the Sōtō Zen sect in Japan, remains an enigma in the intellectual world. While his work is rife with philosophical insight, the prose he uses to convey it is often described as nonphilosophical, as poetic, or as imaginative, if not just downright obscure at times. While this reflects Dōgen's view that Zen practice and the abandonment of conventional reason are necessary for the realization of the "Buddha mind," it poses a conundrum not only for his readers but also for those who try to teach his philosophy. One of Dōgen's great marks in Zen history, however, is that he was perhaps the first to develop a systematic philosophical approach to Zen. The challenge for Western readers is to grasp this systematic aspect in a way that is both faithful to Dōgen and yet meaningful and somewhat clear.

Dōgen's Experience

It is helpful perhaps to recall Dōgen's own initial experiences with Zen teaching. Trained and ordained as a monk in the Tendai sect, then the dominant tradition in Japan, for a brief time at the young and impressionable age of fourteen years Dōgen was also a student of Eisai, the founder of the Rinzai school of Zen. After Eisai's death, Dōgen traveled for three years, eventually coming to study assiduously with Eisai's successor, Myōzen Zenji, for six years at the Kenninji Temple from 1217 to 1223. (His age at this point corresponded roughly to the traditional age of most college students.) Though he had great respect for Myōzen, Dōgen nevertheless felt unsatisfied, and according to tradition he departed to China to study with the Chan (Zen) masters there, receiving the Dharma transmission from Rujing in 1227. Soon thereafter Dōgen returned to Japan and established the Sōtō lineage, which stresses the practice of *zazen* (seated "meditation") as the primary way to realize Buddha nature and hence attain awakening, as opposed to the Rinzai Zen emphasis on kōan (paradoxical statements about the nature of reality) meditation and the *nembutsu* (Name of Buddha prayer or recitation) practice of Jōdo Shin-shū (True Pure Land) Buddhism.

It is altogether significant that Dōgen's first truly authentic experience with Zen teaching was purportedly not in the confines of a monastery, listening to a master's instruction or poring over ancient Buddhist sutras, but through a conversation with an old, rather ordinary monk-cook he met while traveling on a boat during his trip to China in 1223. Dōgen had gone to China seeking deeper understanding because he was unable to reconcile the tension between the Tendai practice of *zazen*, based on the idea that enlightenment is something that is acquired through disciplined cultivation, and the Tendai teaching that one is already enlightened. As the story goes, one day the old monk came aboard the boat as it was docked in the harbor; he was looking for shiitake mushrooms with which to make soup. When asked by Dōgen why he was in such a hurry and could not stay to talk, the monk replied that he had to hurry back to his cooking duties. He regarded them as his lifelong practice of the Way (*Dao*), he said, and therefore he could not leave his practice to others. This confused the young Dōgen, who pressed the old man as to why he did not leave the cooking to the younger monks so that he could spend his time, as befitting his age, studying the sutras and practicing *zazen*. The monk purportedly laughed loudly and declared, "I can see that you are a good man but a stranger here, and therefore perhaps do not understand what the practice of the Way is, nor what the language of the teaching truly is." On hearing this, Dōgen was apparently "suddenly amazed and ashamed." This experience continued to affect his basic understanding of Zen throughout his life—namely, that the Way is open and available to all and essentially realized in the most ordinary and mundane activities and occurrences. As a more mature Dōgen would later write, "What we mean by the sutras is the entire cosmos itself. . . . The sutras are the entire universe, mountains and rivers and the great earth, plants and trees; they are the self and others, taking meals and wearing clothes, confusion and dignity."[1]

What is one to make of Dōgen's amazement and shame? What was conveyed to Dōgen through his encounter with the old cook-monk? In part, it was the awareness of the limitations and pitfalls of relying solely on rationally constructed language to attain realization. In other words, language does not exist either merely to circumscribe or to interpret reality; the true function of language, rather, is to "open up" reality. The profundity of Dōgen's own later language often came to lie in poetic and nonphilosophical expression (much in the way that Heidegger's later language exhibited his famous "turn"), if we understand philosophy here in the sense of striving to determine Buddha nature in a purely cognitive sense.

Dōgen's Dilemma

Dōgen's attention from the time of his ordination as a fourteen-year-old monk until at least the time he received the Dharma was focused on the following observation and question: "Both exoteric and esoteric teaching explain that a person in essence has true dharma nature and is originally a body of 'buddha nature.' If so, why do all buddhas in the past, present, and future arouse the wish for and seek enlightenment?"[2] While there may not be a definitive answer to this query, turning to the history of Mahāyāna Buddhism perhaps provides some insight into Dōgen's dilemma, which is also directly connected to the dilemma with which the present essay is concerned—namely, how to read Dōgen's philosophy without reducing it to a purely rational argumentative standpoint.

Mahāyāna Buddhism has long been concerned with understanding the concepts of original enlightenment (*hongaku*) and acquired enlightenment (*skikaku*). The notion of acquired, or gradual, enlightenment has been present since the earliest teaching of the historical Buddha, Śākyamuni. The concept of original enlightenment, however, is a later development, though its proponents claim that it has always been present in the Buddha's teaching. They say that original awakening is eternal, without beginning or end in time. Following the Mādhyamika (Middle Way) teaching of the great Indian philosopher Nāgārjuna, who realized that *śūnyatā* (emptiness) and *tathatā* (suchness) are fundamentally the same,[3] oppositions such as enlightenment and delusion, being and nonbeing, samsāra and nirvāna, life and death, and the one and the many were able to be negated and thus affirmed in their absoluteness. According to Dōgen, "Though not identical, they are not different; though not different, they are not one; though not one, they are not many."[4] The standpoint of original enlightenment was consequently able to assert the unity of enlightenment and practice, Dōgen's primary concern, by expanding the notice of "practice" beyond that of mere religious discipline to include the much broader range of everyday activity.

So why do buddhas, as already awakened beings, need to practice to attain what is already theirs? Why would an enlightened being need to seek enlightenment and engage in such nonintellectual practice as "just sitting and doing nothing" (*shikantaza*)? Dōgen writes in the first fascicle or chapter of his version (there are actually several versions) of his masterwork *Shōbōgenzō* in what has become a rightly famous passage: "To study the buddha way is to study the self. To study the self is to forget the self. To forget the self is to be actualized by myriad things. When actualized by myriad things, your mind and body as well as the bodies and minds of others drop away. No trace of realization remains, and this no-trace continues endlessly."[5] Here one finds another clue toward possibly grasping Dōgen's later solution to his earlier nagging question. Since all things are continually moving and are impermanent, the self consistently moves to find a place of nonmovement. This is why Śākyamuni Buddha stressed that only "no-self" (*anātman*) is the standpoint from which "one" (and not necessarily the individual one either) realizes the truth of the Dharma as "dependent origination" (*pratītyasamutpāda*). Awakened or enlightened beings continually practice, because practice is itself the Way. To do otherwise, though it too is the Way, is not to "realize" the Way. Without the realization, the mind does not "fall away," and Buddha nature is not "seen."

Realizing Dōgen

While much excellent scholarly work in the modern era has been done on Dōgen (whose name means literally "Source of the Way"), the question remains whether a standard philosophical analysis ultimately conveys to the reader the fullness of Dōgen's realization of the "Zen mind," which is also "no-mind" (*mushin*). How is one to approach and understand, much less teach, Dōgen's philosophy without inadvertently failing prey to the very epistemological assumptions that his thinking calls into question? Is it possible? Or is Dōgen's wisdom, in the end, only graspable with the aid of an acknowledged master? While there are undoubtedly some who would argue that this is the case, I will briefly address the possibility of reading and teaching Dōgen, not from the point of view of overcoming this dilemma, but from the standpoint of the dilemma itself—in other words, from the perspective of ontological and epistemological ambiguity. This ambiguity arises when one understands that for Dōgen any "method" that Zen might imply or entail is determined first and foremost by the experience of the individual seeking realization, and since every individual's experience is unique, what works at one time does not necessarily work at another time, even with respect to the same individual. Only by comparing one's own experience of "reality" and understanding of it with the ideas communicated by a master like Dōgen and, moreover, with one's own changing experiences can a deeper realization of Zen occur.

There is also an inherent danger to a comparative approach, and that is the tendency to interpret the other in terms of one's own conceptual categories. Today Western culture is obviously in a much better position to evaluate, understand, and appreciate the East than it was even less than a century ago, due largely to more accurate translations and cross-cultural interaction. Indeed, only now, one could argue, is it the case that the language of Western philosophy can adequately take up the challenge of reading and grasping a thinker like Dōgen. Contemporary continental European philosophy provides a useful segue in this regard. Its critique of metaphysics and of the hegemony of reason over the past two centuries provided a new philosophical language to *break through* (to use a term found both in Eastern and Western philosophical and religious traditions) the "gateless gate" of Zen, thereby allowing the possibility of new and authentic insight to flourish. Philosophers such as Hegel, Schelling, Kierkegaard, Nietzsche, Heidegger, Merleau-Ponty, Deleuze, and Derrida have provided, in their respective ways, such a language. And the recent works of T. P. Kasulis, John Maraldo, Graham Parkes, Bret Davis, and Jason Wirth, to name just a few, serve as excellent examples of rendering accessible the philosophy of Zen in a sophisticated way using the language of contemporary continental thought.

It is essential to keep in mind that a comparative approach is not limited to or defined exclusively by a cross-cultural intellectual exchange. Dōgen, for example, also employed a comparative method to communicate his understanding of Zen. Certainly he compared the philosophy of Zen to that of the other major Buddhist schools in his day (Tendai, Kegon, and Shingon), though it is important to note that

Dōgen always resisted the contention that he was developing a new school or type of Buddhism—namely, Zen Buddhism. Dōgen thought that "philosophy" was integral to all authentic approaches to Buddhism, but also that greater emphasis needed to be placed on conjoining the nonphilosophical practice of *zazen* with the practice of philosophy. Subtending this emphasis, moreover, is one's common, everyday experience. It is, in fact, a central thesis of Dōgen's Zen that only through an appeal to prereflective ordinary consciousness and experience can one realize the Zen mind and thereby move closer to attaining enlightenment.

Doing Dōgen

The appeal to ordinary experience is the crucial aspect of Dōgen's thinking that needs to be stressed if one is to have any real measure of success in conveying the philosophy of Zen to others. Drawing on my own personal moments of realization, for instance, and considering them in the light of Dōgen's philosophy have enabled me, as a university professor, to better communicate my reading and understanding of Dōgen. Now, I have some formal background in Zen practice and have had (at least according to students' reports and evaluations) some measure of success exposing students to the practice of *zazen* in an effort to more fully convey Dōgen's insistence on its importance. But *zazen* is an arduous and time-consuming practice, and in an institutional setting such as the classroom its effects are assuredly very limited. I also realize that many instructors who are interested in assigning readings from Dōgen in their classes have neither this background nor the desire to lead students in "meditation." I only mention my experience in this regard for those so inclined. More effective, I found, were my efforts in several classes to persuade students to think about Dōgen's philosophy on an existential basis, such as by keeping a daily journal wherein they would reflect philosophically on Dōgen's writings by appealing to their everyday experiences. For a few this has meant attempting to practice *zazen* on their own, but for most it has meant finding time to take a quiet walk in the woods, on the beach, or just around campus, or simply paying closer attention to eating and drinking, or even reflecting on their engagement with various technologies ranging from cars to computers to televisions.[6] The point that I am trying to make is that "reading" Dōgen involves more than simply reading the printed words in a book and reflecting on their meaning. Dōgen invites his readers to "read" the world through the perspective of their concrete life experiences.

Keeping in mind the traditional Zen master who presses his disciples to confront their immediate experience of Zen in the moment, my altogether simple advice would be to read Dōgen not by merely recalling one's past life events in attempting to "find" Zen moments, but rather actively confronting one's present understanding of Zen in and through one's own current experiences. Nevertheless, despite a certain ontological identification, the ordinary prereflective consciousness that is common to everyone, enlightened or not, should not be confused with the extraordinary awakened consciousness. The language, and hence the practice, of Zen philosophy performs a dual function: it makes certain "systematic" propositions regarding the nature of existence while simultaneously cultivating creative responses to existence, therein producing the spontaneity of the Zen mind that allows the originary state of enlightenment or awakening to become existentially manifest and thereby known or recognized. The expression of Zen is the activity of Zen. "Seen" this way, the distinction between original and acquired enlightenment falls away, as Dōgen realizes, thereby resolving both the dilemma of explaining why buddhas and bodhisattvas still practice and the dilemma of how to communicate or teach this realization. Though distinct, original and acquired enlightenment are simultaneously occurring. Taking time, "being time" (*uji*), as Dōgen phrases it, to realize this is the timeless practice of all buddhas. Realizing the insights and merits of Dōgen's own practice—his *zazen* and his thinking—can be effectively understood and communicated if one understands that existence itself is the ultimate text, and that books are not gates to be unlocked but rather only keys with which to unlock the great gateless gate of understanding, and hopefully of awakening.

Notes

1. Dōgen, *Shōbōgenzō*, cited in Hee-jin Kim, *Dōgen Kigen: Mystical Realist* (Tucson: University of Arizona Press, 1975), 97.
2. "Kenzei's Biography of Dōgen," cited in the introduction by Kazuaki Tanahashi, to *Moon in a Dewdrop: Writings of Zen Master Dōgen*, edited by Kazuaki

Tanahashi, translated by Robert Aitken, Philip Whalen, et al. (San Francisco: North Point Press, 1985), 4.

3. Nāgārjuna, *Mūlamadhyamakākarikā* (*The Fundamental Wisdom of the Middle Way*), translated by Jay L. Garfield (Oxford: Oxford University Press, 1995), Chap. 25, verses 18–19, p. 75.

4. Dōgen, *Shōbōgenzō*, cited in Kim, *Dōgen Kigen*, 164.

5. Dōgen, *Shōbōgenzō*, in Tanahashi, *Moon in a Dewdrop*, 70.

6. With regard to this last point, I do try to discourage them from using television viewing as a relevant activity in that it discourages the "nonthinking" activity of Zen by oftentimes stimulating a passive "not thinking" instead. Most students seem to concur with me on this point.

Gereon Kopf

The Absolute Contradictory What: On How to Read the Philosophy of Nishida Kitarō

Nishida Kitarō (1870–1945) was the founder of the Kyoto School of philosophy and one of the first thinkers to stratify a comparative philosophy by combining concepts and arguments from diverse philosophical traditions, especially Buddhism and what is now called Continental philosophy. His main contribution to philosophy and, in my mind, the reason why the study of Nishida's philosophy should be included in any survey course on philosophy, however, is his construction of a nondualist philosophy in systematic form.

The term "nondualism" is used usually to translate the Sanskrit word *advaita*. It is most familiar as part of the name of the philosophical school Advaita Vedanta, which rejects dualism in favor of monism. The term also characterizes a variety of philosophical positions within Buddhism that suggest the middle way between the opposites of, for example, eternalism (the view that human beings have an eternal soul) and annihilationism (the view that nothing really exists). While it is already difficult to subsume the philosophical position of Advaita Vedanta and the various forms of Buddhism under one and the same category, Nishida's philosophy not only differs from the philosophical standpoints akin to that of Advaita Vedanta, but also rejects them. In Nishida's hands, nondualism becomes a philosophical position that subverts any dualism and the dichotomy between dualism and monism. It proposes instead a third and more inclusive position.[1] It is this third position that I will refer to as "nondualism."

The research for this essay would have not been possible without the generous support of the Japan Society for the Promotion of Research, my leave of absence from Luther College, the hospitality of the Nanzan Institute for Religion and Culture, and the feedback of James Heisig and Thomas Kasulis.

Unfortunately, anyone in the English-speaking world who attempts to teach Nishida's philosophy will likely encounter three major difficulties. First, Nishida has (as a glance of his text reveals) a penchant for cryptic terminology. For instance, the key to Nishida's nondualism is the enigmatic concept of the "self-identity of the absolute contradictories" (*zettai mujunteki jiko dōitsu*). This concept has the potential to confound readers who struggle with his dense prose or are unwilling to accept a philosophy that seemingly postulates a contradiction, or paradox, as its primary paradigm. Second, Nishida's philosophy is not monolithic—its foundational paradigm changes slowly from the first blueprint of his philosophical project in the *Inquiry into the Good* (*Zen no kenkyū Inquiry*), published in 1911, to the mature expression of his philosophy in *The Logic of Basho and the Religious Worldview* (*Basho no ronri to shūkyōteki sekaikan*), published in 1945. The works written in the thirty-four years in between gave Nishida an opportunity to refine his nondual paradigm and to elaborate its philosophical implications. Third, many of the key essays are either not translated into English or are no longer in print. The number of commentaries in English on Nishida's philosophy is relatively small.

For the benefit of readers without Japanese language proficiency, I list book-length translations and main commentaries published in English in the bibliography. In addition, James Heisig's *Philosophers of Nothingness* provides a nearly complete list of all works regarding Nishida's philosophy in European languages; and Michiko Yusa's *Zen and Philosophy* contains a bibliography of Nishida and a complete guide to his works. Also to make his ideas more accessible, I will proceed in two steps. First, I will use a key passage from his first completed work, the *Inquiry*, to outline Nishida's main philosophical interest. Second, I will introduce a hermeneutical model to elucidate the key term of his mature work, namely the self-identity of absolute contradictories; this model illustrates some of its implications.

The Key Problem in Nishida's Philosophy

Keiji Nishitani, one of Nishida's students and successors at Kyōto University, reports in a tribute to his teacher that Nishida would tell his students to look for the knack that opens the doors to any particular philosophical system. The key to Nishida's philosophy is his belief that the philosophers of Europe adopted what he calls an antinomical approach. By this he means that the philosophical tradition of Europe provides a conundrum in which there are two opposite and mutually exclusive positions such as "materialism and idealism" or "dualism and monism." Nishida rejects these alternatives and argues for a third position, namely that of philosophical nondualism.

Let me briefly analyze his discussion of ethics in the *Inquiry*. Ethics, to Nishida, comprises the quest for the criteria to distinguish between good and evil or that which is meritorious and not meritorious. His strategy in the *Inquiry* suggests two fundamental ethical positions: "heteronomous" ethics and "autonomous" ethics.[2] The category "heteronomous ethics" includes any ethical theory that identifies an authority external to the self, such as an autocrat or god, as the source for our moral criteria. Autonomism, in contrast, seeks the source of morality inside the self. One model that seems to resist this categorization is the notion of moral law that in some sense is simultaneously immanent in and transcendent to the self, since the moral self does not create but rather discovers this law. However, as I show below, Nishida overcomes this difficulty and de facto subsumes moral law under the category of autonomous ethics. As this brief outline already indicates, Nishida's agenda and strategy differ from traditional ethical approaches; his main concern is to expose the dualistic bias of traditional ethics, at the center of which he identifies the dichotomy between internality and externality, and to advance his own nondualistic position. Thus, it is no surprise that Nishida disavows both heteronomism and autonomism.

Any ethics that bases morality on an external authority reduces morality to power and thus fails to provide an ethics. Furthermore, an ethics claiming that even an external authority is bound by some universal notion of the good locates morality outside of an external authority and thus cannot be called heteronomism. In a wider sense, however, Nishida argues that anything that is external alienates the self and thus cannot qualify as the Good.

The alternative—that is, any moral theory that draws the criteria to distinguish good and evil from sources inside of the self, either from reason or from will—is equally flawed. A rational theory, which locates the criteria for morality in reason, imposes, not unlike heteronomous ethics, an external standard—namely, rationality—onto the self.

The eternal and unchanging nature of the moral law is alien to the self and must be experienced by the self as an external demand and thus cannot provide the criteria for the Good. In addition, the intellectualist approach privileges the rational over the nonrational and the intellectual over the emotive dimensions of the self, and thus rejects fundamental dimensions of the self. On the other hand, hedonism and utilitarianism identify the self's well-being—that is, the well-being of the individual self in the case of hedonism and of the community of selves in the case of utilitarianism—as the standard of moral reasoning. However, each of these theories qualifies pleasure in one sense or another. The hedonist, for example, has to weigh the positive pleasure bestowed by one action against the negative pleasure of another, while utilitarianism is forced to balance the pleasure a course of action bestows on one part of the population with the suffering it incurs on another. Both require a hierarchy of pleasures and, ultimately, a standard to evaluate, rank, and negotiate the various pleasures and displeasures. This standard, however, Nishida argues, is external to the discourse on pleasure itself and, subsequently, indicates the inconsistency inherent in the theory of hedonism and the need for a different moral criterion. Nishida is thus forced to construct his own ethical position of action theory based on his definition of the good as the unifying activity.[3]

In Nishida's view, an ethics—or a theology or an ontology, for that matter—that evokes externality as its primary principle is inherently dualistic and has to be rejected. To avoid any form of dualism, Nishida seems to overemphasize the principle of internality. This becomes especially clear when one examines Nishida's hierarchy of ethical positions. Nishida almost ranks the ethical positions he discusses by the degree of externality they exhibit. For example, an ethical theory based on rationalism constitutes an improvement over a heteronomous ethics, because it locates the criteria for goodness within consciousness and thus resolves the alienation that arises when heteronomous ethics superimposes an external set of criteria on the self. However, insofar as the rational criteria are external to emotion and thus alienate rational thought from nonrational emotion, a rationalist theory of ethics equally fails to provide sufficient criteria for moral theory. While hedonism accounts for emotion, it still requires criteria outside of emotion to distinguish pleasure from pain and to identify various degrees of pleasure. Nishida concludes, "[I]t is clear that the explanation of what is good must be found in the essence of the will itself. Will constitutes the fundamental unifying activity of consciousness; as such it constitutes the energy that unifies the fundament of reality directly. Will does not comprise an activity for the other but for the self."[4] This seems to indicate that Nishida privileges the internal and the nonrational over the external and the rational. Similarly, in the paragraph in his writings prior to the one just cited he seems to endorse the priority of the internal. In that paragraph, Nishida explains that "the basic principles of the Good are to be searched inside of consciousness."[5]

However, it is not the case that Nishida proposes an internalism promoting idealism, pantheism, and autonomism; rather, some of his concepts are highly ambiguous. This ambiguity constitutes almost a trademark of the *Inquiry* and of Nishida's early (1911–30) thought. On the one hand, Nishida strives to overcome the duality between externality and internality; on the other hand, he tends to privilege the internal because his main philosophical goal is to subvert dualism. For example, in the *Inquiry*, the will at the same time constitutes the principle of internality as well as the unifying activity that sublates all oppositions and dichotomies (presumably including internality and externality). Thus defined, the concept of will is highly ambiguous. However, the problem is much deeper, since Nishida's conception of the will affects his definition of internality as well. In fact, the text reveals three different meanings of "internalities." First, Nishida juxtaposes the self with an external authority; then he suggests that reason is external to emotion; and finally he defines the self as the "unifying activity" of "personality," which he equates with the "unity of the totality"[6] and the "unifying power of the cosmos."[7] The first notion of internality coincides with what we today call an individual self, the second with something akin to the unconscious—namely, the place of emotions and instincts—and the third, if taken literally, transcends the distinction of internality and externality altogether (not unlike the Jungian or the so-called cosmic Self). While the former two seem to correspond to the general usage of "internality" in present-day English and Japanese, the third conception cannot be really called internality, since it transcends the distinction between internality and externality. And this seems to be the key to Nishida's thought. (In fact, some fifteen years after the *Inquiry* Nishida distinguishes between a "simple" internality, which is opposed to externality, and a "true" internality, which includes the opposition between a simple internality and a simple externality. Given this distinction, however, the latter one does not deserve the label "internality" anymore but should be called [to use a formula from his later career] the "self-identity of the absolute contradictories of internality and externality.")

One could make the argument that Nishida's attempt both to privilege the concept of internality and to transcend it[8] interferes with Nishida's own attempt to develop a nondual philosophy, since he de facto privileges the internal demand or the internal activity of consciousness over externality and ultimately an autonomous ethics over a heteronomous one. Consequently, Nishida's philosophy as presented in the *Inquiry* has been accused of monism, psychologism, and dogmatism, and he himself abandoned the terminology for more appropriate terms.[9] Nevertheless, the *Inquiry*, especially the chapter on ethics, reveals Nishida's agenda better than any other of his works.

It is interesting and telling that Nishida chooses the alternative of heteronomism and autonomism, and not some of the more traditional ways of categorizing ethical theories, as the focus of his discussion. This choice is made because Nishida is not very interested in ethical theories such as Aristotle's virtue ethics or Kant's deontology per se; rather, he is interested in outlining two prototypical philosophical standpoints, while the ethical positions he assigns to those standpoints are secondary. In short, what Nishida rejects are ethical systems exclusively based, on the one hand, on the principles of externality, otherness, difference, and eternality, and, on the other hand, those based on principles of irrationality, subjectivity, and selfhood. The ethical position he himself promotes has as its goal the elimination of the dualism between self and God or self and society. But at the same time, his position upholds the differences between individuals and even between individual actions, and it upholds the universal dimension that overcomes the notion of the self as a closed system; this universal dimension includes the dimension of the others, such as a Thou, the world, and God, as he argues in his section "Religion." This approach constitutes in raw form the blueprint for his later and more mature nondualistic philosophy.

Nishida's Strategy

In his later work, Nishida developed a three-part argument structure, which existed only implicitly in his *Inquiry*, into a full-fledged system. In a concrete sense, he expands the moments of externality, internality, and their nonduality into a system of three worlds, which I will refer to here as the worlds of objectivism, subjectivism, and history.[10] Nishida's system of the three worlds outlines the process of an ever-deepening self-awareness in his earlier work prior to 1930. This system serves as a model that described, in its original form, three different interpretations of the historical world, and, in its later incarnations, the three dimensions of the historical world itself. In other words, Nishida's threefold model undergoes a slow transition from epistemology to the philosophy of history. I believe that this model can also be employed as a heuristic device to understand the philosophical project of Nishida in general and to demonstrate the structure and implications of his philosophical nondualism in particular. However, the fact that Nishida himself develops three different versions illustrates the complexity of this model, to which I cannot do justice in a brief introductory essay. I will therefore use a simplified version to outline in broad strokes how this model can provide a key to Nishida's philosophy.

Nishida argues that the principle of externality is indicative of the world of objectivism. It is the world in which the self finds itself external to and opposed by other things. Such a world is constructed by objectivism, which proposes that the knower stand outside the self, and even subjectivity is treated as an object of study. The world of objectivism is devoid of subjectivity and constitutes a world of seemingly external individual objects governed by the law of causality and located in a linear temporality. In this world, the self is neither free nor in control of its destiny but rather remains subjected to causes and conditions. The primary characteristics of the world of objectivism are duality (self/world and subject/object), affirmation (the constituents of this world are attributed substance or ontological value), causality, and temporality. In the history of philosophy, the world of objectivism is reflected in philosophical positions such as materialism, dualism, realism, and, positivism.

The principle of internality, in contrast, is created by the subjectivist standpoint. Subjectivism proposes a world of engagement, where the individual members are not eternally separate from one another or from things; instead, they form one dynamic unity. In the world of engagement, distinctions between self and other as well as self and world disappear. According to Nishida, this engagement also collapses the distinctions between past and future and collapses time into the present moment; past and future exist only insofar as they are expressed in—have an effect on—the present. Commentators frequently cite the example of sports or art, where practitioners lose themselves in the movement or the music insofar as their selves no longer constitute isolated entities. Such a worldview emphasizes the dimensions of subjectivity and free will. It postulates the principles of unity and atemporality. This unity is the unity of interaction between self and world, and it negates individuality and externality. The principle of atemporality involves the rejection of a worldview that makes the present contingent on the past and reduces human agency to mere effects of prior causes. This standpoint, Nishida explains, is reflected in various degrees by the positions of idealism, rationalism, monism, and phenomenology.

Faced with these alternatives, Nishida rejects both standpoints in favor of his own nondual one. He especially laments the tendency of each of these standpoints to give an incomplete picture of the human predicament and to exclude moments that are essential to the human experience. I am unable to argue each of these principles in depth in the present essay, but it is helpful to list them in order to understand what motivated Nishida to suggest the route of nondualism in the first place. Nishida concretely criticizes the objectivist standpoint for denying the moments of subjectivity, nonbeing, free will, and the present, because he considers these four fundamental features of human experience. More than likely, Nishida believed that the dualism of the objectivist position symbolizes the principle of difference, reifies the principle of affirmation, supports the law of causality (where the principle is that every phenomenon is contingent on a source outside itself), and maintains a concept of temporality as the principle of continuity. When Nishida argues that the objectivist standpoint is incomplete, he does not reject the principle of differentiation, but rather its reification into a dualism of essences. He does not reject the principle of affirmation, but rather its reification into a metaphysics of being and substances. He does not reject the principle that every phenomon is contingent on a source outside itself, but rather the exclusion of free will and teleology.

And he does not reject the principle of continuity, but rather the abstract conception of linear time that reduces the present to an infinitely small point on the time line that reifies past and future.

Obviously, the case of subjectivism is diametrically opposed to that of objectivism. It seems safe to say that Nishida believes the following about subjectivism: the monism of the subjectivist position emphasizes the principle of unity, which overcomes alienation and is necessary for a dynamic world view; subjectivism rejects the external world through the principle of negation; teleology is necessary to conceptualize free will; and the concept of atemporality reifies the notion of the present. Nevertheless, Nishida rejects subjectivism, because it denies the principles of difference, continuity, and affirmation that objectivism affirms. At the same time, it is important to note that Nishida does not reject the principle of unity, but rather its reification into one all-encompassing totality. He does not reject the principle of negation, but rather the denial of individuality and plurality. He does not reject the concept of free will, but rather a teleology in which the future unilaterally determines the present and the world unilaterally determines the individual. And he does not reject the concept of the present, but rather the denial of change. In short, Nishida suggests a philosophical standpoint that includes both moments of objectivism and subjectivism, causality and free will, as well as difference and identity.

The Historical World

While the preceding section has clarified the considerations that motivated Nishida to develop the nondual principle and to conceive of the historical world, how this historical world is to be stratified still needs to be addressed. In what follows, I apply the model of the three worlds to the discourses of epistemology and the philosophy of history in order to elucidate Nishida's conception of the historical world.

In his lectures entitled "Religious Studies" Nishida suggests the analogy of a play to apply the threefold model to the epistemological discourse. He compares the objectivist position to the audience at a play, which occupies a removed standpoint of seeming objectivity. The subjectivist standpoint functions analogously to "actors" who actively and subjectively engage in the performance of a play. From the standpoint of the audience, the performance of the play is not only distant and unattainable, but also an object, which is perceived and can be analyzed and interpreted, but which ultimately is irrelevant to the life of the individual viewer. The actors, in contrast, do actively participate in the performance and "sink into their role." Their participation eliminates the abyss the audience perceives between themselves and the performance. Thus, the performance is meaningful to the actors, and they are also involved in the unfolding of the performance itself. However, their absorption in the play makes it impossible for them to perceive the performance and to "experience the unfolding of the totality" of the play.[11] The play in this example illustrates the world in Nishida's philosophy.

The actors cannot understand this "unfolding" in which they participate, much in the same way a person may be fluent in his or her native tongue but may be unable to explain the intricacies of its grammar to a novice. To be able to explain the grammatical rules of language, the removed perspective of a teacher or a scholar trained in linguistics is necessary. Yet, it is clear that a really proficient person is one who possesses both skills. Similarly, the ideal position for Nishida is one that encompasses the standpoint of the audience and the actor; this position includes the experience of and the participation in the unfolding of the totality. Nishida thus argues that the human predicament is ambiguous insofar as human beings simultaneously engage in and perceive the world and therefore concludes that the notion of the unity of subject and object is necessary. To express this ambiguity inherent in human existence or the necessity of two seemingly mutually exclusive paradigms, Nishida uses paradoxical concepts (often appearing contradictory) as indicative of his nondual paradigm. Thus, Nishida replaces with his nondualism the objectivism that expresses the separation between audience and performance and the subjectivism that dissolves this difference.

In the historical world, the objectivity of human existence can be found in the conditionality of the subjective agent. To Nishida, concepts such as causality, past time, and objectivity signify the condition of the individual. Even as subjective agents we are not free to choose the basic condition of our existence. We do not choose the year and country of our births or our parents. These facts are given to us. Our bodies further reflect this conditionality; this conditionality is of course a product of our past actions as well as the actions of the world around us. If, for example, someone were to cut off my leg today, this action would determine my abilities and choices tomorrow. Every individual is faced with a certain set of givens that are inevitable.

Right now I cannot change the fact that I am sitting in my office in Nagoya in front of my computer. Unlike the first set of conditions, I can transform this latter set, but even any actions to negate this narrow set of conditions, such as going to the airport to take the next plane to Fiji, still cannot deny the presence of conditionality. In order to get to Fiji, I will first have get up from my computer, leave my office, and go to the airport. Once I am in Fiji, or even on the plane, where I start regretting my impulsive decision to quit my job, I am now faced with a new set of conditions. This conditionality, which expresses itself in my environment—that is, my body, my office, the political state of affairs in Japan and the world in March 2004, and the expectations of my colleagues who look at me with surprise as I hastily make my way out of the institute—Nishida refers to as "the created." Every moment I inherit a body that I then change through activities, whether it is drinking sake or engaging in running meditation (*kaihōgyō*) on Mt. Hiei, I engage in these moments. In the historical world, that which is created and that which creates are not separate; they determine each other. The body I have right now enables me to engage in certain activities, or prevents it. By the same token, the activities I engage in determine what kind of body I do have. The subjective dimension of this existence, in contrast, lies in the fact that I now can transform what I am, and also what the world is. Of course, I cannot undo my country of birth, my mother tongue, the year in which I was born, and so forth, since I am stuck in these conditions. But at the same time, I do have a limited set of options from which I can choose. Human individuals can to varying degrees make plans and choose their activities; they are creative. The historical world, consequently, must be the world that is given-and-yet-transforms-itself, and that transforms-itself-and-yet-is-given.

The Self-Identity of Absolute Contradictories

To conceive of the human predicament as the ambiguity between the worlds of knowledge and engagement as well as between the worlds of conditionality and transformation, Nishida employs the concept of the self-identity of absolute contradictories. He introduces this concept in his *Philosophical Essays Volume 2* (*Tetsugaku ronbunshū daini*) in the context of his discussion of the historical world to distinguish the historical world from the worlds of objectivism and subjectivism. And this concept is ultimately the key to understanding Nishida's nondualism. Nishida does not employ his nondual paradigm to replace previous paradigms, but rather to include them into his system. In this sense, he does not reject dualism or monism, but simply identifies their roles and limitations. For example, Nishida does not, as it is assumed frequently, reject formal logic. He believes that logic is necessary to construct the world of knowledge, but, at the same time, fails to capture the world of engagement as well as the ground of philosophy. By the same token, monism provides the hermeneutic model for the world of engagement, but fails to provide a worldview that can accommodate phenomena such as multiplicity and change. The role of the nondual paradigm is neither to organize the world of knowledge nor to provide a key to the world of engagement, but is rather to contextualize the various ways of knowing into one system that does justice to the human predicament.

Nishida illustrates this three-world approach in a seldom-cited passage of his lectures on religion where he exemplifies the worlds of objectivism, subjectivism, and their nonduality as scholarship, morality, and religion. In this lecture, Nishida argues that science and religion do not have an antagonistic relationship; anyone who believes that does not understand the role of either. They cannot be at odds, because knowledge about the world falls into the domain of scholarship and engagement with the world belongs to the realm of morality, whereas one's place within the world and the existential ambiguity of the individual within this world are essentially religious matters. Conflicts between these realms arise only when religion is mistaken as a source of knowledge about the world and scholarship is used as a tool to avert spiritual and existential crises. In other words, religion does not have either the competence or the authority to regulate knowledge or morality. Nishida neither surrenders religion to scholarship—that is, any systematic form of knowledge—nor vice versa. Scholarship is devoted to an understanding of the world, morality to the actions of subjective agents, religion to the Kantian awe that motivates both and the piety that unites them.

In addition to this inclusive aspect, however, Nishida's nondualism also exhibits a subversive dimension as well. One should not forget that, in Nishida's philosophy, the worlds of objectivism and subjectivism fulfill an important rhetorical function. As shown above, whenever Nishida discusses a particular philosophical dilemma, he sets up the objectivist and the subjectivist standpoints as two exclusive alternatives and then proceeds to argue the untenability of both. Following R. N. Ghose's terminology, one could call these two exclusive alternatives "counterfactuals."[12] This term indicates not so much that Nishida argues against straw men but that he considers these standpoints, even the subjectivist one, to be abstract and incomplete. In addition, the term "counterfactuals" implies that not only the philosophical concepts and position Nishida discusses are in need of a methodic subversion and sublation by his philosophy, but also that the very standpoints of subjectivism and objectivism are indeed contrary to the facts and need to be subverted and revised in an infinite process.

In the end, Nishida's nondualism, if read in the light of the three-world model, provides an exciting philosophical system that accommodates different ways of thinking and promises a solution to all perennial philosophical conundrums that have been framed as the alternative between two mutually exclusive paradigms. A prime example of such a conundrum is the mind-body problem, which not only has been given attention by philosophers but also has had profound influence on science and social science. The mind-body problem generally frames the alternative as between materialistic monism (there is only one substance—namely, matter—and consciousness constitutes nothing but an epiphenomenon of physical processes) and dualism (consciousness constitutes a nonphysical substance). Nishida, of course, reads these two positions as the reification of the two fundamental aspects of human existence. In addition, Nishida's philosophy provides a critical method that prevents the philosopher from resting on one particular philosophical position, including the nondual one. This, if nothing else, makes the study of Nishida's philosophy worthwhile.

Notes

1. Conceptually, Nishida's nondualism is closer to Rāmānuja's Viśiṣṭādvaita Vedanta or Sri Aurobindo's criticisms of Śaṅkhara than to Śaṅkhara's Advaita Vedanta.
2. Similarly, he suggests two possible theological alternatives (theism and pantheism), two metaphysical positions (materialism and idealism), and two approaches to epistemology (intellectualism and voluntarism).

3. According to the *Encyclopedia of Philosophy* published by Iwanami Shoten in 1922, the term *katsudōsetsu* Nishida uses to identify his own position was borrowed from the Japanese translation of *Aktionstheorie*. The theory was developed by the German psychologist Hugo Munsterberg (1863–1916) in the late nineteenth century.
4. Nishida, Kitarō, *Nishida kitarō zenshū* (The Collected Works of Nishida Kitarō). Tokyo: Iwanami Shoten, 1988), 1:143.
5. Ibid., 1:142.
6. Ibid., 1:148.
7. Ibid., 1:152.
8. A similar tension can be detected in his discussion of "spirit," which he describes as opposite to nature, on the one hand, and as the unifying activity transcending all opposites, on the other, and in his treatment of the relationship between God and creation.
9. As I have noted in my "Between Identity and Difference: Three Ways of Reading Nishida's Non-dualism," *Japanese Journal of Religious Studies* 31, nos. 1–2 (2004), two of the main critics whose criticisms motivated Nishida to improve his philosophy are Satomi Takahashi and Hajime Tanabe. Keiji Nishitani's *Nishida Kitarō* and Heisig's *Philosophers of Nothingness* are two of the English-language publications that discuss the exchange between Nishida and his critics.
10. Nishida's model of the three worlds develops slowly in roughly three major steps. In his 1928 article "The World of Intelligibility," Nishida refers to these three worlds as the "universal of judgment" (*handanteki ippansha*), the "universal of self-awareness" (*jikakuteki ippansha*), and the "universal of intelligibility" (*eichiteki ippansha*). In his 1937 *Philosophical Essays Volume 2* (*Tetsugaku ronbunshū daini*), he discusses these three worlds in slightly modified form as the "world of physical laws" (*butsuriteki sekai*), the "world of living organisms" (*seibutsuteki sekai*), and the "world of history" (*rekishiteki sekai*). Finally, in his 1939 *Philosophical Essays Volume 3* (*Tetsugaku ronbunshū daisan*), Nishida exchanges the terminology of the three worlds for what he refers to as "the created" (*tsukurareta mono*), "the creating" (*tsukuru mono*), and their dialectic. Nishida developed the early terminology to address fundamental epistemological issues, the middle-period terminology to discuss our understanding of the historical world, and the later terminology to discuss the historical world itself. Since it is the most inclusive of the three, I will focus here on his later terminology.
11. Nishida, *Nishida kitarō zenshū*, 15: 291.
12. R. N. Ghose, "The Modality of Nāgārjuna's Dialectic," *Journal of Indian Philosophy* 15 (1987): 288.

Suggested Reading

Carter, Robert E. *Nothingness beyond God: An Introduction to the Philosophy of Nishida Kitarō*. St. Paul, MN: Paragon House Publishers, 1998.
Ghose, R. N. "The Modality of Nāgārjuna's Dialectic." *Journal of Indian Philosophy* 15 (1987): 285–307.

Heisig, James. *Philosophers of Nothingness*. Honolulu: University of Hawaii Press, 2001.

Heisig, James, and John C. Maraldo, eds. *Rude Awakenings: Zen, the Kyoto school, and the Question of Nationalism*. Honolulu: University of Hawaii Press, 1995.

Huh, Woo-Sung. "The Philosophy of History in the Late Nishida: A Philosophical Turn." *Philosophy East and West* 14, no. 3 (1990): 343–74.

Kopf, Gereon. "Between Identity and Difference: Three Ways of Reading Nishida's Non-dualism." *Japanese Journal of Religious Studies* 31, nos. 1–2 (2004): 73–103.

———. *Beyond Personal Identity: Dōgen, Nishida, and a Phenomenology of No-Self*. Richmond, UK: Curzon Press, 2001.

Maraldo, John C. "Nishida Kitarō." In *Routledge Encyclopedia of Philosophy*, 7:13–16. New York: Routledge, 1988.

Nakamura Yūjirō. *Nishida tetsugaku no datsukōchiku* [The Deconstruction of Nishida Philosophy]. Tokyo: Iwanami Shoten, 1987.

Nishida Kitarō. *Nishida kitarō zenshū* [The Collected Works of Nishida Kitarō]. Tokyo: Iwanami Shoten, 1988.

Nishitani Keiji. *Nishida kitarō*. Translated by Seisaku Yamamoto and James Heisig. Berkeley and Los Angeles: University of California Press, 1991.

Yusa, Michiko. *Zen and Philosophy: An Intellectual Biography of Nishida Kitarō*. Honolulu: University of Hawaii Press, 2002.

Translations of Works by Nishida Kitarō into English or German

(In chronological sequence of publication of original)

1911. *Zen no kenkyū* [Inquiry]. Translated by Masao Abe and Christopher Ives as *An Inquiry into the Good*. New Haven, CT: Yale University Press, 1990.

1917. *Jikaku ni okeru chokkan to hansei* [Intuition and Reflection in Self-Consciousness]. Translated by Valdo H. Viglielmo as *Intuition and Reflection in Self-Consciousness*. Albany: State University of New York Press, 1987.

1923. *Geijutsu to dōtoku* [Art and Morality]. Translated by David Dilworth and Valdo H. Viglielmo as *Art and Morality*. Honolulu: University of Hawaii Press, 1973.

1926. "Basho" [Place]. Translated by Rolf Eberfeld in *Die Logik des Ortes: Der Anfang der Modernen Philosophie in Japan*. Darmstadt: Wissenschaftliche Buchgesellschaft, 1999.

1928. "Eichiteki sekai" [The World of Intelligibility]. Translated by Robert Schinzinger in *Intelligibility and the Philosophy of Nothingness: Three Philosophical Essays*. Honolulu: East-West Center Press, 1966.

1932. "Watakushi to nanji" [I and Thou]. Translated by Rolf Eberfeld in *Die Logik des Ortes: Der Anfang der Modernen Philosophie in Japan*. Darmstadt: Wissenschaftliche Buchgesellschaft, 1999.

1933. *Testgaku no kompon mondai* [The Fundamental Problems of Philosophy]. Translated by David Dilworth as *Fundamental Problems of Philosophy: The World of Action and the Dialectical World*. Tokyo: Sophia University, 1970.

1938. "Zettai mujunteki jikodōitsu" [The Identity of Absolute Contradictories]. Translated by Robert Schinzinger in *Intelligibility and the Philosophy of Nothingness: Three Philosophical Essays*. Honolulu: East-West Center Press, 1966.

1945. "Basho no ronri to shūkyōteki sekaikan" [The Logic of Place and the Religious Worldview]. Translated by David Dilworth in *Last Writings: Nothingness and the Religious World View*. Honolulu: University of Hawaii Press, 1985. Also translated by Michiko Yusa as "The Logic of Topos and the Religious Worldview." *Eastern Buddhist* 19, no.2 (1986): 1–29, and 20, no. 1 (1987): 81–119.

Jason M. Wirth

"The bottom of my soul has such depth that neither joy nor the waves of sorrow can reach it": An Introduction to the Kyoto School

European nihilism teaches us to return to our forgotten selves and to reflect on the tradition of oriental culture. This tradition has, of course, been lost to us moderns, and is thus something to be rediscovered. There is no turning back to the way things were. What is past is dead and gone, only to be repudiated or subjected to radical criticism. The tradition must be rediscovered from the ultimate point where it is grasped in advance as "the end" (or eschaton) of our westernization and of Western civilization itself. Our tradition must be appropriated from the direction in which we are heading, as a new possibility . . .

—Nishitani Keiji

This essay seeks to introduce the Kyoto School (*Kyōto-ha*) as one of the most distinctive and provocative philosophical movements of the twentieth century. As James Heisig recently reflected, the Kyoto School "is not an eastern thought diluted for foreign consumption, nor is it a simple transference that assumes a background in the history of oriental ideas. It makes an unsolicited contribution to world philosophy that both respects the traditions of philosophy and expands them. In this

I thank my editors David Jones and Ellen Klein for their generosity with this project. Early and somewhat protean ideas for this paper were first generated at an Asian Studies Development Program Conference on which Dr. Jones and I collaborated. It was a three-day faculty development workshop entitled "Buddhist Environmental Values and the Challenge for Technological Responsibility," held September 22–24, 2000, at Oglethorpe University in Atlanta. I also thank my good friend the late Dr. Ron Carlisle for his many fine and insightful comments on an earlier draft of this essay.

respect, the development of the school from Nishida to Tanabe to Nishitani is a rising crescendo. Never has the west produced an intellectual movement whose contribution to the east can compare with what these three thinkers offer the west."[1] What, then, makes the Kyoto School more than either a Japanese imitation of a Western invention or an introduction to Western philosophy for a non-Western audience? Where does one locate its manner of discourse as it asserts itself as a distinctively Japanese contribution to world philosophy?

On Not Letting Integrity Get the Last Word

Before attempting to answer these questions, one must first arrive at some sense of what is at stake in philosophy itself. Before one can speak of a Japanese philosophical contribution to world philosophy, one must have some sense of what one is talking about when one talks about philosophy. And here, suddenly, we are immediately at the crux of the problem. There is much healthy and laudable philosophical debate about the nature of philosophy itself. No doubt, some American philosophy departments have developed the uncharitable propensity of denigrating forms of philosophy with priorities and values alien to their own as somehow not properly philosophical.[2] This, I submit, is not an intrinsic failure on the part of philosophy per se, but on the part of some of its practitioners, regardless of their own personal philosophical commitments. In the big picture, however, such enmity can sometimes spark genuine debate about what is properly philosophical about philosophy itself and hence, in a way, philosophy's restless identity crisis therefore testifies to its strength, not to its decadence.[3] As the celebrated African philosopher Paulin Hountondji has argued:

> Philosophy can be regarded as the most self-conscious of disciplines. It is the one discipline that involves by its very nature a constant process of reflection upon itself. This process of self-reflection, inherent in the nature and practice of philosophy, bears not only upon its purposes, objectives, and methods, upon its relation to the world and to human experience in its multiple expressions, upon its status among other disciplines and forms of intellectual pursuit and discourse, but also, most radically, upon its very nature as an activity and as an enterprise.[4]

Furthermore, the question of introducing the Kyoto School to Western philosophical tastes and habits already risks immediately obscuring the problem. Questions of the form, "What does so and so tradition say about *X*?" or its other variations ("Does said culture even have a philosophy?" or "What does said culture *X* have to say about the really important concept *Y*—for example, God, justice, truth, ethics, and so forth?") assume the domain of epistemic judgment as *fundamental*. Despite the heterogeneous composition of the Western philosophical tradition, there is a marked propensity to insist on the primacy of the *what* question (το τι εστιν, *quid sit*, what is the nature of *X*?). This is not to say that questions of epistemic judgment (What can and do I know?) are not valuable or that they could be avoided. They rightly mark some of the great philosophical triumphs of large parts of the Western philosophical canon and they belong—with due esteem—to part of any philosophical endeavor. Yet to insist on their *value* is not necessarily to have insisted or determined that they are *fundamental*. To ask, "*What* does the Kyoto School think about the nature of philosophical discourse?" is already to have assumed a posture in which one cannot hear or fully appreciate the philosophical stakes of the Kyoto School.

Thomas P. Kasulis, in his book *Intimacy or Integrity: Philosophy and Cultural Difference*, provides some helpful philosophical shorthand in this respect. Kasulis describes the Western propensity for the primacy of epistemic judgment, in which beings are isolated and analyzed in order to determine their natures, as a culture of integrity. "The Latin '*integritās*' is related to '*integer*,' meaning an indivisible whole."[5] Again, this is a propensity, and not an ironclad law of cultural determination. A culture of integrity is a culture that tends to take logic and discursive analysis very seriously. "In short: integrity means being able to stand alone, having a self-contained identity without dependence on, or infringement by, the outside."[6] The integrity paradigm is the provenance of both classical logic and the underlying metaphysical commitment to the sense of being in which it can successfully operate. The formal rules of reasoning, at least in their classical sense, assume the primacy of discernment, because they assume even more primordially an ontology of discrete and discernible entities. As such, this would immediately contrast with the Buddhist tradition's insistence on "dependent co-origination" (*pratītya-samutpāda*).

The Kyoto School, however, epitomizes the critical limits of an integrity-based ontology. For the Kyoto philosophers, not only can one not properly speak of integral things, one cannot speak of a substantial foundation that secures things in their respective natures. Nishida Kitarō,[7] the progenitor of the Kyoto School, argues forcefully for a manner of thinking that does not have recourse to a fundamental ground. There is no ground in the positive sense (in the metaphysical sense of substance, ουσια, *substantia, ens per se*). That is, in marked contrast to the Aristotelian tradition, there is no master subject persisting through its various predications, but unable to take itself as its own predicate (no ὑποκειμενεν, that is, *subjectum* or *suppositum*).[8] As Aristotle famously argued in book zeta of his *Metaphysics*, being is a pure subject, "being not what is said of a subject, but being the subject of whatever is said" (1029a).[9]

For the Kyoto philosophers, there is also no ground in the negative sense, as if nothingness were somehow a ground or a hole or empty space. This is not philosophy oriented to and secured by ground, nor is it errantly capricious in the absence of ground. It does not produce a foundationalist discourse nor a discourse governed reactively by the tragic lack of a ground, as if it were a Buddhist version of Sartrean existentialism. Rather, to use Nishida's terse formulation, "the absolute must relate to itself as a form of contradiction. It must express itself by negating itself."[10] There is no subject of being. Rather, in the subject position, being self-negates—that is, it withholds itself and withdraws, in order to self-predicate. Every predicate expresses the absolute nothingness that haunts the subject position. Yet no predicate determines it in any way. This is doubtless a rather terse formulation, and it is certainly not the kind of language that one would ever find in the classical Mahāyāna tradition; it is an appropriation and creative transformation of the language of the German philosophical tradition. The Kyoto school's texts can be quite dense, and they would probably appear well-nigh inaccessible to someone without at least a little exposure to the texts and practices of the Continental philosophical tradition.

The Kyoto School, first emerging toward the end of the Meiji period and therefore in part reflecting the Japanese appropriation of the European university, was immersed deeply in the German philosophical tradition. It does not follow, however, that the Kyoto School is merely a Japanese version of German idealism, Nietzsche, and Heidegger.

Rather, the Kyoto School recognized in some of these figures new ways to articulate ancient East Asian philosophical insights and experiences, especially those of the Buddhist tradition. In these figures, the Kyoto School found new language to help rejuvenate and reinvigorate and hermeneutically retrieve philosophical possibilities that in some cases exceed the German tradition that enabled their rearticulation.

In this German tradition, beginning with Kant's famous Copernican Revolution, which barred thinking from discerning adequately either the integrity or the ground of things, another, more primordial question began to emerge. In order to preserve its relationship to the *what* question (the question of integrity), I will call this primordial question "the *who* question." *Who* I am exceeds *what* I am, such that one might say that there are two ways in which one can be *what* one is. (1). Who one is is simply what one is. (The *who* is a particular instantiation of a general *what*.) (2). More primordially: *what* I am is the one that can be *who* I am. (The *who* transcends the *what* within which it first appeared.)[11] Heidegger in *Being and Time* famously argued for this distinction. "With the expression of 'self,' we answered the question of the *who of Dasein*. The selfhood of Dasein was defined formally as a way of existing, that is, not as a being objectively present [*ein vorhandenes Seiendes*]. *I myself* am not for the most part the who of Dasein, but the they self [*das Man-selbst*] is."[12] *Das Man*, the impersonal pronoun of cultural ideologies, makes me *what* I am. It constitutes me as something, as some quiddity, as present and available to myself. The *who* of Dasein, the questionability—indeed its question-worthiness [*Fragwürdigkeit*]— that pursues and troubles Dasein at the core of Dasein's being is what the *subjectum* of ontological integrity denies. Dasein is to itself most properly a question, a future, an irresolvable site of possibilities, a singular *who* emerging out of the impersonality of its original *what*.

Heidegger's insight, despite its justly celebrated forcefulness, was not entirely new to the German philosophical tradition. Kant's third critique, *The Critique of Judgment* (1790), dismantled the hylomorphic[13] propensity of classical Christian aesthetics. For Saint Thomas, for example, the hylomorphism that made possible the beauty of something was linked to the formed matter's proximity to its *integritās*. The εἶδος or *integritās* of a thing, the form of its matter (ὕλη), became beautiful in direct proportion to its capacity to be *what* God intended it to be. Saint Thomas reflected that "we call mutilated people ugly, for they lack the required proportion of parts to the whole."[14] Mutilated people and freaks fall unsettlingly short of their proper idea, and we respond with disapprobation and revulsion.

For Kant, however, beauty is found in the union of the true (the *what*) and the good (the *who*). It is not merely that something is what it is, as if beauty were merely the purity of a thing's integrity. Beauty is the grace of the free play of form, in which aesthetic judgment simultaneously unites both a thing's freedom and its form. German idealism, especially that of Schelling, extended Kant's insights into the progressive movement of nature as a movement of the contraries of freedom (the absolute) and form. Nature's progression is the irresolvable life of its contrary forces, the inseparable life of the *who* and the *what* of nature.

The insights of German idealism also explosively reappear in the grand music of Nietzsche's thinking. Already in his first major work, the *Birth of Tragedy* (1871), Nietzsche wrote of the vital struggle between Dionysus (the *who*, the freedom otherwise than form) and Apollo (the austerity of form, the *what*) that can be resurrected in the sublime musicality of tragic drama. In tragic drama, the early Nietzsche argued, the preeminence of identity is exposed as illusory. Later, Nishitani Keiji, another of the Kyoto School's most luminous lights, admitted that Nietzsche decisively reopened the portal to Japanese Zen for him.[15]

Of course, one could write many books cataloguing the many lines of intersection and divergence within the majesty of the German philosophical tradition. More humbly, it is my intention here merely to indicate briefly the opening (a language of integrity deployed in the retrieval of intimacy) that the Kyoto School seized and transformed.

Integrity Language as a Kind of Fundamental Practice and *Upāya* to Invoke the Primacy of Intimacy

There are several fine thinkers associated with the Kyoto School. Some of them, such as Abe Masao, Hisamatsu Shin'ichi, and Miki Kiyoshi, simply exceed the range of this introductory essay. In what follows, I restrict my comments to its three most renowned members: Nishida Kitarō (1870–1945), the lifelong friend of Suzuki Daisetz and perhaps the most important Japanese philosopher of the twentieth century;

Tanabe Hajime (1885–1962), who studied in the early 1920s with both Heidegger and Husserl and who later embraced Shinran (1173–1262) and the True Pure Land sect of Buddhism (Jōdo Shin-shū); and Nishitani Keiji (1900–1990), a student of Nishida who studied with Heidegger during the period of his Nietzsche lectures. I also do not want to give the impression that there are not rich and productive differences and disagreements and shifts of focus between these three thinkers. Just as wanton generalizations about German philosophy are futile, so are ones about the Kyoto School.

Since the purpose of this essay is to provide a philosophical and pedagogical opening to the Kyoto School, I will content myself with a single generalization that I will pursue in what follows. The Kyoto School deployed the fissure that opened within an integrity tradition in order to rejuvenate an ancient tradition that integrity obfuscates. German philosophy, with its retrieval of the primacy of the who question, provided the Kyoto school with a kind of *upāya*, or "skillful means,"[16] to reinvigorate its own, increasingly neglected tradition.

The dizzyingly rapid period of modernization at the onset of the Meiji Restoration all but severed many of the great Dharma lineages. As such, they needed to be retrieved in a language and a tradition that was quite foreign to these increasingly obscure traditions. Yet the new language of Continental philosophy had been inherited in a superficial manner. Nishida later recalled his early exposure to the Japanese "appropriation" of the Western philosophical tradition: "Japan's attitude in adopting European culture was problematic in every respect. The Japanese did not try to transplant the roots of the plant, but simply cut off eye-catching flowers. As a result the people who brought the flowers were respected enormously, but the plants that could have produced such blossoms did not come to grow in our country."[17] Japanese philosophy would need to master fundamentally a new philosophical tradition in order to resuscitate its own philosophical past. Nishitani Keiji was later to insist upon the urgency of this unrecognized crisis: "From the perspective of political history, Japan's being cast on to the stage of world politics during the Meiji Restoration was the greatest change in the history of the nation. But if we look at the change from the point of view of spiritual history, the greatest spiritual crisis was also taking place. What is more, we went through the crisis without a clear realization that it was a crisis; and even now the crisis is being compounded by our continuing lack of awareness of our spiritual void."[18] In other words, the Kyoto philosophers attempted to counter the growing philosophical obscurity of their own tradition by deploying the language of integrity in order to retrieve and articulate what Kasulis called the tradition of intimacy and its emphasis on interrelatedness and interdependence (and even "dependent co-origination"). They recovered—if I might borrow here Heidegger's phrase—"the other beginning"[19] that has been obscured by a manner of thinking that originates with the freestanding subjectum and its world of similarly discrete entities.

This "other beginning" was dramatically evident in a passage from Nishida's 1927 work, *From the Actor to the Seer*:

> It goes without saying that there are many things to be esteemed and learned from in the brilliant development of western culture, which regards form [εἶδος] as being and formation as the good. However, at the basis of Asian culture, which has fostered our ancestors for over several thousand years, lies something that can be called seeing the form of the formless and hearing the sound of the soundless. Our minds are compelled to seek for this. I would like to give a philosophical foundation to this demand.[20]

The Kyoto School, in attempting to retrieve a more primordial, albeit at first always obscured, beginning, provides a searing critique of self-integrity, which comes to us in the Western tradition as the will to live, the will to self-enhancement and preservation, and the insatiable appetites of the ego. Self-integrity, a thing's insistence upon itself, its conation, is what Spinoza, following both Hobbes and an ancient tradition, called the *conatus*. As Spinoza defined it in proposition 7 of part 3 of the *Ethics* (1677): "The *conatus* with which each thing endeavors to persist in its own being is nothing but the actual essence of the thing itself."[21] The conation of being is its insistence on itself, on its integrity. Such a drive is more familiarly dubbed "the will to life" (Schopenhauer) or the will to survive. Somehow we conceive our desire as fundamentally underwritten by a drive to protect and enhance ourselves. In a sense, the Buddha's Four Noble Truths challenge what seems to be the most obvious truth of our genetic composition (that we are hardwired to survive at almost all costs). In this sense, to live "naturally" in an enlightened fashion, one must take on the question of "nature" itself.

In order for the "other beginning" to be retrieved, the beginning that has already begun must somehow be unbegun. The other beginning has to be unleashed from its obscurity within an initial beginning. The call for the retrieval of the other beginning by the deconstruction (*abbauen*) of what already has begun does not issue from simple neglect. It is not that we were too indolent or parochial to have begun at the other beginning. It belongs deeply to the Buddhist tradition that in meditation *we cannot begin at the beginning*. The other, more primordial beginning has first to be retrieved, and hence the Buddhist insistence on a fundamental practice that breaks through the affective distress of our initial mode of being and thinking. Indeed, the first opening to the other beginning is the realization that our modes of thinking and being are out of accord and full of turmoil or *duhkha*.[22]

Hence, the Kyoto School reiterated the Mahāyāna call for the Great Death. As Nishitani argued in his magnum opus *Religion and Nothingness* (1949), the Great Death is born of the Great Doubt. Such a doubt is not the Cartesian doubt in which I find myself in an epistemic crisis. It is an experience of what the Kyoto School called "absolute negation." In the Great Doubt, the doubting self doubts so consummately that it ceases to be a self. It does not preserve itself as the conation of doubting. The Great Doubt even consumes the doubting subject, unlike Cartesian doubt, which secures the doubting subject as the *res cogitans*, even amid a universe of dubitable objects. In Cartesian doubt, the doubting subject adequately takes itself as its own object. The Great Doubt, on the other hand, "is like a bean whose seed and shell break apart as it ripens: the shell is the tiny ego, and the seed the infinity of the Great Doubt that encompasses the whole world."[23] The absolute negation of the Great Doubt is therefore an experience of the death of the ego, the cessation of myself as a *subjectum*.

This is why it can be called the "Great Death." There are numerous Zen sayings referring to that conversion in such terms, for example: "In the Great Death heaven and earth become new," and "Beneath the Great Death, the Great Enlightenment." As in the case of doubt, this enlightenment must be an enlightenment of the self, but at the same time it must signal a "dropping off" of the mode in which "self" is seen as agent. It is something that presents itself as real from the one ground of the self and all things. It is the true reality of the self and all things, in which everything is present just as it is, in its *suchness*.[24]

The Great Doubt and the Great Death usher forth the other beginning, and in this sense they retrieve the clarity that had been heretofore obscured by the initial beginning. In Nishida's stunning final essay, "Nothingness and the Religious Worldview" (1945), this is articulated as the retrieval of an original self that "object logic"—the sway of integrity—obfuscates. "As the Buddhists say, it means to see our essential nature, to see the true self. In Buddhism, this seeing means, not to see the Buddha objectively outside, but to see into the bottomless depths of one's own soul. If we see God externally, it is merely magic."[25] Indeed, Nishida was quite fond, even in his calligraphy, of evoking the famous Zen phrase that proclaims, "The bottom of my soul has such depth that neither joy nor the waves of sorrow can reach it."[26] The self "knows that it has been born to die eternally."[27] This is not to say that it dies and then is reborn into an otherworldly eternal life. Once someone "dies, a person is eternally dead. The individual never returns."[28] Rather, Nishida adheres, as did all of the Kyoto School, to the saying of the Zen master Bu-nan: "While alive be a dead man. Be thoroughly dead, and behave as you like: all will be well."[29]

The Great Death is not, however, the attainment of some kind of plateau upon which thinking comfortably houses itself as if it had reached the promised land. Tanabe was especially strong on this point, arguing for the discontinuous movement of *metanoesis* (*zangedō*), in which one repents the betrayal of each and every arrival, peregrinating in the endless cycle of death and rebirth within thinking itself. For the Kyoto philosophers, Dasein becomes a koan, a mysterious and vital union of contraries, and a dynamic and progressive coincidence of opposites.

This death that reveals the other beginning was already at stake in the first work of the Kyoto School—namely, Nishida's watershed study, *An Inquiry into the Good* (*Zen no kenkyū*) (1911). As Nishida initially struggled to articulate the retrieval of a lost primordial ground, he relied on a term, "pure experience," which he borrowed from William James and to which he linked Schelling and Fichte's intellectual intuition. Prior to the realm of "object logic" and discrete judgments, prior to the grand sway of integrity, Nishida retrieved the realm of what the Mahāyāna Buddhist tradition preserved with the word "suchness" (*tathatā*). In pure experience "there is no distinction between subject and object in any state of direct experience—one encounters reality face to face"[30] As such, direct experience precedes any denotative realm in which the *subjectum* experiences and judges discrete objects. Pure or direct experience is an intuition that the realm of object logic or integrity has been abstracted from a pure state of awareness that transcends judgment. Meaning emerges *from* pure experience, but it is fundamentally not *of* pure experience. "A truly pure experience has no meaning whatsoever; it is simply a present consciousness of facts just as they are."[31] Meaning, while critical, necessarily diminishes the other beginning, which, in its bottomless self, evades the very meanings it grants: "Meanings or judgments are an abstracted part of the original experience, and compared with the original experience they are meager in content."[32]

Finally, the retrieval of the other beginning does not amount to a correction of thinking's initially misguided ontology. It is fundamentally a radical and ethical change of orientation in thinking. As Heisig rightly claims, "For the Kyoto philosophers, thinking either transforms the way we look at things in life or it is not thinking in the fullest sense of the word."[33] Thinking sheds its (self-)obsessive tendencies, repenting its ontological fallenness, and continually converts in love and affirmation to exteriority. The unleashing of the abyss of interiority is simultaneously the birth of exteriority, of what the Buddhist tradition called the Great Compassion (*mahākarunā*). As Nishida had argued right from the beginning, "The more we discard the self and become purely objective or selfless, the greater and deeper our love becomes. We advance from the love between parent and child or husband and wife to the love between friends, and from there to the love of humankind. The Buddha's love extended even to birds, beasts, grasses, and trees."[34]

It is no longer the case of an insatiable *subjectum* and its inexhaustible interests. This is the very crux of Schopenhauer's misunderstanding of the Buddhist and Hindu traditions. He thought that Being itself is an expression of the incessant and agonizingly insatiable strivings of a fundamental will (absolute subject) and its perpetual yet vain self-predications (or representations, *Vorstellungen*). The Kyoto School thinks instead that in exteriority the Good as such, beyond its abbreviation into *my* Good, is liberated. Philosophy as an experience of solar generosity, thousand-armed giving, honey sacrifices, prodigality, and dharmic pot-latches emerges from the ashes of intellectual stinginess. As Nishitani reflected, "The sun in the sky makes no choices about where to shine its rays and shows no preferences as to likes or dislikes. There is no selfishness in its shining. This lack of selfishness is what is meant by non-ego, or 'emptiness' (*śūnyāta*)."[35]

Notes

1. James, Heisig, *Philosophers of Nothingness: An Essay on the Kyoto School* (Honolulu: University of Hawaii Press, 2001), 272.
2. By this statement I do not wish to be construed as taking a position on the lamentable debate in the United States between the analytic and Continental philosophy camps. At their most philosophical, both traditions should have trained us better to eschew such ad hominem attacks. Nonetheless, the fact remains that in practice we too often hastily label our opponents not even as wrong but as not even practicing philosophy. Such cheap shots imply that the proper practice of philosophy is reducible to one's own current activities. In the eyes of the Kyoto School, for example, such propriety would be exposed as part of the incessant and shameless greed of the ego. The human condition has never been particularly prone to philosophy. I submit that it is unfortunate if we cannot learn to profit from our various disagreements. After all, as Aristotle reminds us, philosophy is not ideology but an experience born of wonder.
3. For a further and in-depth discussion of such issues in relationship to African philosophy, please see my "Beyond *Black Orpheus*: Preliminary Thoughts on the Good of African Philosophy," in *Race and Racism in Continental Philosophy*, edited by Robert Bernasconi with Sybol Cook (Bloomington: Indiana University Press, 2003), 268–285.
4. Paulin J. Hountondji, *African Philosophy: Myth & Reality*, translated by Henri Evans with Jonathan Rée (Bloomington: Indiana University Press, 1996), 7.
5. Thomas P. Kasulis, *Intimacy or Integrity: Philosophy and Cultural Difference* (Honolulu: University of Hawaii Press, 2002), 25.
6. Ibid., 53.
7. Please note that throughout this essay I respectfully adhere to the East Asian practice citing the family name prior to the given name.
8. As Heidegger articulates it in *Being and Time* (1927), the *subjectum* is "something self-same in manifold otherness." Martin Heidegger, *Being and Time*, translated by Joan Stambaugh (Albany: State University of New York Press, 1996), 108 (sec. 25).
9. Aristotle, *Metaphysics*, translated by Richard Hope (Ann Arbor: University of Michigan Press, 1960), 133.
10. Nishida Kitarō, "Nothingness and the Religious Worldview," in *Last Writings*, translated by David A. Dilworth (Honolulu: University of Hawaii Press, 1987), 68.

11. This is also a theological distinction. Thomas Merton, for example, located this distinction within the Christian contemplative tradition: "And Christ has granted us His Friendship so that He may in this manner enter our hearts and dwell in them as a personal presence, not as an object, not as a 'what' but as a 'Who.' Thus He Who is, is present in the depths of our own being as our Friend, and as our other self." *New Seeds of Contemplation* (1961; reprint, Boston: Shambhala, 2003), 157. For Merton, the *Who* of Christ—in excess of the *What* of Christ—opened us contemplatively to the *Who* within every person. Whether or not one subscribes to Christ's exclusivity in providing such an opening, Merton is attentive to the barrier of the ego (the *What* of humanity) and its obfuscation of the Who that the great Chan master Linji called the "true person of no rank."

12. Martin Heidegger, *Being and Time*, 247 (sec. 54).

13. "Hylomorphism" refers to the Aristotelian tradition in which a thing is a shape of matter.

14. In Umberto Eco, *Art and Beauty in the Middle Ages*, translated by Hugh Bredin (New Haven, CT: Yale University Press, 1986), 78.

15. See Graham Parkes's introductory essay to his translation (with Setsuko Aihara) of Nishitani Keiji, *The Self-Overcoming of Nihilism* (Albany: State University of New York Press, 1990), xix.

16. This is a classic term in the Buddhist tradition that names the art of discoursing in the prevailing idiom. It is the art, if I may take a liberty here, of somehow speaking true lies. I do not speak on my own terms, but in the terms of the other. In a very radical sense, there are two senses of *upāya* in play in the discourse of the Kyoto School. The first would be the *upāya* of providing a discourse of intimacy in the prevailing discourse of integrity. The second is the even more profound sense that all discourse is in its own way *upāya*. For a further discussion of this in relationship to Tanabe, see my "Death and Resurrection as the Eternal Return of the Pure Land: Tanabe Hajime's Metanoetic Reading of Nietzsche," in Södertörn Philosophical Studies 2 (Stockholm: Södertörns Högskola, 2006).

17. Quoted in H. Gene Blocker and Christopher I. Starling, *Japanese Philosophy* (Albany: State University of New York Press, 2001), 124–25.

18. Nishitani, *Self-Overcoming of Nihilism*, 175.

19. See Martin Heidegger, *Beiträge zur Philosophie (Vom Ereignis)*, ed. Friedrich-Wilhelm von Herrmann (Frankfurt am Main: Vittorio Klostermann, 1989), 55. "This confrontation [*Auseinandersetzung*] is originary when it is of the beginning [*anfänglich*], but is necessarily as such as *another* beginning" (translation mine).

20. Quoted in Abe Masao, introduction to Nishida Kitarō, *An Inquiry into the Good* (New Haven, CT: Yale University Press, 1990), x.

21. Spinoza, *Ethics*, translated by Samuel Shirley (Indianapolis: Hackett Publishing Company, 1982), 109.

22. This is part of the First Noble Truth in which everything (that is, the five *skandhas* or aggregates) is declared to be suffering or turmoil (*duhkha*; or Pali, *dukkha*). The root of all *duhkha* is the infinite thirst of the ego.

23. Nishitani Keiji, *Religion and Nothingness*, translated by Jan van Bragt (Berkeley and Los Angeles: University of California Press, 1982), 21.

24. Ibid.

25. Nishida, *Last Writings*, 77. "For the self to face God is to die" (ibid., 68).

26. Nishida's calligraphic inscription of this phrase is reproduced in *Intelligibility and the Philosophy of Nothingness*, trans. Robert Schinzinger (Tokyo: Maruzen, 1958).

27. Nishida, *Last Writings*, 87.

28. Ibid.

29. Ibid., 101.

30. Nishida Kitarō, *An Inquiry into the Good*, trans. Abe Masao and Christopher Ives (New Haven, CT: Yale University Press, 1990), 31.

31. Ibid., 4.

32. Ibid., 9.

33. James Heisig, *Philosophers of Nothingness: An Essay on the Kyoto school* (Honolulu: University of Hawaii Press, 2001), 14.

34. Nishida, *Inquiry into the Good*, 174. In Zen meditation, the first of the four vows that one chants indicates the Great Compassion: "Sentient beings are numberless. I vow to save them all."

35. Nishtani, *Religion and Nothingness*, 60.

For Further Reading and Research

Nishida Kitarō

Principal works in English translation

Art and Morality. 1924. Translated by David Dilworth and Valdo Viglielmo. Honolulu: University of Hawaii Press, 1973. (Currently out of print.)

Fundamental Problems of Philosophy—The World of Action and the Dialectical World. 1933–34. Translated by David Dilworth. Tokyo: Sophia University Press, 1970. (Long out of print.)

Intelligibility and the Philosophy of Nothingness. Translated by Robert Schinzinger. Tokyo: Maruzen, 1958. Reprint, Westport, CT: Greenwood Press, 1973. (Currently out of print.)

An Inquiry into the Good. 1911. New Haven, CT: Yale University Press, 1990. Completely and provocatively reworked by Abe Masao and Christopher Ives, this is the second and much improved translation. The first version was translated by Valdo Viglielmo as *A Study of Good* (Tokyo: Japanese Government Printing Bureau, 1960) and is long out of print.

Intuition and Reflection in Self-consciousness. 1917. Translated by Valdo Viglielmo with Takeuchi Yoshinori and Joseph S. O'Leary. Albany: State University of New York Press, 1987. (Currently out of print.)

Last Writings: Nothingness and the Religious Worldview. 1945. Translated by David Dilworth. Honolulu: University of Hawaii Press, 1987. An alternative translation of the main essay in this book, Nishida's final summation of his philosophy, appeared as "The Logic of *Topos* and the Religious Worldview," translated by Yusa Michiko, *Eastern Buddhist* 19, no. 2 (1986): 1–29 and 20, no. 1 (1987): 81–119.

Selected secondary sources

Botz-Bornsein, Thorsten, *Place and Dream: Japan and the Virtual.* Amsterdam: Rodopi, 2004. Contains some important chapters on Nishida, as well as two on Kuki Shūzō (1888–1941).

Carter, Robert E. *The Nothingness Beyond God: An Introduction to the Philosophy of Nishida Kitarō.* New York: Paragon House, 1989.

Elberfeld, Rolf. *Kitarō Nishida: Moderne japanische Philosophie und die Frage nach der Interkulturalität.* Amsterdam: Rodopi, 1999.

Nishitani Keiji. *Nishida Kitarō.* Translated by Yamamoto Seisaku and James Heisig. Berkeley and Los Angeles: University of California Press, 1991.

Tremblay, Jacynthe. *Introduction á la philosophie de Nishida.* Paris: L'Harmattan, 2007. This is an indispensible introduction by a leading French-Canadian Nishida scholar.

Wargo, Robert J. J. *The Logic of Nothingness: A Study of Nishida Kitarō.* Honolulu: University of Hawaii Press, 2005. This is a strong study.

Yusa Michiko. *Zen and Philosophy: An Intellectual Biography of Nishida Kitarō.* Honolulu: University of Hawaii Press, 2002. This is a fine study of Nishida's life and thought, with a magisterial bibliography.

Tanabe Hajime

Principal work in English translation

Philosophy as Metanoetics. 1946. Translated by Takeuchi Yoshinori. Berkeley and Los Angeles: University of California Press, 1986. This still ranks as one of the finest translations of a Kyoto school text.

Selected secondary sources

Unno Taitetsu, and James W. Heisig, eds. *The Religious Philosophy of Tanabe Hajime: The Metanoetic Imperative.* Berkeley, CA: Asian Humanities Press, 1990. (Currently out of print.)

Nishitani Keiji

Principal works in English translation

The Self-Overcoming of Nihilism. 1949. Translated by Graham Parkes with Aihara Setsuko. Albany: State University of New York Press, 1990.

On Buddhism. Translated by Yamamoto Saisaku and Robert E. Carter. Albany: State University of New York Press, 2006. These are late lectures given during the 1970s and they provide an interesting engagement with Zen from the perspective of contemporary social needs.

Religion and Nothingness. 1962. Translated by Jan van Bragt. Berkeley and Los Angeles: University of California Press, 1982.

Nishida Kitarō. Translated by Yamamoto Seisaku and James Heisig. Berkeley and Los Angeles: University of California Press, 1991.

Selected secondary sources

Stambaugh, Joan. *The Formless Self*. Albany: State University of New York Press, 1999.

Unno Taitetsu, ed. *The Religious Philosophy of Nishitani Keiji: Encounter with Emptiness*. Berkeley, CA: Asian Humanities Press, 1990. (Currently out of print.)

General Studies on the Kyoto School

Abe Masao. *Zen and Western Thought*. Honolulu: University of Hawaii Press, 1985.

Franck, Frederick. *The Buddha Eye: An Anthology of the Kyoto School*. New York: Crossroad, 1982.

Heisig, James. *Philosophers of Nothingness: An Essay on the Kyoto School*. Honolulu: University of Hawaii Press, 2001. This is the best general introduction to the Kyoto School.

Heisig, James, and John Maraldo, eds. *Rude Awakenings: Zen, the Kyoto School, and the Question of Nationalism*. Honolulu: University of Hawaii Press, 1994.

Heisig, James, ed. *Japanese Philosophy Abroad*. Nagoya: Nanzan, 2004.

Ōhashi Ryōsuke. *Die Philosophie der Kyoto Schule*. Freiburg: Karl Alber, 1990.

Ōhashi Ryōsuke. *Japan im interkulturellen Dialog*. Munich: Iudicium, 1999.

Waldenfels, Hans. *Absolute Nothingness: Foundations for a Buddhist-Christian Dialogue*. Translated by James Heisig. New York: Paulist Press, 1980.

III

Contexts

FRAMEWORKS

John A. Tucker

History as a Vehicle
for the Universal

"World history," "world civilizations," and "global history" can be differentiated abstractly, but they typically overlap in practice. Critics often see "world history" and "world civilizations" courses as "Eurocentric," with token additions of non-European national histories such as those of India, China, and Japan as concessions to demands for multiculturalism. Global history, by comparison, emphasizes the construction of global perspectives.[1] In this essay I will take a pragmatic approach, recognizing that most colleges and universities have courses such as "world history" and "world civilizations" that constitute working paradigms for modification. Rather than a wholly new program of study, this essay moderately advocates a "more global approach" to the teaching of world history. The notion "civilization" has been criticized as elitist, especially when the criteria for it have led historians to exclude large swaths of the past because they somehow did not meet the standards on all counts. Even worse, "world civilizations" courses often are little more than "Western civilizations" courses, either privileging the West or focusing exclusively on it. Here, "civilization" refers to a high level of human culture characterized by, most completely, the presence of cities, socioeconomic diversification, systems of writing, and sophisticated political, legal, and religio-philosophical systems. Ideally, a "world civilizations" course should leave no major pattern of cultural development with significant historical duration unmentioned. The call for "more globalism" is meant to highlight developments that are not tied to national histories, but instead have a metanational importance. Herein the emphasis is on incorporating Asia into world history courses by way of focusing on Asian philosophical systems.

I would maintain that the future of history lies, in part, with the exploration of "mentalities," or "popular visions of the world"[2] that go beyond narrowly defined nation-states and their distinct ideological interests. Examining world civilizations through the exploration of world mentalities—here understood in terms of widely embraced philosophical systems rather than the often remote ideas of "great man" philosophers—enables students of world history to transcend the limited interests of "area studies wars,"[3] pitting, for example, East Asianists against South Asianists, and so forth, while empowering students with a more universalistic (albeit hardly universal) grasp of global history, one serving more the interests of humanity than of colonial regimes. As Norman Wilson explains in *History in Crisis*, one reason for the study of history is that "history cures us of provincialism by showing that change is the only constant."[4]

While affirming history as the prime vehicle for the formulation and reformulation of philosophy, I would question Aristotle's claims about the particularistic character of history. Without history and the medium of historical hermeneutic, philosophy would lack the temporal dimension, and thus remain a static subject, impossibly out of time. Most importantly for the approach to teaching world civilizations advocated here is that major systems such as those of Judaism, Greek philosophy, Hinduism, Buddhism, Confucianism, Daoism, Christianity, and Islam transcend national histories and the narrow confines of their schemes of periodization, and so provide students with broader horizons, in time and space, for understanding the intellectual foundations of history. Thorough integration of world philosophical mentalities within narratives of world history enables the latter to escape the dustbins of past particulars, and approach the realm of, if not universals (a questionable category), then levels of generalization about humanity, nature, logic, and the cosmos that give history greater vitality, meaning, and significance.

What is advocated here is hardly unprecedented: Howard Spodek's *The World's History, vol. 1, To 1500* does an impressive job of spotlighting the rise of "world religions" (Hinduism, Buddhism, Judaism, Christianity, and Islam) and "ideologies of empire" in Chinese history (Legalism, Daoism, and Confucianism).[5] Yet Spodek offers no systematic account of the rise of philosophical thought, apart from the religious and ideological angles, and in offering the latter does not situate coverage of those themes in the most meaningful periods historically. More disappointingly, Spodek does not examine Confucianism and

Daoism, for example, as philosophical systems relevant to East Asia generally, instead preferring to treat them as ideological developments characteristic of China. While the "world" character of religious systems is affirmed, these same systems generated significant philosophical visions that are equally important, and equally metanational, in historical character.

Admirably, in *The Heritage of World Civilizations*, by Craig et al. features in its opening chapter, "The Coming of Civilization," extended examination of "the four great revolutions in thought and religion," highlighting the rise of philosophy in China, religion in India, religion among the Israelites, and Greek philosophy.[6] Other texts, such as Duiker and Spielvogel's *The Essential World History*, treat world philosophical systems here and there, but typically as subnarratives to nation-based surveys of historical development. For example, Confucius is discussed in the account of the dawn of Chinese history, as a crucial figure in the production of its "civilization."[7] Missing is a more systematic grasp of Confucius, the *Analects*, and Confucianism in terms not only of Chinese history, but that of Korea, Japan, and all of East Asia. It is the latter kind of comprehensive, systematic vision of the vital philosophical past that I would advocate, one situating philosophical systems not in the register of "great man" genealogies, nor in the "legacies" column of national histories, but rather as historical processes defining mentalities of significant global regions.

One way for new world histories to address the past more globally is through the study of the rise of distinctly Asian philosophical systems, including those of Hinduism, Buddhism, and Confucianism. The first two are often treated as world religious systems, which no doubt they were, but they also require exploration as systems of ethical, epistemological, and metaphysical importance, not just of faith and soteriology. These systems are important to a more global understanding of world history and civilizations because each transcends national boundaries, having a relevance for, at the very least, an entire region, and in the case of Confucianism, Hinduism, and Buddhism, over time, a considerable portion of humanity and the world. Equally compelling is that these systems of religion and/or philosophy have not vanished, as is true with so many objects of historical study. Although they are hardly the same entities, their evident resilience in the modern world ensures that they will be elements in future intellectual landscapes, and makes them certain subject matter for any history of world civilizations recognizing the present as "a reconfiguration of forces that have been shaping the world for centuries."[8]

Numerous approaches to these systems might be valid. One possible approach is the "systems through texts" method, or an introductory approach to world philosophies through the study of pivotal texts in translation, which makes intimate engagement with the relevant literature possible for undergraduates. Of course, the "systems through texts" strategy must be accompanied by wider readings in introductory textbook accounts of the systems that the individual texts helped define. Intensive class discussions of the texts, critically and yet sympathetically, is de rigueur if their full value is to be appreciated. While it is not a wholly satisfactory means of coming to terms with any world philosophical system, unless students are expected to read at least one major work per system they will remain compromised in their understandings, reliant on secondary materials in assigned texts and lectures. To use Plato's analogy, they will know little more than shadows. Reading, for example, the *Bhagavad Gītā* in translation, while still leaving students several levels removed from the ideas communicated in the Sanskrit text, nevertheless provides a more authentic experience of the system.

In the remainder of this essay, I would like to offer three textual strategies for the "systems through texts" approach, first in relation to Hinduism, then Confucianism, and finally Buddhism. In each case, rather than presenting the system as a national development, or as the monument of genius philosophers, the suggested emphasis is on the cumulative tradition that the text or texts issued from and in turn gave rise to. Rather than interpret philosophical systems as distinctive to a single national entity, such as China with Confucianism and India with Hinduism, we should highlight texts that lend themselves to understanding systems cross-culturally over time.

For the study of Hinduism, the recommended text is the *Bhagavad Gītā*, the "exemplary text of Hindu culture for centuries." Long renowned as one of the most popular pieces of sacred literature in India, the *Gītā* has also impacted, as Barbara Miller notes, much of the remainder of Asia as well, not to mention Western thinkers such as Henry David Thoreau, Ralph Waldo Emerson, and T. S. Eliot, just to mention a few luminaries.[9] The origins of the *Gītā* are uncertain, though it is safe to say that it crystallized between 400 BCE and 400 CE, along with the *Mahabharata*, the great Sanskrit epic of ancient India of which the *Gītā* is one part. The *Gītā* seems to date, along with other portions of the *Mahabharata*, from around the first century. Despite ambiguities surrounding its beginnings, the *Gītā* is most certainly an expression of the Indo-Aryan peoples who entered the Indus Valley around 1000 BCE and established themselves as dominant formulators of what later came to be called Hinduism. As such, the text can easily be read as a mythic reflection of history, especially insofar as it is set on a battlefield, Kurukshetra, just as a war between relatives of the legendary king Bharata was about to begin. Realizing that he must fight his cousins, Arjuna, one of the key warriors of the Pāndava forces, becomes hesitant. The main text of the *Gītā* conveys the philosophical insights offered to Arjuna by his charioteer, Krishna. Ultimately, Krishna reveals himself as none other than Vishnu, Brahman, and the syllable om of the Upanishads—that is, as the most holy and supreme creator/destroyer of the entire cosmos, past, present, and future. Before doing so, however, he explains to Arjuna that the true self, the *atman*, is something that cannot be destroyed, even in warfare. Rather than worry about killing anyone, Krishna advises Arjuna to fulfill his dharma—that is, do his duty as a warrior, not with thoughts of reward or fame, but as acts of selfless devotion to him, Krishna, the divine Vishnu incarnate. If he can go into battle in this way, then Arjuna will have acted in an exemplary fashion. Though not a work of systematic philosophy, the *Gītā* does allude to, in a most dramatic way, the Hindu philosophy of the self (*atman*) in relation to the divine (*Brahman*), thus providing ample opportunities for a textual exploration of the system of Hinduism within the context of a world civilizations class. Moreover, the text had abiding historical relevance: it was both extolled by Gandhi, who admired its teachings of selfless devotion, and appealed to by his assassin, who believed that in murdering Gandhi he was doing his duty. Finally, while the *Gītā* relates most directly to Indian religio-philosophical culture, its impact extended, in ancient times, into Indo-China, and in modern times, has spread into the West, making it one of the most exceptional texts of all time.

For the study of Confucianism, reading of the *Analects* is recommended. Of course, one reason for choosing this text is that it defines the literary starting point of the development of the Confucian mentality, especially as described in relation to Confucius and his disciples in dialogue—Zilu, Zixia, Zigong, Yanhui, and others. However, from my perspective, the fact that the *Analects* "came first" is not the prime reason for its selection. Rather, what makes the *Analects* valuable is the fact that it was not written by Confucius, but rather compiled over generations by his disciples, their followers, and subsequent editors, and then interpreted by commentators in China, Korea, and Japan over the last two millennia. It was also among the first Chinese works translated by Jesuit scholars attempting to communicate the nature of imperial Chinese culture to Rome in the late sixteenth and seventeenth centuries. The very composite and yet seminal nature of the text makes it valuable, since it discourages an approach to Confucianism as the work of a philosophical prodigy, Confucius, and instead reveals it as a system of thought formulated through dialogue, personal study, engagement, and reflection. Reading of the *Analects* also reveals that the Confucianism of early Confucians was a work in progress, typically subject to revision and reformulation on the basis of subsequent discussion and study. The text also belies the stereotype that Confucianism was inherently supportive of rulers, serving well their ideological needs. Instead, the *Analects* portrays Confucius as a wandering teacher who occasionally found himself in situations that frightened his followers. Yet their teacher was never personally perturbed, nor for that matter ever patronized by a lord or elevated to high station by a ruler. Indeed, the presentation of Confucius and Confucianism in the *Analects* defies, at nearly every turn, misleading clichés that secondary sources often serve up to students.

Finally, the *Analects* is a key text for teaching world philosophy in a world civilizations course because it communicates much that was distinctively Chinese, and yet relates notions that most importantly came to define much ethical, political, and religious discourse in the greater East Asian region. Had Confucius and the work that purports to relay his original teachings been nothing more than of consequence to the Chinese, it would not be suitable for a world history survey. But in fact the *Analects* was read throughout Asia, and often served as the basis for the articulation of new expressions of thought. One example will suffice: in Tokugawa Japan, seventeenth-century scholars such as Itō Jinsai and Ogyū Sorai, living some two millennia after the *Analects* first crystallized, expounded their philosophical visions, expressions of the Confucian mentality, via extended lexicographic studies of the

Analects. So pivotal was this anonymous text that it continued as a key ingredient in the East Asian curriculum well into contemporary times. While it hardly exhausts the parameters of the system of Confucianism, its seminal quality is evident in the seemingly unending series of commentaries and studies it has prompted over the ages by East Asians and those seeking to understand them. Using the *Analects*—a brief work, available in any number of English translations—as the touchstone, instructors can also supplement their survey of Confucianism as an East Asian system by comparing and contrasting it with a host of other important texts, such as the *Zhuangzi*, the *Daodejing*, the *Mencius*, the writings of Dong Zhongshu, and the works of the Neo-Confucians.

For the study of Buddhism, various texts might be useful. The *Dhammapada* (*The Way of Righteousness*), for example, provides an excellent statement of early Buddhist moral thought. However the *Dhammapada* was not as influential outside of India as were later texts such as the *Vimalakīrti Sutra*, "one of the most popular of [the] Asian classics for about two thousand years."[10] The latter is valuable insofar as it expresses a widely endorsed approach to the problem of lay practice within the context of Mahāyāna Buddhism, the more universalistic variety that ultimately spread from India into Central Asia, Southeast Asia, and East Asia. Yet as Wing-tsit Chan once remarked, "No one can understand the Far East without some knowledge of the teachings of the *Lotus Sutra*, because it is the most important scripture of Mahāyāna Buddhism, which cuts across the entire Far East."[11] What makes the *Lotus Sutra* (*Saddharma Pundarīka*) most compelling is that, like the *Vimalakīrti*, it was presumably the product of various Indian and/or Central Asian Buddhist scribes who formulated a universalistic, soteriological version of the early philosophical teachings that was capable of doctrinal flexibility and yet steadfast in affirming that all sentient beings will attain Buddhahood in either this lifetime or in a future life. Equally dramatic, though at another level, the *Lotus Sutra* is presented as the last sermon of the historical Buddha, thus making it a purported "final" teaching within its tradition. The *Lotus* also explains in detail the compassionate nature of the bodhisattva, most poignantly illustrated through its accounts of Guanyin (Jpn., Kannon), the bodhisattva of mercy. Full of engaging, fascinating, and often fantastic parables, the *Lotus* is hardly a dull read. Yet in its pages, complex doctrines such as the Buddhist two-level theory of truth are adumbrated. Moreover, issues related to women and their place in Buddhism are addressed, albeit in disturbing ways. Finally, the *Lotus* offers a unique explanation of the end of Siddhartha Gautama's physical existence on earth, portraying him ascending to the heavens in a bejeweled pagoda, flanked by another Buddha, Prabhūtaratna, manifesting the total body of the Buddha.

There are literary and philosophical weaknesses in the *Lotus,* such as its systematic repetitiveness and its tendency to address matters of "faith, hope, and love," more than purely philosophical issues.[12] Nevertheless, there is no denying that the *Lotus Sutra* does communicate a great deal of the philosophical mentality of Buddhism as it developed throughout Asia, and as it has come to be understood in the West; thus, it could easily be used by instructors as an appealing means of relating philosophical issues to the colorful contents of soteriological literature. More than the *Analects*, the *Lotus Sutra* is of uncertain origins: even the language in which it was first written is not known. As a result, teaching the *Lotus* necessarily bypasses the "great man" approach so common in the study of philosophical ideas. Most virtuously for the study of world history, however, is that the *Lotus* was an exceptionally important text in China, Korea, and Japan, communicating in each area of East Asia the essential message of universal attainment of Buddhahood, which in turn became a staple feature of the traditional East Asian mentality. Additionally, in China and Japan, the *Lotus* was the subject of repeated commentaries. In Japan, the *Lotus* was a crucial text for several of the major schools of Buddhism, including most especially those of Tendai and Nichiren. And as the scholarship of Willa and George Tanabe has shown, the *Lotus* has inspired a prodigious amount of artistic and cultural allusions to its narratives and the teachings communicated therein.[13] Study of the *Lotus Sutra*, then, provides an understanding of the teaching as it penetrated the various realms of Asia and East Asia, providing a key ingredient in the philosophical and religious mentality of the region as a whole.

Notes

1. Raymond Grew, "On the Prospect of Global History," in *Conceptualizing Global History*, edited by Bruce Mazlish and Ralph Buultjens (Boulder, CO: Westview Press, 1993), 3.

2. Michel Vovelle, *Ideologies and Mentalities*, translated by Eamon O'Flaherty (Chicago: University of Chicago Press, 1990), 4–9.
3. Neil L.Waters, ed., *Beyond the Area Studies Wars: Toward a New International Studies* (Hanover, NH: University Press of New England, 2000).
4. Norman Wilson, *History in Crisis: Recent Directions in Historiography* (Upper Saddle River, NJ: Prentice Hall, 1999), 139.
5. Howard Spodek, *The World's History, vol. 1, To 1500* (Upper Saddle River, NJ: Prentice Hall, 2000), 257–369.
6. Albert M. Craig et al., *The Heritage of World Civilizations, vol. 1, To 1650* (Upper Saddle River, NJ: Prentice Hall, 2002), 15–28.
7. William J. Duiker and Jackson J. Spielvogel, *The Essential World History, Comprehensive Volume* (Belmont, CA: Wadsworth, 2002), 48–49.
8. Arif Dirlik, Vinay Bahl, and Peter Gran, eds., *History after the Three Worlds: Post-Eurocentric Historiographies* (New York: Rowman and Littlefield, 2000), 3.
9. Barbara Stoller Miller, introduction to *The Bhagavad-Gītā: Krishna's Counsel in Time of War* (New York: Columbia University Press, 1996), 1.
10. Robert A. F. Thurman, "The Teaching of Vimalakīrti," in *Approaches to the Asian Classics,* edited by William Theodore de Bary and Irene Bloom (New York: Columbia University Press, 1990), 232.
11. Wing-Tsit Chan, "The Lotus Sutra," in *Approaches to the Asian Classics,* edited by William Theodore de Bary and Irene Bloom (New York: Columbia University Press, 1990), 220.
12. Ibid., 25.
13. Willa J. Tanabe and George J. Tanabe, Jr., eds., *The "Lotus Sutra" in Japanese Culture* (Honolulu: University of Hawaii Press, 1989).

Suggested Readings

Abu-Lughod, Janet. *Before European Hegemony: The World System, A.D. 1250-1350.* New York: Oxford University Press, 1989.
Brooks, Bruce, and Taeko Brooks. *The Original Analects: Sayings of Confucius and His Successors.* New York: Columbia University Press, 1998.
De Bary, William Theodore, and Irene Bloom, eds. *Approaches to the Asian Classics.* New York: Columbia University Press, 1990.
Hall, David, and Roger T. Ames, *Thinking Through Confucius.* Albany: State University of New York Press, 1987.
Lau, D. C., trans. *The Analects.* By Confucius. New York: Penguin Books, 1979.
Legge, James. *Confucius: Confucian Analects, The Great Learning, and The Doctrine of the Mean.* New York: Dover, 1971.
Said, Edward. *Orientalism.* New York: Pantheon, 1978.
Waley, Arthur. *The Analects of Confucius.* New York: Vintage. 1938.
Ware, James R. *The Sayings of Confucius.* New York: Mentor, 1955.
Watson, Burton, trans. *The Lotus Sutra.* New York: Columbia University Press, 1993.

Francis Brassard

Asking the Right Questions

Once the Buddha was asked ten questions. Some dealt with the nature of the world, some were related to the soul, and others pertained to the fate of the awakened person. According to the Buddhist scriptures, he did not answer. His legendary silence is often explained with the notion that, because the ten questions will only lead to fruitless speculations, they are not conducive to spiritual progress. In other words, from the Buddha's perspective and concerns, these questions were not worth answering. A similar idea was expressed using the simile of the arrow. In this simile, a man, who had just been shot by an arrow, was only interested in discovering who shot the arrow. Concerned with knowing the caste and other details of the social status of the aggressor, the man did not worry in the least about getting rid of the arrow nor about saving his own life. Like the ten questions posed to the Buddha, the man's questions were not pertinent to the problem at hand. In other words, they were out of context.

These two stories taken from the Buddhist canon are often used to show that the teachings of Buddhism need to be understood in the light of a specific context—that is, as a means to bring about spiritual transformation. Outside this context, they have no meaning whatsoever. In both cases, however, despite the fact that the questions asked missed the point, they somehow provide us with hints or directions for further inquiry. Asking questions thus becomes a means of revealing the context in which an idea, a system of thought, or even a spiritual practice is to be understood.

In the present essay, I discuss how asking questions may facilitate the integration and infusion of Asian philosophical and religious materials into Western disciplines. I believe that asking the right questions is likely to expose the presuppositions and the assumptions underlying any philosophical discourse or religious practice. As such, it enables us to dig more deeply below the surface of the expressed ideas and, hopefully, to identify a basis for comparison and common understanding. Because asking the right questions eventually has to do with identifying the concerns and the motivations that give rise to a system of thought, it makes it possible "to see" ideas from the perspective of those who developed them and of those who still advocate them.

Before presenting some examples of this approach, let me first discuss what it means to "ask the right questions." A question is above all a research and investigative tool. If it allows us to make some sense of the unknown, it already is a good question. If it permits us to see in a new light something apparently known, it is an even better question. A good question is therefore judged on the results it yields. To some extent, one never knows the value of a question before one has tested it. My first practical suggestion would therefore be that one should not worry so much, at the beginning, whether one's question is the right question. The first step is to simply formulate a question and work with it.

This understanding is not much different from what the Buddha, and eventually Buddhism, conceived as the value of spiritual practices and even of claims of truth. Through his own experience the Buddha was able to identify, from all the questions circulating during his time, those that were truly productive. In a similar way, people studying the fields of religions and foreign cultures have come to formulate questions that are revealing by bringing together pieces of puzzling situations. Not only are their questions able to make more sense but also, like a good scientific model usually does, they help us predict the ways a community of believers will behave under certain conditions.

The questions I wish to discuss in the present essay were not originally conceived by me. I am, however, very happy to be given the opportunity to share them. They were "given to me" by Professor Charles Adams, a renowned scholar of Islam, while I was a graduate student of religious studies at McGill University. I have been using them in many of my classes on Eastern religions and philosophies as a way to shed new light on elements believed to be well known or understood by my students. In other words, I use them as tools to reveal contexts. My discussion of these questions is in many ways a tribute to Charles Adams.

In an article entitled "Islam and Christianity: The Opposition of Similarities," Adams suggested a set of three related questions to make us aware that elements that appear similar can, in fact, be quite different due to the contexts in which they are articulated. The first question deals with how the human problem or the human situation that calls the religious response into existence is understood and formulated. The second question is related to the means by which the human problem is solved. The aim of the third question is to reveal what it means for an individual—and in some cases, for a community—to apply the given solution. To put the matter differently, one could ask: What is the nature of the state one reaches when one has solved the human problem? Note that these questions reflect the assumption that religious practices are performed and beliefs are held for a purpose. As such, these questions clearly echo the Buddhist attitude toward their spiritual teachings as well as toward any other system of thought aiming at salvation or spiritual emancipation. To begin, let us now ask these three questions to both Muslims and Christians and compare their responses.

For Muslims, the human problem is related to the fact that we are beings created by Allah—in short, that we are creatures. The concept of "creature" implies that, when contrasted to that of a creator, creatures have limitations. Apart from not being able to fly like birds or to remain under water like fish, the most important limitation for any human being is his or her lack of knowledge regarding what is the right thing to do. To use another simile, we are very sophisticated machines that do not exactly know how to operate ourselves in an optimal way. To make the best use of us, therefore, we need guidance. This is the solution to our most basic problem. And where do men get guidance? According to the Muslim faith, guidance was given to us in the form of revelations, the last and most complete being the one transmitted through the prophet Muhammad. Thus, the main thrust behind most Muslim intellectual endeavors has to do with making this revealed guidance more and more explicit in our daily lives—that is, to know the way Allah expects us to behave.

When Muslims apply the revealed guidance to their lives, when they act in an optimal way, the only thing to expect is a great sense of optimism and eventually success in all enterprises of life. Lack of success can consequently be explained as a failure to follow Allah's guidelines. When this failure is caused by such conditions as domination by foreign powers, the result is an acute sense of humiliation and eventually of aggressiveness toward those powers. Given this context, the desire to use the Shari'a, or Muslim law, as the only code to regulate society is not, in the minds of those Muslims who advocate it, a backward move at all. Indeed, for them it means the same as the idea of "restoration of democracy" does for those who promote what they believe to be the best possible world to live in.

Christians, on the other hand, whose faith is believed to be related closely to that of Islam and Judaism, will give entirely different answers to the three questions just asked. For a start, the main problem of humanity has nothing to do with the status of being a creature. In Christianity, God has created men, but Christians do not draw the same conclusions from this belief as Muslims do. For them, the idea of being created by God is secondary. What is primary is the fact that men became sinners. The idea is not that they do sinful actions, but that they are intrinsically sinners. This is their nature. Because of this nature, whatever they do is tainted by sin. There is nothing they can do by themselves to change this situation. It is only through the redemptive act of Jesus, by dying on the cross, that they will be forgiven—that is, that their nature as sinners will be transformed. Jesus is thus the only true solution to the human problem as viewed by Christians. In theory, a Christian should therefore experience a deep sense of peace. Their sinful nature has not been erased, but forgiven. To some extent, an accomplished Christian is aware of two things at the same time: his sinful nature and the forgiveness of God. In fact, and in a somewhat puzzling way, the more one is aware of one's sinful nature, the more the redemptive act of Jesus becomes important and increases this deep peace of mind.

In this context, any type of action, especially social, is possible. Because the world still remains marked by sin, one may think that it is not worth spending time changing it. A life of seclusion, cut out from society as much as possible, may be considered the ideal life. Striving to become an ideal model of Christian life may be viewed as the ultimate act of love toward all beings. On the other hand, one may feel that one should relieve men of their temporary suffering, following the example of Jesus, who also cured sick people. But however much effort they make, there will still be poor and sick people. They cannot really change this situation. What this means is that for a Christian, and contrary to the Muslim view, success in life should not be important. Poverty and lack of success are not humiliating. On the contrary, these experiences or conditions help Christians understand their condition as sinners and eventually make them accept the gift of God's forgiveness. One can thus understand why most of the Eastern Orthodox churches, which put great emphasis on the mystic teachings of Jesus, have had a limited influence on social development and have very rarely opposed any form of government in their respective countries. Also, one can see why the "theology of liberation," developed by some members of the Catholic Church, had limited success and was in fact opposed by the so-called conservative theologians of Rome. Social action to improve the lot of people is ultimately a secular concern. Thus, the idea of the separation of the church and the state goes well with the presuppositions of Christian theology. This is not the case with Islam, where state and religion are one.

The contexts that have been revealed through the above three questions admittedly provide only impressionistic pictures of Christianity and Islam. Nevertheless, I think that they are clear enough to help us understand some of the ideas, practices, and attitudes of the believers of these religious traditions. For example, why is it that Muslims, as opposed to Christians, are very reluctant to subject their holy texts to critical analysis? Very often, Christians, in an attempt to show their openness, contrast their own attitude with that of Muslims, which, from this particular point of view, appears closed and "fundamentalist." On the basis of the contexts revealed, this comparison is false. Indeed, because the sacred scriptures of Islam, especially the Qur'an, are the solution to the human problem, they should be compared to what is considered the Christian solution to the human problem—namely, Jesus. Thus, the reluctance of the Muslims to analyze critically the Qur'an is probably equivalent to the attempt to subjugate the host and wine to various scientific tests, at the moment of their consecration, just to see whether they are really transformed into the body and blood of Christ. This would be, from a Christian point of view, ludicrous and unacceptable. Similarly, if the most intense religious experience for some Christians is the Eucharist, for Muslims it is the recitation of the Qur'an, which brings them closest to the creator. In this regard, many Muslims learn the entire Qur'an by heart, without even knowing Arabic, the language in which it was written. Again, why is it that any translation of the Qur'an is no longer considered to be the true Qur'an? It was because Arabic was the language Allah chose to reveal his guidelines to us. Any translation is already an interpretation. This is no longer the word of Allah. To put it in simple terms, Christians can read the Bible in English, French, or Latin, but what Muslims can read in these languages are only, at best, commentaries or, at worst, false interpretations of Allah's revelations.

Although the three questions suggested to me by Charles Adams have been used to highlight the major differences between Islam and Christianity, I have adapted them to help students understand the contexts in which the major ideas and practices of Buddhism are articulated. These ideas and practices are often contrasted with those of Hinduism or Jainism, which, as philosophical systems aiming at emancipation or liberation, may be considered very close to Buddhism.

An interesting example of such contrast or comparison is the idea of "dharma." Teachers of Asian religions know very well the variety of meanings this term assumes on the basis of its context of use. For instance, the notion of dharma principally means "duties" in the context of Hinduism, whereas in Buddhism it designates, among other things, the teachings of the Buddha. However, when dharma qua duties is used within the framework of the Yoga of Action (*karma yoga*), its function resembles that of the practice of *zazen*, as conceived in its wider sense by Dōgen, the founder of the Japanese Sōtō Zen school of Buddhism. Indeed, for the practitioner of the Yoga of Action, the basic problem of life can be defined as an inability to decide the right course of action. One of the main presuppositions underlying this system of spiritual practice is that all our actions are based on a dualistic perception of reality. Because of that very limited outlook, one cannot know what is really beneficial to us, to the community, and to the world in general. The solution is then to act according to a set of guidelines or rules that are not based on one's egoistic self, or anyone else's "self" for that matter. Thus, the duties prescribed by dharma, in addition to being a way to regulate social relationships, have been infused with a new meaning: they now serve as a set of rules by which one regulates one's life without regard to the outcomes of one's actions. To reinforce the nondualistic nature of these rules, it may be natural to attribute them to a higher authority, such as that of a supreme and all-encompassing God. Thus, in this context, theism becomes an important component of the religious outlook, and the fundamental nature of one's spiritual effort is to do whatever is required with an attitude of complete renunciation, or surrender, to this higher authority.

For Dōgen, the basic problem of life is also related to the dualistic nature of our decisions and our behavior. Because our true nature, the Buddha-nature, is clouded by our desires, we live in a constant state of anxiety as to what ought to be done. To recover our true and nondualistic nature, we have to do *zazen,* or sitting meditation. For Dōgen, however, *zazen* was more than just sitting in a meditative posture for a certain amount of time while focusing our attention on a single point. Rather, *zazen* means to give ourselves up to a strict and all-embracing code of behavior. In that way, desires, even if they are present in the mind, will not interfere in the course of our actions. If, in the case of the Yoga of Action, a supreme authority is giving weight to the mandatory nature of our actions, in the context of Dōgen's understanding of the practice of *zazen* it is our immediate experience of reality as it is that is supreme. By giving undivided attention to such trivial actions as brushing one's teeth or washing one's cup, one has to be able to force one's mind to follow, or embrace, reality in whatever form it presents itself. The purpose of the strict code of regulated, simple behavior, which is part of the Zen monk's daily routine, is to create the best possible conditions to support one's efforts. Although it may be difficult to describe what is going on in the mind of the Zen monk engaged in the practice of *zazen*, one may point out the similarity between the role of the phenomenal world in Zen and that of the supreme deity in Yoga. Both are used to eliminate the egoistic self in order to make room for a nondualistic mode of behavior. By following one's dharma as closely as possible, it is hoped that one will eventually understand the "mind" of the intelligence that created it—that is, that one will experience God. Similarly, in modeling one's behavior on reality as it is, one wishes to experience its true nature—that is, the Buddha-nature that is in everything.

It is often said that there is no God in Buddhism, but what does this mean? Frankly speaking, it means nothing as long as we have not put this idea in its proper context. I tried to show in the previous example that a spiritual system affirming the existence of a supreme God may very well be based on assumptions similar to that shared by an apparently different system negating the existence of such a God. The three questions discussed earlier thus allow us to go beyond the cultural expressions of these systems of belief and practices. Similarly, these questions may be used to identify basic differences in places where one would expect likeness. The Indian notion of karma is a good example of this.

Although *karma* is translated broadly as "action," the ways to get rid of its negative effects differ depending on the spiritual context in which it is articulated. For the Jains, for instance, karma is viewed as a kind of spiritual dust accumulated on the soul. To free the soul from it, one has to perform penance that takes the form of extreme abstinence. The amount of karma-dust accumulated and the amount of penance to be performed are almost equivalent. In the Buddhist context, however, because knowledge is believed to be an important factor in the process of liberation, the relationship between accumulated karma and the amount of spiritual practices required is altered significantly. Incidentally, karma is no longer viewed in the Buddhist context as dust but rather as latent tendencies to act in specific ways. Thus, the problem for Buddhists is no longer to match their efforts to the quantity of karma accumulated but rather to find a way to eradicate the cause of its accumulation. Once it has been eliminated, no more karma accumulates, and the already accumulated karma, except that which gave rise to the present body, instantaneously disappears. Some Buddhists would even say that at this point one realizes that karma never existed in the first place. Such realization is the true liberation from karma.

Because I have taught Buddhism to students coming from a Western cultural environment, I also use the three questions to compare Buddhist ideas with those of Western religions, particularly Christianity; for instance, I discuss the role of scriptures or the nature of devotional practices. One comparison I like to discuss with my students is the one between the Buddhist notion of reincarnation and the Christian idea of resurrection. For some in the West, reincarnation or rebirth has become popular because it allows one many chances of acquiring salvation. But Christians are likely to reject this idea because, among other things, it minimizes, or even negates, the role of Jesus in one's salvation. Whatever the reasons given in favor of or against reincarnation, it appears that it cannot be compared to the idea of resurrection. Indeed, within the Buddhist context, reincarnation is used to define and explain the nature of the human problem, whereas resurrection, from the Christian point of view, is part of the solution of what they perceive to be the human problem. Thus, a more appropriate comparison would be between resurrection and the Buddhist idea of *nirvāna*. In fact, a more appropriate comparison is likely to make religious interdialogue more interesting and fruitful. Not only does asking the right questions yield more insight into the workings of a foreign religious tradition, it also creates bridges by which one can reach out to the believers of other religions.

Building bridges is what asking questions is all about. Our questions are produced from our presuppositions. These presuppositions somehow determine the initial alignment of the bridge that is to be built in order to reach the other shore. If this initial alignment is flawed, to the extent that it would make the bridge end up in the middle of the river, then a new alignment must be made. That is, a new question has to be formulated because the previous one was not appropriate. This new question is still based on one's presuppositions, but this time the fruitless attempt has now been integrated and processed. At this point, even failure reveals something of the unknown. Thus, by a process of trial and error, questions become better and more refined. In this process, new contexts are revealed and explored. Once our bridge has found a firm footing on the other shore, communication is possible.

Suggested Readings

Adams, Charles J. "Islam and Christianity: The Opposition of Similarities." *Mediaeval Studies* 6 (1984): 287–306.

Denny, Frederick M. *Islam and the Muslim Community*. New York: Harper San Francisco, 1987.

Gethin, Rupert. *The Foundations of Buddhism*. Oxford: Oxford University Press, 1998.

Gombrich, Richard. *Theravāda Buddhism: A Social History from Ancient Benares to Modern Colombo*. London: Routledge, 1988.

Küng, Hans, Josef van Ess, Heinrich von Stietencron, and Heinz Bechert. *Christianity and the World Religions: Paths of Dialogue with Islam, Hinduism and Buddhism*. Garden City, NY: Doubleday and Company, 1986.

Smith, Wilfred Cantwell. *The Faith of Other Men*. Toronto: CBC Publications, 1962.

Williams, Paul. *Mahāyāna Buddhism*. London: Routledge, 1989.

Shigenori Nagatomo

A Sketch of the *Diamond Sutra's* Logic of Not

"When one side is illuminated, the other side remains in darkness."
—Dōgen, "Genjōkōan"

The topic of this essay is the logic that is used in the *Diamond Sutra* (Skt., *Vajraccedhikāprajñāpāramitā*), which is called the "logic of not" (Skt. *na pṛthak*).[1] This logic is formulated as: "*A* is not *A*, therefore it is *A*." Since this statement appears to be contradictory, or paradoxical at best, I wish to explain the philosophical reasoning of this formulation proposed in the *Diamond Sutra* to counter what some might dismiss as nonsensical or meaningless. In order to articulate the philosophical reasons for this contradictory formulation, I will advance the thesis that as long as one understands the "logic of not" in light of Aristotelian logic by assuming a dualistic, either-or egological stance, it remains contradictory, and to understand it properly one must read it by effecting a perspectival shift to a nondualistic, neither-nor, nonegological stance. Only then can one see that it is not contradictory, and therefore not nonsensical.

Before delving into a philosophical articulation of the meaning of this "logic," let me briefly provide some background information. The *Diamond Sutra* appeared at an early phase in the development of Mahāyāna Buddhism, and it belongs to a group of literature that Buddhologists call the "perfection of wisdom" (*prajñāpāramitā*). Wisdom (*prajñā*) is characterized in this literature as severing "all doubt and attachment" like a "diamond that cuts well."[2] The "diamond" designates metaphorically the transparency of the mind, while "cutting" is a metaphor for the nondiscriminatory activity of the mind. And

I wish to express my appreciation to Dr. John Krummel of Temple University for repairing my English and for his insightful comments.

when the nondiscriminatory activity is realized as knowledge, it is called wisdom (*prajñā*). In this respect, *prajñā* is demarcated from the kind of knowledge Aristotle proposes in his *Metaphysics* in which a universal is singled out as its genuine form.[3] Because the sutra does not treat *prajñā* as theoretical knowledge, it envisions it to be practical and experiential in nature. The experience of it is achieved through the practice of meditation. The perfection of wisdom that the sutra thematizes, then, is a practical ideal to be achieved and embodied for those who have not achieved it. The sutra assigns this practical goal to the bodhisattva. The bodhisattva is a person who is intent on the achievement of enlightenment for his or her own sake as well as for the sake of benefiting others. The sutra formulates the bodhisattva's perfection of wisdom in the propositional form: "*A* is not *A*, therefore it is *A*." My goal in this essay is to make this statement intellectually intelligible by philosophically reconstructing the *Diamond Sutra*'s standpoint.

The Conceptual Structure of the *Diamond Sutra*

The conceptual structure of the *Diamond Sutra* can be sketched by contrasting the characterizations given to the bodhisattva with those whom the sutra identifies as the "foolish, ordinary people" (*bālaprthag-janā*). According to the sutra, the "foolish, ordinary people" are said to "seize on the idea of the self,"[4] whereas the bodhisattva does not. What demarcates the foolish and ordinary person from the bodhisattva, then, is whether or not one attaches oneself to the idea of the self. This demarcation conceals a difference in their respective epistemological stances. In the case of the foolish and ordinary person, the operation of the epistemological stance is framed by a structure in which the act of grasping (*grāha*) is correlative with that which is grasped (*grāhya*); there is a mutual, interdependent relationship between them. But foolish and ordinary people do not realize this interdependency. In its ontogenesis, the idea of the self arises in them by virtue of the act of grasping. In fact, this grasping-grasped correlative relationship is operative for anything appearing in the field of consciousness by virtue of the act of grasping, such as the material object, the object of sensory perception, or the object of the mind,[5] as long as it is constituted from within the everyday standpoint. Whenever any of these objects is grasped—

that is, constituted as an (intended) object of consciousness—a discriminatory and oppositional relationship is *structurally* established between that which grasps and that which is grasped. This relationship is dualistic, because the relationship is established in virtue of the separation and the opposition between the act of grasping and that which is grasped. Moreover, it is egological because the act of grasping is rooted in ego-desire. The reason why people are called "foolish" and "ordinary," then, is that they are *not aware* that their cognitive activity is structurally framed by the dualistic, egological, and epistemological structure.

On the other hand, the *Diamond Sutra* maintains that the bodhisattva does not seize the object that is dualistically and egologically constituted; instead, the bodhisattva is said to embody a stance of nonattachment. To explain this stance logically, the sutra states that the bodhisattva does not seize "either *dharma* or no-*dharma,*"[6] where we can take "dharma" to mean a thing-event observed in the world. Seizing either dharma or no-dharma involves accepting the linguistic activity of either affirming or negating dharma as the standard for making judgments and understanding reality. And this presupposes either-or logic as its modus operandi. Either-or logic is a stance that prioritizes one over the other by dividing the whole, usually by saving the explicit at the expense of the implicit; the result is the one-sidedness of "seizing either *dharma* or no-*dharma*" as it celebrates the exclusion. To gather together what has been observed, the sutra deems that either-or logic results in the *egological* constitution of the object, whatever the object may be, when it is tied to the dualistic standpoint of the foolish and ordinary person.

This is a formula for creating, and accepting as true, various kinds of dualism such as mind/body (matter), and good/evil, along with a host of others. What is troublesome is that the either-or logical structure appears "natural and reasonable" to foolish and ordinary people as long as they remain unaware of the epistemological structure in which there is mutual interdependence between the act of grasping and that which is grasped when constituting an object. This occurs because it appears to be "obvious" to their sensory perceptions and rational minds. By contrast, the *Diamond Sutra* advocates the stance of neither affirming nor negating. One of the important points that deserves special attention in this connection is that the neither-nor propositional form allows a *holistic* perspective to emerge as an alternative to either-or logic, and this perspective does not admit the dichotomization of the whole as a way of experiencing and understanding reality, as does either-or logic. What is important to note is that the holistic perspective follows the cardinal principle of knowing, for to know means to know the whole, whatever the whole may be construed to mean. The sutra characterizes this holistic perspective, when realized as a form of knowledge, as "nondiscriminatory" wisdom.

The Meaning of Affirmation and Negation in the Sutra

What makes us judge the statement "*A* is not *A*, therefore it is *A*" as contradictory or paradoxical is the presence of the word "not." If it were not for the occurrence of this word, it would simply make an identity statement that reads: "*A* is *A*, therefore it is *A*" to the effect that "*A* is identical with itself" or "*A* is the same as itself." There will be no problem in understanding it, or at least so it seems. However, this statement is vacuously true, since it is tautological—that is, it does not give us any additional information about *A*. The *Diamond Sutra* obviously does not want to make a statement that is vacuously true. Instead, it maintains that *A* is *A* if and only if *A* is not *A*. In light of Aristotelian logic, this would be judged contradictory. It is also paradoxical in that it goes counter to common opinion. It seems, then, that the intelligibility of the statement "*A* is not *A*, therefore it is *A*" lies in understanding the meaning of negation as it is used in the sutra. A question is now raised: How does the sutra understand negation?

Here, it may be appropriate to review the idea of contradiction and the excluded middle that Aristotle formulates in his *Metaphysics* along with his correspondence theory of truth.[7] In this book, he maintains that *A* cannot be both *A* and not *A* at the same time; otherwise contradiction occurs. When he makes this assertion, we must keep in mind that the contradiction in the statement arises through our linguistic activity. *A* as a thing-event and *A'* as realized in the statement, according to Aristotle, must "correspond" to each other. That is, *A'* as a sign in the statement must refer to *A* as a thing-event. This is the reason why Aristotle maintains a correspondence theory of truth. When he proposes this theory of truth, he makes a very important move. He assumes that A as a thing-event stays the same in spite of the passage of time. However, when A is realized as a linguistic sign (A') in the statement, A as thing-event becomes frozen into an atemporal conceptual space. A question we need to raise here is: Does A' so realized continue to "refer" to A in spite of the temporal change extralinguistically—that is, outside of language—while maintaining the idea of self-sameness? Suppose, for example, I leave my briefcase in a garden for five thousand years. Does the briefcase remain the same briefcase? Obviously, it does not, since it will decay and decompose.

This raises the question of the scope and status of Aristotle's correspondence theory of truth. While he wants to maintain this theory of truth as the correspondence between a thing-event and its linguistic sign, he severs this tie when he introduces the idea of self-sameness into the discourse. He does this by invoking the idea of substance (*ousia*) in order to guarantee the idea of self-sameness in spite of temporal changes. To legitimate the validity of the law of the excluded middle, Aristotle flees into language. Accordingly, he advocates the idea of substance in a thing-event that is captured through the linguistic sign. This is an intellectual or theoretical move. To use the previous example, if the briefcase is left in a garden for five thousand years, no substance remains except as an intellectual abstraction. According to Aristotle, the primary substance remains the same in spite of the temporal changes we observe in nature. What changes are only attributes of the substance. He assumes that nature, including everything in it, does not change in its essential characterization. This is true only in a linguistic space and within a certain language-game as long as the speaker's interest remains. What this analysis suggests about Aristotle's correspondence theory of truth is that Aristotle takes a *homocentric* view in understanding reality. To borrow Nietzsche's phrase, it is "human, and all too human."

Insofar as the *Diamond Sutra* makes the contradictory statement in the form of "A is not A, therefore it is A," it must provisionally accept either-or logic. Otherwise, we cannot understand the practical and logical necessity of the sutra's negation of A. On the other hand, insofar as it makes a contradictory statement in understanding what A is, we must also recognize that it does not take either-or logic as the proper way of expressing what A is. This is clear by the insertion of "not" in the identity statement "A is A, therefore it is A." This suggests that the sutra does not accept the idea of self-sameness as its essential characterization in recognizing what A is. Here we need to question why the sutra does not accept the idea of self-sameness. According to the sutra, this rejection is because the idea of self-sameness arises due to attachment. The foolish and ordinary *attach* themselves to it; that is, the idea of A as being self-same arises from the epistemological stance inherent in the grasping-grasped relationship when constituting an object.

At this point, we need to examine the structure out of which A is singled out as A. A occurs in a domain—that is, within the natural environment—and in order for A to be singled out as A in this domain, there must be not-A. On the other hand, if A can occur without reference to a context—for example, a domain of discourse—it implies that A can "stand on its own" without dependence on anything else. The sutra takes this to be unreasonable, because there is no A apart from not-A and conversely there is no not-A apart from A. For both A and not-A to occur, there must be a place or a domain for them to appear. Contrary to Aristotle's position, they are intralinguistically defined when they are realized as linguistic signs. In other words, the being of A is established only in opposition to the non-being of A, where the meaning of the being of A is defined relative to the meaning of the nonbeing of A. That is, both A and not-A logically presuppose each other in their being and meaning. Therefore, the sutra reasons that it is a mistake to ascribe to A an absolute meaning by virtue of its self-sameness, where the absolute meaning of A connotes that A is self-contained and self-sufficient in and of itself. However, as the preceding analysis shows, A cannot "stand on its own" in its being and meaning, and so the sutra concludes that if self-sameness is ascribed to A, it must be relative and not absolute. A must be understood in relational terms. (This analysis would also apply to A as a linguistic sign.)

In fact, the *Diamond Sutra* makes a stronger claim: the idea of A as self-same is a linguistic illusion or fiction, and as such is not real. In order to see if this claim holds true or not, we need to look at the logical structure inherent in the act of affirming A. The sutra asks us to examine how the act of affirmation is established when recognizing A as A, as a thing-event of the world that is realized as a grammatical subject in the subject-predicate structure of language. The sutra maintains that when one performs an act of affirming A, whatever A may be, it cannot do so unless it simultaneously and logically presupposes an act of negation.

And, when one affirms A, the act of affirmation implicitly negates all that is not-A in order for it to be realized as an act of affirmation. In other words, the act of affirmation is an affirmation qua negation. There is no affirmation pure and simple. Both affirmation and negation presuppose each other; they are dependent on and relative to each other. In other words, the act of affirmation is an identity of contradiction.

But why do the foolish and ordinary people, the sutra asks, think there is an affirmation pure and simple? The sutra reasons that it is due to the either-or logic embedded in the act of affirmation. Either-or logic states one must either affirm or negate A, and hence there can be no "middle" between them. According to Aristotle's either-or logic, this is recognized as the law of the excluded middle. We can see that the *Diamond Sutra* goes against common opinion. It criticizes this stance because it falls into one-sidedness. When it is used in making a knowledge claim, it is bound to be partial and becomes even prejudiced. It prioritizes either affirmation or negation in virtue of its intrinsic feature of exclusion. Prioritization dichotomizes the whole, and the sutra's criticism comes from its observation that reality cannot be discerned unless the whole is understood.

By rejecting either-or logic, the *Diamond Sutra* offers a neither-nor propositional form in its place. This alternative is advanced to avoid the extremes that arise when foolish and ordinary people accept either-or logic as *the* standard of experiencing and judging the thing-events of the world. Furthermore, the "neither-nor" propositional form offers a third alternative that either-or logic fails to recognize. It is offered as a way of achieving a holistic perspective by avoiding the substantialization of A, whether in eternalism or nihilism. The purpose is to see A holistically as a relational term by means of the knowledge of the context or place in which A occurs, which leads us to examine the standpoint of nonattachment.

The sutra, however, offers a stance that cannot be embodied by logically or intellectually negating either-or logic or by taking a neither-nor attitude. Suppose we attempt to negate logically either-or logic to arrive at the stance of nonattachment. When we attempt to negate it, there remains the affirmation of what is being negated. That is to say, there arises an affirmative judgment in the mind of those who have negated either-or logic, and this affirmation becomes an object of attachment. In order to embody the stance of nonattachment, we must also negate this act of affirmation. However, this process creates an infinite regress, and therefore the process of logical negation does not enable us to embody the stance of nonattachment. The same problem arises when intellectually *taking* the neither-nor propositional attitude in order to embody the stance of nonattachment, because by taking this attitude there remains the affirmation of this act, and consequently this act must be negated. This process can go on ad infinitum. The sutra reasons that this infinite regress occurs because there is a positing of an ego in consciousness. In other words, in order to embody the stance of nonattachment, the ego that posits the act of grasping must disappear. For this reason, the sutra states that the bodhisattva must "depart from all thought" by realizing that "all things are without a self."[8] This is a nonegological stance.

"Departing from all thought" is an existential project that is carried out through the practice of meditation. The *Diamond Sutra* mentions a meditative state that is identified as "neither image nor no-image" as the initial experiential foundation for advancing the neither-nor propositional form. This meditative state is the standpoint of the "middle" in which "*A* is not *A*, and it is neither *A* nor not *A*." It suggests a practical transcendence vis-à-vis the meditation experience that effects a de-substantialization of *A* contrary to the way the "foolish, ordinary people" want to have it. De-substantialization means that *A* is empty of any conceptually fabricated substance. That is, when there is no act of grasping, there is no *A* as that which is grasped. Insofar as both *A* and not-*A* are empty of substance, they are one. Because they are one in this respect, they are nondualistic; *A* is nondualistically related to not-*A*. Hence, this oneness is not an undifferentiated indistinguishability. To indicate where this oneness occurs—that is, its experiential correlate— the sutra states that "*A* is neither *A* nor not *A*." This is a description of the context or the place in which both *A* and not-*A* occur. As such, it transcends both *A* and not-*A* without departing from either *A* or not-*A,* because it is the ground upon and in which both *A* and not-*A* occur.

In order for this to occur, the mind of foolish and ordinary people must become, to use a Zen Buddhist term, no-mind. No-mind does not mean a mindless state, much less losing the mind, nor does it mean the mind's disappearance. Rather, no-mind means a disappearance of the mind's *discriminatory* activity; there is no operation of the mind's dualistic, either-or egological activity. In the state of no-mind, the named is nameless and the discriminated is nondiscriminatory, for in this case the object alone shines forth—there is no longer the belief that there is a "real" object corresponding to a linguistic activity, since there is no concern with no-mind to substantialize or reify it. Nonetheless, no-mind mirrors desires, ideas, and/or images as they are, for there is in no-mind no superimposition of categories and concepts, nor is there a projection from the unconscious. They are mirrored against the background that is nothing, which is the no-mind. Yet, each individual thing that is mirrored is acknowledged to be an individual thing qua individual thing with the sense of equality that is owed to other individual things. No-mind is a free mind that is not delimited by any idea, desire, or image. Moreover, no-mind is a no-place in which both A and not-A occur. It is nothing, but this nothing is not a relative nothing. It is *absolutely* nothing in the sense that it cuts off any polarized concept. Where there is absolutely nothing, there is no determination whatsoever except its own self-determination via negation. Here we can have a glimpse of what it means to achieve "perfection of wisdom" in which discernment occurs via nondiscernment—that is, nondiscriminatory knowledge.

Concluding Remarks

To conclude, I would like to make a brief observation about how the "logic of not" assists us to reevaluate the dualistic—either-or, egological epistemological structure—when it is applied to the self's understanding of itself, its interpersonal relationship to others, and its ecological relationship. The logic of not offers us a holistic perspective on these issues that are based on its nondualistic and nonegological stance.

Take as an example the Socratic dictum "Know thyself." In attempting to know "one's self," we ordinarily appeal to reflection. In a reflective mode of reasoning when knowing oneself, there occurs a consciousness that does the reflecting and a consciousness that is reflected on. It is performed within an epistemological structure between the reflecting consciousness and the reflected consciousness, wherein one can readily discern a dualistic structure. We may pose questions regarding this activity. Is the reflecting consciousness the same as the reflected consciousness? Can one know one's self in toto by appealing to this method? The goal of "knowing one's self" is to capture the reflecting consciousness in its act, but not the reflected consciousness, because the reflected consciousness is a shadow or a second image of the reflecting consciousness. This knowing cannot be achieved in toto, because in the dualistic structure the reflecting consciousness is distanced from and opposed to the reflected consciousness. More importantly, reflection experientially renders opaque the reflecting consciousness when attempting to know the ground of one's self, because the consciousness that performs reflection is rooted psychologically in the unconscious and physiologically in the body. The reflection is incapable of addressing the ground of a person. Unless we capture the self in its act (its ground), there occurs no genuine and authentic knowing of one's self.

The preceding analysis can be extended to knowing others from the perspective of an "I." When we accept the dualistic, either-or, egological epistemological standpoint as the standard for knowing others and apply this to understanding the relationship between the "I" and "others," the "I" and the "others" are as distant from and opposed to each other as the "I" and its self are, which may occur either ideally, really, or both. For this reason, the problem of other minds occurs. To approach this problem by introducing empathy—for example, as Husserl does in his *Cartesian Meditations*[9]—does not constitute a real solution. The problem of other minds is a quasi problem that surfaces when accepting the dualistic, either-or, egological epistemological standpoint. Or we might say that it arises in such a way that it responds to the structure of this epistemological standpoint. By contrast, if we assume a holistic perspective that the "logic of not" exhorts us to employ, this problem does not occur, for the holistic perspective demands a knowledge of a *grounding place* in which both "I" and "others" occur—wherein "I" is "others" and vice versa, and wherein both are held in "betweenness"[10] in terms of their intersubjectivity and intercorporeality.

The dualistic, either-or egological stance is a theoretical stance, as is exemplified by Aristotle's move into language. This stance defines the human being as a "being-outside-of-nature,"[11] for it enables the human being to observe (*theōria*) nature from the outside by assuming a discursive mode of reasoning and ignores the fact that the human being is also a being-in-nature—he or she is born from and returns to nature—for he or she is an *incarnate* being. The various environmental problems we face today on the global scale are consequences of accepting the view that human beings are simply beings-outside-of-nature. The theoretical stance objectifies nature, turning it into a thing of manipulation and control for the purpose of gratifying capitalistic ego-desire instead of considering nature as a place of cohabitation and coexistence. Today we stand helpless, unable to solve environmental problems arising from the contradiction between the "being-outside-of nature" and "being-in-nature" (the contradiction framed by the dualistic, either-or, egological epistemological structure). Being-outside-of-nature is represented by the methodological stance of natural science, particularly when it is tied (as in the contemporary period) to technology as scientific technology. Being-in-nature is represented by the everyday experiential standpoint. No solution is forthcoming, however, as long as we adhere to this epistemological stance as *the* standard for understanding reality, whether it pertains to knowing one's self or to dealing with others and nature. Such a formula is unfailing in its creation of oppositions and conflicts. Even if a "solution" is proposed from this stance, it will create another problem or conflict, because it arises out of the oppositional stance presupposed by this structure.

As the preceding cursory observations suggest, the dualistic, either-or egological stance presents us with theoretical difficulties and contradictions when we attempt to understand the self, the relationship between the "I" and the "other," and our ecological relation with nature. A sketch of the *Diamond Sutra*'s "logic of not" has been provided to envision a way out of such problems and contradictions.

Notes

1. For an extended discussion on this logic, see Shigenori Nagatomo, "The Logic of the *Diamond Sutra*: A Is Not A, Therefore It Is A," *Journal of Asian Philosophy* 10 (2000): 213-244.
2. Nakamura Hajime and Kino Kazuyoshi, trans. and eds., *Hannyashinkyō, Kongō-hannyakyō* (*The Heart Sutra and the Diamond Sutra*). (Tokyo: Iwanami Shoten, 1996), 195. Since doubt and attachment are issues of depth-psychology for the ego-consciousness, I shall not deal with them in this essay.
3. Richard McKeon, ed., *The Basic Works of Aristotle* (New York: Random House, 1941), chap. 1.

4. Edward Conze, *Buddhist Wisdom Books* (New York: Harper Torch Books, 1958), 34.
5. Ibid., 53.
6. Ibid., 34.
7. McKeon, *Basic Works of Aristotle,* chap. 1.
8. Conze, *Buddhist Wisdom Books* 53, 59.
9. Edmund Husserl, *The Cartesian Meditation* (The Hague: Martinus Nijhoff, 1973), 104.
10. Watsuji Tetsurō, *Watsuji Tetsurō's "Rinrigaku": Ethics in Japan*, translated by Seisaku Yamamoto and Robert E. Carter (Albany: State University of New York Press, 1996).
11. Yuasa Yasuo, *"Wasurerareta Dekaruto"* (Forgotten Descartes) in *Complete Works*, vol. 4 (Tokyo: Hakuha shobō, 2003), 263.

Suggested Readings

Conze, Edward. *Buddhist Wisdom Books*. New York: Harper Torch Books, 1958.
Husserl, Edmund. *The Cartesian Meditation*. The Hague: Martinus Nijhoff, 1973.
McKeon, Richard, ed. *The Basic Works of Aristotle*. New York: Random House, 1941.
Nagatomo, Shigenori. "The Logic of the *Diamond Sutra*: A Is Not A, Therefore It Is A," *Journal of Asian Philosophy* 10 (2000): 213–44.
Watsuji Tetsurō. *Watsuji Tetsurō's "Rinrigaku": Ethics in Japan*. Translated by Seisaku Yamamoto and Robert E. Carter. Albany: State University of New York Press, 1996.
Yuasa Yasuo. *"Wasurerareta Dekaruto"* [Forgotten Descartes]. In *Complete Works*, Vol. 4. Tokyo: Hakuha shobō (2003): 231–269.

ART

Harriette D. Grissom

Names and Forms: The Paradox of Embodiment in Indian Art

Nameless and Formless Thou art, O Thou Unknowable. All forms of the universe are Thine: thus Thou art known.
— Devi Mahatmya, cited in Diana Eck,
Darsan: Seeing the Divine Image in India

For students browsing through art history books or looking at slides in survey classes, erotic temple sculptures are often the first experience of Indian art—and a sensational experience this is. Supple *yakshas*, sensual *mithuna* couples, and copulating figures suggest a culture whose puzzling spirituality is wonderfully more sensual than that of the West, or else a religion so barbarous that it celebrates every manner of perversity. Both of these misconceptions lodge readily in Christianized consciousness, impressed as it is by a strict division between spirituality and sexuality that pervades all but the most esoteric aspects of Western Christianity. Christ has a mother and God has a son, but neither of these deities have wives or consorts, and to propose that they could have is to create a popular upset of major proportions.

Thus, the notion of deities who couple publicly in religious settings is at once a source of a great fascination and a potential stumbling block for Westerners attempting to understand the embodiment of the sacred in Indian art. The sensuality of much Indian religious art is especially confusing in light of the asceticism and restraint of the senses advocated by significant Hindu texts such as the *Bhagavad Gītā*. How is it that a religion that advises adherents to "withdraw the senses from sensuous objects" "like a tortoise retracting its limbs"[1] represents its deities with such visceral enthusiasm?

Apologists, some of whom appear to be still answering to shocked British colonialists, can lead or mislead the student through a warren of theories and explanations, none of which is quite satisfying: the art reflects the decadent tastes of the aristocracy who commissioned it; the art represents the union of abstract masculine and feminine principles; the art is designed to engage ordinary people in spiritual contemplation by appealing to them at a "basic" level; the art is supposed to offer sex education; the art represents the rise in popularity of tantric cults in medieval India.[2] While each of these explanations is somewhat valid, they fail to address a larger paradox that permeates not only sacred Indian art but sacred art in general: *How is the divine to be embodied and represented, and how far shall this embodiment go in materializing spiritual beings?*

In Indian philosophies, as in Western philosophies, the relationship between ultimate reality and material manifestation is a pervasive and problematic issue. In some ways, art addresses this issue more eloquently and persuasively than philosophical discourse. It speaks of the paradox from the heart of the paradox, insofar as religious art is precisely a struggle to capture in material form that which cannot be captured in material form.

However, art does not *resolve* the philosophical dilemma of embodiment so much as it tends to illustrate it and expand the discourse. While consideration of the importance of embodiment in Indian sculpture can provide an excellent occasion to discuss the complexity of Indian philosophy with regard to this topic, art is ultimately a different kind of discourse than philosophy. Its statements are inevitably overlays built on a rich archaeology of visual traditions that cannot be set aside as readily or refuted as summarily as one can set aside certain ideas or theoretical formulations. Just as the site of an ancient city informs the shape of all the cities to come on that site, visual vocabulary tends to incorporate and extemporize upon the ancient as well as to produce novel images and interpretations. As Lannoy points out in *The Speaking Tree*, in art one may regress in order to move forward.[3] Artistic production brings with it a colorful ancestry of compelling icons, images, and symbols, heedless of their philosophical implications.

Understanding the significance of delight in the human figure in Indian sacred sculpture thus calls for a two-pronged investigation: In addition to examining the issue of embodiment from various philosophical perspectives, it is also necessary to look at more mythic, pre-philosophical (or perhaps extraphilosophical) themes and tropes that pervade Indian aesthetics and iconography. We must look at what

Lannoy calls "primeval" influences. Among these influences are ideas about the relationship between microcosm and macrocosm that inform Indian art and culture. In addition, we must consider the primacy of dance as an art form in Indian culture.

Microcosm and Macrocosm: The Cosmic Man

In their impressive *Kalatattvakosa, a Lexicon of Fundamental Concepts of the Indian Arts,* the contributors use etymological analysis to reveal the depth of ideas in Indian art and to demonstrate their connections with a wide range of sacred texts. One of the concepts they examine is that of the *purusa*, or the cosmic man, a figure that emerges as a central symbol of the continuity and analogical connection between humanity and divinity.[4] Understanding the significance of this figure in Indian culture, as well as the pervasive perception that the microcosm of the human body is an analogue of larger cosmic principles, is a good place to begin explaining the significance of the human form in Indian religious art.

In his earliest, mythic form the *purusa* is a cosmic urfigure whose body is the source of all that exists. The *Rig-Veda* tells us,

> The moon was born from his mind; the Sun
> came into being from his eye;
> from his mouth came Indra and Agni,
> while from his breath the Wind was born.
> ... the Earth from his feet, from his ear the four directions.
> Thus have the worlds been organized.[5]

An ancient precedent thus exists for envisioning the infinite source of creation in human form, for the same word that describes the cosmic urfigure also describes a human being. The figure "reveals the archetypal Man, the origin and personification of the universe and society who is coextensive with the universe and yet transcends it."[6]

Purusa brings forth a feminine being, *vraj*, who becomes his consort, so that the cosmic man has as his counterpart a cosmic woman. In addition to the ancient image of the cosmic man and his consort, Indian iconography further rests upon the ancient heritage of Harappan civilization, which yields an extensive array of voluptuous female figures. Whether these figures are seen as fertility goddesses or emblems of a matriarchically oriented culture, they captured the imagination of visual artists, informing later representations of goddesses.[7]

As one who creates out of the destruction of his own body, *purusa* is also a sacrificial figure represented by an abstract man-figure on the Vedic altar. In the *Vastusastra*, which sets forth the principles for building a temple, *purusa* becomes a powerful demon who is subdued beneath the structure. Each part of the *purusa*'s body defines an architectural and ritual aspect of the temple. Buddha was sometimes considered a *mahapurusa*.[8] *Purusa* is identified with Visnu and Krisna in the *Bhagavad Gītā* and the *Ramayana*, and with Siva in other texts.[9] In iconography, the *purusa* and his consort are evident in the early representations of nature spirits—*nagas* and *yakshas*—as well as in the *mithunas* or auspicious couples, the Siva Nataraja, the Siva lingam shrine of Elephanta, and the Visnu *anantasayin* of the Dasavatara temple.

In the *Upanishads,* the concept of the *purusa* becomes spiritualized to represent the inner being or the soul.[10] The Samkhya philosophers carry this tendency to its logical extreme, creating an unbridgeable distinction between *purusa*, which is seen to be spirit or pure consciousness, and *prakriti*, which is material nature. From the Samkhya point of view, there can be no true interpenetration between spirit and matter. Though Indian philosophers will continue to grapple analytically with the problematic relation between material manifestation and pure spirit, iconographic traditions remain drawn to the powerful image of the cosmic body, and artists seem less troubled by the apparent paradoxes of spirit and matter. In fact, one might argue that artistic representation, with its capacity to express ambiguity meaningfully, articulates the paradox eloquently. Whatever the metaphysical implications, the supreme force that underlies the universe is profoundly creative, and its activity is mirrored in artistic pursuit.

The Subtle Body

Stella Kramrisch in her work on Indian art notes a passage from the *Visnudharmottara* that states it is not possible to understand the rules of

Indian painting without an understanding of dance traditions.[11] As a dancer, this great interpreter of Indian traditions was profoundly aware of the dynamic quality of the figure in Indian art. She acknowledges the widely asserted view that dance is the foundational art form of Indian culture, and that the unity of Indian sculpture, architecture, and painting can be traced to dance.[12] She writes:

> Visual art in India is movement precipitated into measured lines and volumes. Breath was known to be the principle of all living, moving form. It was the criterion of a good painter that he painted figures as if breathing. The figures of Indian art are modeled on breath. . . . By concentrated practice of breathing, an inner lightness and warmth were felt to gather into themselves the heaviness of the carnal body and to dissolve it in the weightless "subtle body" built of movement only and emotion. . . . The "subtle body" is given concrete shape by art, in planes and lines of balanced tension and unimpeded flux.[13]

The art of dance is fundamentally an embodiment of spiritual awareness, a transformation of the material body through self-discipline and careful cultivation of the principles of the *Natyasastra,* which are designed to render the body a vehicle for subtle and transformative communication.

Taking the art of dance as a cue, the plastic artist strives to convey the "subtle body" as both a metaphor and a medium for spiritual reality that eludes the senses and resists materialization. The body represented in classical Indian sculpture is a transformed body. This is apparent in a vocabulary of symbols, an intensity of emotion, a multiplicity of arms, and a vibrant form that demonstrates the sculptor's ability to capture the moods, atmospheres, and dynamic potential of the body the same way a dancer might.

This transformation of the body through sculpture is achieved in two ways: the first is close adherence to the canons specified in works like the *Vishnudharmottara.* The canons or *sastras* are highly prescriptive, indicating what color the deity should be, how many arms it should have, what sort of clothes it should wear, and what symbols and images must be present to propitiate adequately the divinity and invite its presence in the image. It is surprising that this degree of prescriptiveness can yield such robust work. One might expect the opposite—namely, a wooden, lifeless depiction. However, the analysis offered in the *Kalattvakosa* demonstrates that the specificity of the canons of Indian art is not an empty formalism, but rather the result of a meticulous effort to maintain the integrity of the correspondence between the spiritual macrocosm and the material microcosm.

Equally important in sculptural execution is the idea of *rasa*. Central to Indian aesthetics, *rasa* signifies a refinement and intensification of emotion that infuses not only the deity but also the heart of the artist creating the deity. This fragrance or savor of emotion is a crucial element both in artistic production and in the satisfactory experience of a work of art.[14] Just as the dancer uses a vocabulary of gestures and facial expressions to create the essence of an emotion, so the sculptor uses the vocabulary of symbols and attributes to evoke a lived emotion that is compelling, profound, and appropriate for the deity he or she is representing.

Transformation of the body through artistic process is most readily understood through tantric philosophies that propose the body can be a quintessential medium for spiritual realization. The body is potentially an instrument of bliss. According to Abhinavagupta in the *Tantraloka*, "When the body that is filled with the divine that shines in the core of the universe, is being viewed like this, it is to be meditated upon, to be worshipped, to be propitiated and the one who becomes fully possessed of it, gets liberated."[15] But this view of the body as an instrument for achieving liberation is far from universal in Indian philosophy. Indeed, most branches of Indian religious philosophy see the body as a hindrance, if not a complete obstacle, to liberation. Is there any way within the philosophical perspectives of Indian religion, outside the unique realm of tantric tradition, to account for the centrality of the body in the depiction of divinity?

Philosophical Views of Embodiment

In his article "Human Embodiment: Indian Perspectives," John Koller explains several of the most significant positions on the question of spiritual truth and the material realm in various streams of Indian philosophy.

Presenting these different views to students and examining how they are borne out in Indian religious art not only gives depth to the understanding of the art, but also illuminates the multidimensionality of Indian philosophy, which is too often seen by casual Western observers as a homogeneous whole.

Even a cursory look at the theme of embodiment reveals the complexity of Indian philosophy with regard to the relation between spirit and matter. Carvakans deny the existence of an "ultimate [spiritual] self" apart from the mind-body experience. Samkhyas, meanwhile, hold a dualistic view that proposes a complete disconnection between "pure consciousness," which they believe can never exist in material form, and the "physical-mental" experience, which is bound by its objective, material nature. Advaita philosophers, on the other end of the spectrum from the Carvakans, claim that only spirit, the ultimate Self of Atman/Brahman, is real, and that the experience of embodiment and the whole material world is in fact an illusion, *maya*.[16] These divergent strategies to explain the relationship between the spiritual and material realms are reflected in a range of ideas about image-making, the artist, and the art object.

In the dualistic Samkhya philosophy, material phenomena (*prakriti*) can be illumined by the light of pure consciousness (*purusa*). This illumination can occur when the material realm is sufficiently refined, when it assumes a sattvic form and is thus able to "catch the light" of *purusa*. Through this refinement, the material realm of *prakriti* becomes an instrument of the pure light of *purusa*. Art-making provides precisely this kind of refinement to the material realm.

It is important to note that in Indian philosophies the mind is not necessarily privileged over the body, as if one were spiritual and the other material. Mind and body are both seen as material manifestations. Unlike Western philosophers who suppose that the mind is more akin to spiritual reality, Indian philosophers regard mind and body as accomplices in the creation and perpetuation of delusion and ignorance.[17] It stands to reason that if both mind and body are equally alienated from the *purusa* of ultimate consciousness, both are equally susceptible to sattvic refinement.

One word for the religious icon in India is "vigraha." In her book *Darsan: Seeing the Divine Image in India,* Diana Eck tells us this word "means 'to grasp, catch hold of.' The *vigraha* is that form which enables the mind to grasp the nature of God."[18] Eck stresses the importance of having sight of the divine and of being seen by the divine. *Darsan* is a kind of blessing that occurs from beholding the divine and being in its presence. The experience of seeing the divine makes a transformative impression on the soul of the viewer. In addition to providing a visual narrative to convey stories and attributes of the deities, icons of the divine also offer an occasion to receive a glance of the divine.

The capacity of the religious icon to provide a material accommodation for the presence of a god is very much dependent on the manner of its creation. As noted earlier, Indian craftspersons observe closely codified rules, *sastras,* that specify how images will be created, what attributes of the deities must be portrayed, their proportions, their positions, their emblems, and so forth. The goal is to create a beautiful and appropriate image that will appeal to the deity and invite it to reside there. Deities are not the same as their images; on the contrary, they are "visitors" present through the image. Eck points out that often in worship rituals, the deity is invited to inhabit the image at the beginning of the ceremony and allowed to leave at the end of it through rituals of "bidding" and "dismissal."[19] This perspective accommodates the dualism of Samkhya, insofar as it respects the fleeting nature of this interaction between *purusa* and *prakriti.*

In addition to observing formal rules that prescribe the qualities of the image, image-makers also undergo a certain amount of meditation, ritual purification, and austerity as they make an image to ensure the sattvic nature of their creation. "This," writes Stella Kramrisch, "with the most creative type of artist, amounts to a true inner vision and an identification of the self with that vision; in less favored cases, however, the well-fixed tradition itself about the appearance of the image yields a solid and reliable framework with the help of which the religious experience is evoked . . . "[20] Finally, the image must be consecrated with appropriate rituals. Until the consecration ceremony is completed, the eyes of the image remain covered; when they are finally opened, the deity is believed to be "in residence" in the image. Thus, great care is taken in the creation of images to make the material fit for divine habitation. Just as an individual calms and clears the mind in hope of recognizing the hidden spark of divine consciousness, so the artist refines and cleanses the material through ritual process and concentration, thereby conferring upon *prakriti* the potential to reflect *purusa.*

From the perspective of Advaita philosophers, the entire material condition, including all aspects of thought processes and emotions, is illusory, and only the unmanifested, pure consciousness, which lies beyond all names and forms, is real. To describe the true nature of the Self (*atman*), Koller quotes from a text by Sankara, the Indian philosopher who offers the most orthodox Advaitan position: it is "ever free, pure, transcendentally changeless, invariable, immortal, imperishable, and thus always bodiless."[21] The condition of embodiment, like all other material conditions, is simply our delusion.

How and why does this delusion arise? Sankara posits a scheme of evolution in which material manifestation arises as a kind of "froth" from the true, unmanifested condition and progresses to the complexity of human awareness. Koller cites a passage from the Upanishads that compares the world of appearance to a spider's web, plants growing from the earth, or hair growing from a human body.[22] Other sources describe the material condition as the dream of Brahma or the play (*lila*) of the ultimate.

In *Darsan*, Eck seems to suggest that divine images, *murti,* are somewhat like elemental forms of this manifestation. She states, "[T]he term itself suggests the congealing of form and limit from that larger reality which has no form or limit."[23] Here the paradox comes full circle: the *murti* are elemental forms of the formless, invoking ultimacy but not altogether participating in it by virtue of their material nature.

In order to penetrate fully the paradox of embodiment in India's sacred art, however, we must ultimately address the paradox of divinities altogether. If ultimate reality is beyond names and forms, what is the role of divinities that are described with images and thrust into the web of maya, and who are therefore less than ultimate from the perspective of several of India's major philosophical traditions? Gerald J. Larson speaks to this issue in "Indian Conceptions of Reality and Divinity." He explains that just as the Indian sense of personhood is radically different from that of the West, so the concept of deity is radically different. He points out the existence of a "psychology of interpersonal plurality" that accounts for the transmigration of the self into various human and animal forms over the aeons of reincarnation. Rather than identifying solely with the genetic inheritance of parents, individuals find a deeper level of identity through "a transmigrating 'subtle body' which enlivens the gross physical embryo at or shortly after the time of conception."[24] Ultimately, a sense of "individuality" associated with personhood in the West is replaced by what Larson describes as a "fluidarity" that is shaped and defined by the caste system.

Larson contends that the multiplicity and interchangeability of the Indian pantheon in which "every god is every other god" parallels "the psychology of intrapersonal plurality and the social anthropology of interpersonal plasticity" that prevails in India.[25] He explains that even the boundaries between the human and the divine are permeable in Indian traditions. Whereas the descent of God into a human form was an extraordinary and singular occurrence in the Christian tradition, gods readily assume human and even animal form as avatars in Indian traditions. Vishnu descends into the forms of Krisna and Rama, the Great Goddess appears in village *devis* throughout India, and gurus offer the sight of the divine. In medieval bhakti traditions that emphasize devotion as a means of obtaining *moksa* or liberation, God is also seen as the beloved and worshipped as such. The result, says Larson, is "an ease of access, a spontaneous emotional rapport, an absence of separation in kind from the polymorphous divine that appears to be unique to the Indian context."[26]

In the tenth and eleventh teachings of the *Bhagavad Gītā,* Krisna reveals to Arjuna the breadth, depth, and totality of his divinity:

> Arjuna, see my forms
> in hundreds and thousands;
> diverse, divine,
> of many colors and shapes.
>
> See the sun gods, gods of light,
> howling storm gods, twin gods of dawn,
> and gods of wind, Arjuna,
> wondrous forms not seen before.
>
> Arjuna, see all the universe,
> animate and inanimate,
> and whatever else you wish to see;
> all stands here as one in my body.[27]

Divinity, like humanity, is not so much a matter of definition as it is a matter of recognizing that all the dazzling and terrible names and forms are in fact manifestations of the "One."

This realization is, however, mind-boggling: Arjuna's "inner self quakes," and he is deeply relieved when Vishnu resumes his "gentle human form" as Krisna.[28] Krisna advises Arjuna that "devotion alone" gives true knowledge of divinity. The tangible form of the gods thus becomes a kind of grace that spares humans from the overwhelming and unassimilable experience of perceiving divinity directly, allowing us instead to know divinity through the much more human experience of devotion.

Intimacy with the deity is accomplished through daily ministrations either in the temple or in home altars. Rather than remaining distant and untouchable, images of the gods are dressed, bathed, fed, and treated to incense to ensure their comfort and pleasure during manifestation. In his article "Lives of Indian Images," Richard Davies states: "The physical specificity of the god's presence in an icon or image might lead the devotee to glimpse beyond it Siva's more all-encompassing nature. The icon was in this sense translucent. . . . It also allowed the viewer . . . to glimpse with a devotional eye through it—imperfectly, since all human encounters with transcendence will be limited—to the transcendent reality of the deity as well."[29] The devotion afforded through interaction with a particular image of the god becomes a vehicle for experiencing the aspect of the god that is "beyond names and forms."

But if the One comprises so many manifestations, how is the devotee to know which form of the One to worship? Eck explains that rather than being a polytheistic religion in which different deities are assigned different spheres of influence, as in the Greek pantheon, in Indian religion "each is exalted in turn." She continues: "Each is praised as creator, source, and sustainer of the universe when one stands in the presence of that deity. There are many gods, but their multiplicity does not diminish the significance or power of any of them. Each of the great gods may serve as a lens through which the whole of reality is clearly seen."[30] Krisna tells Arjuna: "In whatever way people approach me, in that way do I show them favor."[31]

A Close-up of Kailasanatha at Ellora

The Kailasanatha Temple at Ellora exemplifies the layering of images and ideas that must be considered in an effort to unravel the paradox of embodiment in Indian art, and for that reason it can serve as an interesting example to consider in teaching situations. The entire architecture is hewn from a mountain, and the Kailasanatha Temple was completed only after 150 years of meticulous labor. The temple is a representation of Mt. Kailasa, the mythical home of the god Siva and a site sacred to a variety of religions since prehistoric times. Some believe that Mt. Kailasa is the prototype for Mt. Meru, which denotes the center of the universe. Buddhist stupas and Hindu temples are ritual re-creations of sacred mountains.[32] Thus, the image of the mountain as a sacred place is deeply and pervasively established in the religious imagination of India.

The image of the cave within the mountain is replete with archetypal, religious, and philosophical symbolism.[33] Caves were places of retreat deep within the earth. Going into a cave is like going into the womb or going to the heart of the matter. Speaking eloquently of the significance of the cave temples, Lannoy describes their "labyrinthine plasticity," which he says is "man's most natural artistic mode of expressing inner richness and a yearning for self-realization in a severely inhibited setting. The cave sanctuaries impose precisely these very restricted limitations."[34] The artist working in the medium of rock likewise chooses the densest form of material to transform into a spiritual accommodation. The stone carver goes to the obdurate heart of materiality to perform the alchemy of transformation. According to Rajan, "Kailasa was thus not 'created' but 'exposed' or 'revealed' out of matter, as an embodiment of the monistic philosophy of Sankara. . . ."[35]

Lannoy also makes connections between the interior cave of the stupa and the temple and the neolithic tumuli revered by certain hill tribes.[36] He points out that at the much later time when the great complexes were created, in about the eighth century, Indian urban dwellers sought refuge in the purity and simplicity of the countryside in order to renew their spiritual energies, much as the British and German Romantics did. The idea of retreating to the wilds of the mountains like Lord Siva had a romantic appeal then as it does now. Lannoy proposes that

Sculptured panel of Ravana under Kailasa, with Shiva and Parvati above. Cave XVI (Kailasanatha, Ellora). Photo by Henry Cousens. Used by permission of the British Library. Photo 40/(90),90.

Brahmin priests, in an effort to rewin the loyalties of those drawn to Buddhism, consciously appealed to the iconography of antiquity to create a more rugged, "primitive," indigenous sort of image.

The image of Siva subduing Ravana is a striking feature of Kailasanatha Temple. The scene depicts an incident in which the demon Ravana, imprisoned in Mt. Kailasa to pay homage to Siva, is offended by the fact that Siva is making love to his consort, Parvati. Ravana creates an earthquake to express his anger, but Siva quells it with nothing more than the pressure of his toe on the ground. The scene shows Siva and Parvati inclined toward each other in a sensuous pose on an upper story, while on a lower level Ravana whirls dramatically with his many arms to create a disturbance.

The depiction evokes Siva's paradoxical dual nature as a fiercely powerful ascetic and an accomplished master of sexual Tantra. The demon Ravana's objections to Siva's lovemaking seem to suggest the narrowness of the "small self" upon whom Siva Nataraja, in another depiction of the deity, dances. Likewise, it is only Siva's mastery that sublimates the demonic churning of desire (also represented by Ravana); he creates equipoise via masculine and feminine energies.

With his many arms and his fierce energy, the image of Ravana can also be seen to mirror Siva Nataraja, suggesting that the disruptive energy of the demon and the confident quelling-energy of the master are complements. Ravana is further reminiscent of the demon Purusa confined beneath the Vedic temple—a kind of energetic resource that must be contained to preserve the order of the universe but that is nevertheless at the core of its sacredness.

The couple Siva and Parvati recapitulate fertility figures that have graced Indian art and culture from the most ancient times—the yakshas and yakshis. The brilliance of the sculpture lies in part in its ability to capture a moment in time: Parvati and Siva have been relaxing together, but Parvati, apparently startled by the sudden shaking, seems to grip Siva's arm in alarm. Despite Siva's ability to forestall the earthquake, the deities are affected by this rumbling within the depths of the earth—from the bowels of the material world. Like the devil in much Christian-inspired literature, Ravana seems to steal the show.

The body with its vitality and energy is central to the spiritual endeavor insofar as it is basic to the human condition. Through art—whether that of the sculptor, the dancer, or the yogi—the body becomes dynamic and subtle. This transformation appears to be at once real and illusory, momentary and eternal, a spiritual and a material phenomenon. Philosophers find it hard to rest in the presence of such contradiction. From the perspective of the artist or the one who enjoys the art, however, the gripping nature of art may lay precisely in its capacity to revel in such paradoxes at the experiential level, and, in doing so, to render philosophical solutions less urgent.

Notes

1. Barbara Stoler Miller, *Exploring India's Sacred Art: Selected Writings of Stella Kramrisch* (Philadelphia: University of Pennsylvania Press, 1983), 37.
2. L. N. Pachori, *The Erotic Sculpture of Khajuraho*, (Calcutta: Naya Prokash, 1989), 180–92.
3. Richard Lannoy, *The Speaking Tree: A Study of Indian Culture and Society*, (London: Oxford University Press, 1971), 38.
4. Kapila Vatsyayan, ed., *Kalatattvakosa*, vol. 1. (New Delhi: Indira Gandhi Centre for the Arts, 2001), 29–50.

5. Ibid., 33.
6. Ibid., 32.
7. Lisa B. Safford, "Water, Wood and Women: The Persistence of Ancient Traditions in Modern India," paper delivered at the Asian Studies Development Program National Conference, Kansas City, April, 2004.
8. Vatysayan, *Kalatattvakosa,* 41.
9. Ibid., 40.
10. Ibid., 36.
11. Miller, *Exploring India's Sacred Art,* 266.
12. Ibid., 272.
13. Ibid., 29.
14. Eliot Deutsch, "Reflections on Some Aspects of the Theory of Rasa." In *Studies in Comparative Aesthetics,* Monograph No. 2 of the Society for Asian and Comparative Philosophy (Honolulu: University of Hawaii Press, 1975), 1.
15. Vatysayan, *Kalatattvakosa,* 106.
16. John M. Koller, "Human Embodiment: Indian Perspectives," in *Self as Body in Asian Theory and Practice,* edited by Thomas P. Kasulis et al. (Albany, New York: State University of New York, 1993), 47–48.
17. Ibid., 65.
18. Diane Eck, *Darsan: Seeing the Divine Image in India* (New York: Columbia University Press, 1998), 38.
19. Ibid., 49.
20. Miller, *Exploring India's Sacred Art,* 209.
21. Koller, "Human Embodiment," 52.
22. John M. Koller, "Humankind and Nature in Indian philosophy," in *A Companion to World Philosophies,* edited by Eliot Deutsch et al. (Oxford: Blackwell Publishers, 1999), 283.
23. Eck, *Darsan,* 38.
24. James Gerald Larson, "Indian Conceptions of Reality and Divinity," in *A Companion to World Philosophies,* edited by Eliot Deutsch et al. (Oxford: Blackwell Publishers, 1999).
25. Ibid., 253.
26. Ibid.
27. Barbara Stoler Miller, *Bhagavad Gītā* (New York: Bantam, 1986), 98.
28. Ibid., 101, 108.
29. Richard Davies, "The Lives of Indian Images," in *Religion, Art, and Visual Culture,* edited by Brent Plate (New York: Palgrave, 2002), 180.
30. Eck, *Darsan,* 26.
31. Miller, *Bhagavad Gītā,* 46.
32. George Michell, *The Hindu Temple: An Introduction to Its Meaning and Forms* (Chicago: University of Chicago, 1998), 70.
33. Wendy Doniger O'Flaherty, *Other Peoples' Myths: The Cave of Echoes* (Chicago: University of Chicago Press, 1998), 33–37.
34. Lannoy, *Speaking Tree,* 38.
35. K. V. Soundara Rajan, *Rock-Cut Temple Styles, Early Pandyan Art and the Ellora Shrines* (Mumbai: Somaiya Publications, 1998), 160–61.
36. Lannoy, *Speaking Tree,* 39.

Suggested Readings

Banerjea, J. N. *The Development of Hindu Iconography*. New Delhi: Munshiram Manoharlal, 1974.

Coomaraswamy, A. K. *The Dance of Siva*. New York: Farrar Straus and Co., 1957.

———. *The Transformation of Nature in Art*. New York: Dover Press, 1956.

Craven, Roy C. *Indian Art, A Concise History*. London: Thames and Hudson, 1997.

Davies, Richard. *The Lives of Indian Images*. Princeton, NJ: Princeton University Press, 1997.

Dissanayake, Wimal. "The Body in Indian Theory and Practice." In *Self as Body in Asian Theory and Practice,* edited by Thomas P. Kasulis et al., 39–44. Albany, New York: State University of New York, 1993.

Gerow, Edwin. "Indian Aesthetics: A Philosophical Survey." In *A Companion to World Philosophies*, edited by Eliot Deutsch et al., 304–23. Oxford: Blackwell Publishers, 1999.

Kramrisch, Stella. *The Hindu Temple*. Delhi: Motilal Banarsidass, 1976.

———. *The Presence of Siva*. Princeton, NJ: Princeton University Press, 1981.

Shah, Priyabala. *Shri Vishnudharmottara, A Text on the Ancient Indian Arts*. Ahmedabad: Sadma Society, 1990.

Staal, Frits. "Indian Bodies." In *Self as Body in Asian Theory and Practice*, edited by Thomas P. Kasulis et al., 59–102. Albany: State University of New York, 1993.

Vatsyayan, Kapila, ed. *Kalatattvakosa*. Vol. 2. New Delhi: Indira Gandhi Centre for the Arts, 2001.

Waghorne, Joanne Puzo, and Norman Cutler. *Gods of Flesh, Gods of Stone: The Embodiment of Divinity in India*. New York: Columbia University Press, 1996.

Zimmer, Heinrich. *Myths and Symbols in Indian Art and Civilization*. New York: Harper and Row, 1965.

Stephen J. Goldberg

Philosophical Reflection and Visual Art in Traditional China

In teaching the art (or philosophical and religious texts) of Asia, we are ever mindful of our twin desires for *presence* and *distance*: for bringing distant works of art—works distant in geography and generation—closer to us and, at the same time, for respecting the cultural and historical differences that distance them. The temporality of our engagement with the other, observed Emmanuel Levinas, "opens up the meaning of otherness and the otherness of meaning."[1]

This essay examines the relevance of the classical tradition of Confucian philosophical reflection for the study of Chinese visual art. It offers a philosophically informed understanding of Chinese art that supports an inquiry into the relationship between art and the question of sociocultural authority in traditional China. This will require a reassessment of the fundamental cultural assumptions upon which the status of the artist, the intended recipient, and the work of art are predicated, thus challenging the very categories and terms of our engagement.

Through an explication of selective passages from the *Lunyu*, or Confucian *Analects,* we will be led to a conception of the traditional practice of art, especially among the Chinese *wenren*, or Confucian scholar-gentlemen, as not simply a form of self-expression or mimetic representation, but rather as an aesthetic means of "self-presentation," fashioned within a particular milieu of social relations. This aesthetic means, in turn, will necessitate a radical reformulation of our notion of "style" as no longer merely a formal property of the material art object

This essay is a revision of "Art and Authority of Excellence in Traditional China" (paper presented at Le Colloque International, "La Question de l'Art en Asia," held at the Centre de Recherche sur l'Extrême Orient de Paris-Sorbonne [CREOPS], on February 19, 2004).

but rather—to treat it in its communicative function as a mode of visual address—what Mikhail Bakhtin termed "addressivity, the quality of turning to someone."[2] This reformulation will then enable us to examine the contribution of the visual arts to preservation of the existing social hierarchy and relations of privilege in given periods of Chinese history.

I shall begin, as noted, with an explication of several passages from the *Analects* that shed light on the structures and rationalities of socio-cultural authority, particularly as they relate to our understanding of the later art of the *wenren*. This will then be brought to bear on a reading of three works of art by the fifteenth-century scholar-painter Shen Zhou (1427–1509).

Confucianism and the Dao of Man

"The Master said: Set your sights on the way [*dao*], sustain yourself with excellence [*de*], lean upon authoritative conduct [*ren*], and sojourn in the arts [*yi*]."[3] This passage from book 7 of the *Analects* is a most concise articulation of sociocultural authority and the role of art within a Confucian ethos—a way of conducting and comporting oneself, and the dispositions valued by a community. It encompasses four philo-sophical concepts that are of fundamental importance in establishing the original status and significance of the arts in traditional China: the way (*dao*), excellence (*de*), cultural authority (*ren*), and the practice of art (*yi*).

Whereas the focus in Daoism is on a cosmological account of *dao* as *dahua*, the "great transformational process of existence," for Confucians *dao* is primarily limited to *ren dao*, the "*dao* of man," and has ethical implications for fostering social harmony and maintaining the continuities of tradition. This is best expressed by *li*, or "observing ritual propriety," something that ultimately is to be accomplished: "[*L*]*i* actions are embodiments or formalizations of meaning and value that accumulate to constitute a cultural tradition. . . . Ritual actions, invested with the accumulated meaning of the tradition, are formalized struc-tures upon which the continuity of the tradition depends and through which a person in the tradition pursues cultural refinement."[4] It is thus tradition and not history that serves as the principal interpretative con-text in premodern China.

Roger T. Ames and Henry Rosemont, Jr., in their philosophical translation of the *Analects* of Confucius, characterize *rendao* as "'a way of being consummated and authoritatively human.'" They continue, "As [*Analects*] (15.29) tells us: 'It is the person who is able to broaden the *way*, not the *way* that broadens the person.'"5 The Confucian *dao* thus constitutes an ethos of "excellence" (*de*), the communal expectations concerning one's personal conduct, disposition, and comportment, with a view to becoming an "authoritative person" (*ren*). Art (*yi*), within this Confucian context, is thus conceived as a personal means of self-presentation, indicative of one's consummate sense of appropriateness of conduct in deference to the circumstances that occasion it. In this respect the Confucian notion of art is fundamentally performative, a "co-creative process in which one shapes and is shaped by one's environing circumstances."6 This notion of art differs markedly with traditional occidental aesthetics and its emphasis on mimesis.

In *Analects* 6.30 we are given the basis upon which to formulate a notion of cultural authority: "Authoritative persons establish others in seeking to establish themselves and promote others in seeking to get there themselves. Correlating one's conduct with those near at hand can be said to be the method of becoming an authoritative person."7 An authoritative person is thus one who conducts himself through *patterns of deference*, or *shu* (deferring to others in one's own environing conditions), and through *ritualized patterns of reverence*, or *jing* (revering of others within the received tradition of exemplary acts of one's predecessors), for the purpose of establishing an effective and fruitful social *integration* with others, while at the same time fully disclosing one's own integrity (*cheng*) as a particular person (that is, the achieved quality of one's relations to others). "Integrity is consummatory relatedness."8

Implicit in the Confucian notion of creativity is that it is always reflexive; "thus creativity is both *self*-creativity and *co*-creativity."9 This notion, as we shall now see, has important implications for an understanding of authorship of a work of art in traditional China. It necessitates the formulation of a model of the aesthetic-communicative act, particularly for the Confucian literati (*wenren*), which triangulates the production and reception of art in terms of a relationship of cocreativity between artist, intended recipient, and a venerated master of the past.

This brings us finally to the specific use of the phrase *you yu yi*, to "sojourn in the arts." To "sojourn" does not here mean merely "to wander aimless or unfettered," as a Daoist aesthetics might have it, nor does it mean to "dwell," as is the case with a professional artist; "to sojourn" is "to stay for a while," "to reside temporarily at a place." Accordingly, to "sojourn in the arts" means that one is always en route to another destination, a perpetual leave-taking. Art, within a traditional Confucian context, is thus never a final destination, an end in itself, but a *going toward* a larger purpose. The arts, understood as ritualized actions, are authorized discourses of aesthetic practice upon which the continuity of tradition depends and through which a person, operating from within the tradition, pursues cultural refinement or excellence (*de*) indicative of a consummate sense of appropriateness in their interpersonal relations.

Within the high or elite social domain of Confucian scholars, the arts came to play a vital role in their abiding concern for legitimation of authority and the maintenance of social order, characterized by hierarchal patterns of social behavior defined not in terms of personal motivation, ego, and emotion, but rather in terms of social status (based on education, kinship, and gender), as well as group affiliation, individual loyalty, and personal obligation. The driving force behind this all-important social practice is the perennial desire of the literatus for "recognition" (*zhi*) of his value, with a view to achieving sociocultural authority. This is expressed in two phrases in ancient China: *zhiyin* (one who knows the sound) and *zhiji* (a person who knows one's inmost self).[10]

Our brief discussion of the Confucian ethos represents an attempt to lay bare a number of fundamental social and cultural "assumptions about the world," the "cognitive environment" essential to what it is we are to *attend to* in an appreciative understanding of traditional Chinese art.[11] Our perspective here is cognitive rather than epistemological. These manifest facts and assumptions can be understood to constitute the common source domains of social and cultural cognitive resources mutually shared by artists and beholders. They are the unspoken cognitive frames of experience elicited in the reception of traditional Chinese art (that is, the culturally distinctive modes recognition, attention, and inference central to the discernment of the depicted subject, its meaning, and its significance).

If, in the eighteenth-century Europe of the Enlightenment, the French naturalist Georges-Louis Leclerc, comte de Buffon (1707–88), could say, "Le style c'est l'homme même" ("Style is the man himself"),[12] in fifteenth-century China, especially within the elite *wenren* or literati circles of Suzhou, it be may said, "Style is the relationship." Artistic style—or more precisely, the style or mode of visual address, what Mikhail Bakhtin termed "addressivity"—is an index or cue to the *intentional rapport* of the artist to his recipient or addressee: (a) the closeness and intimacy or distance of relationship; (b) the formality or informality of the occasion; and (c) the mutuality in the comprehension of implicit allusions to styles and themes of the past and references to present contextual circumstances.

The style of visual address is thus surface evidence indicative of underlying expectations about the recipient's contextual knowledge to infer what is meant by what is depicted or inscribed, the nature of artist-recipient relationship, and how the artist senses and imagines the force of its effect and anticipates the addressee's response. This acknowledges that the reception of art is never a passive process, but rather an "actively responsive understanding."[13]

In fifteenth-century Ming China, there is one figure who stands out as an exemplar of the Way (*dao*) of excellence (*de*) and cultural authority (*ren*) in the arts (*yi*): the scholar-painter Shen Zhou, founder of the Wu school of literati painting. I shall now conclude with a brief comparison of three paintings by Shen Zhou, executed in different periods in his life and under very different circumstances. Particular attention will be paid to the role of the recipient and specific occasion as determinants of artistic decisions as to the appropriate style or visual mode of address.

Lofty Mount Lu is a hanging scroll, dated 1467, in the National Palace Museum in Taipei (figure 1). A long inscription written by the artist when he was forty years of age gives poetic expression to the intent of the painting. According to Richard Edwards, "His poem is a rather elaborate and didactic one which, first of all, describes the wonders of the mountain and then relates this magnificence to his teacher, Ch'en Hsing-an [Chen Xing'an]."[14] The following is an excerpt from the conclusion of the poem:

> I was one who loitered about his door;
> Looking up at his lofty eminence
> Mount Lu is no longer high.[15]

Fig. 1. Shen Zhou, *Lofty Mount Lu*. Dated 1467. Hanging scroll, ink and colors on paper, 193.8 × 98.1 cm. Used by permission of the National Palace Museum, Taipei.

Fig. 2. Detail from figure 1.

A visual correlation and, thus, metaphorical equation is drawn between the small but perfectly erect figure of Shen Zhou's teacher, represented in the lower foreground of the painting, and the lofty, towering magnificence of Mount Lu, upon which he gazes (figure 2). *Lofty Mount Lu* is appropriately rendered in a style befitting its recipient, Shen Zhou's venerable teacher, Chen Xing'an; it makes reference to the tall, colorful, richly inked, and densely textured landscape paintings of Wang Meng (ca. 1308–85), one of the Four Great Masters of the preceding Yuan dynasty. To this Shen Zhou brought his own vigorous brushwork and strong sense of structural arrangement. *Lofty Mount Lu* bears a strong similarity in style and composition to Wang Meng's *Su'an Retreat* (also known as *The Simple Retreat*), in The Metropolitan

Museum of Art in New York (figure 3). The latter is a work that in turn alludes to both the tenth-century master Dong Yuan, founder of the lite-rati tradition of landscape painting, and the monumental landscape paintings of the Northern Song, such as *Early Spring*, dated 1072, by Guo Xi (1001–ca. 1090), in the National Palace Museum in Taipei.[16]

For Shen Zhou, embodying this earlier master's style within his own personal mode of visual address was not simply a matter of stylistic influence. Rather, it was an implicit expression of cultural *reverence* for Wang Meng, thus asserting his artistic affiliation with the literati tradi-tion of scholar-painters, and a sign of *deference* to the intended recipient of *Lofty Mount Lu*, his "lofty" teacher, Chen Xing'an. In the inscription, Chen is poetically described as "a yellow crane that rises high and meets the breath of heaven," a felicitous symbol of longevity and loftiness of character that also establishes a link with Wang Meng, whose *hao* or pen name is "Yellow Crane Mountain Woodcutter" (*huangheshanqiao*).

Reverence for tradition and deference to individuals and the ever-changing circumstances of the present is given metaphorical expression in the following passage from the *Analects*: "The master said, 'The wise (*zhi*) enjoy water; those authoritative in their conduct (*ren*) enjoy mountains. The wise are active; the authoritative are still. The wise find enjoyment; the authoritative are long-enduring.'"[17] This statement is an instantiation of a correlative style of reasoning in which the mountains and waters come to symbolize, respectively, constancy or persistence (*tong*) and change (*bian*), and, by correlative extension, observance of tradition and its creative appropriation to meet the ever-changing cir-cumstances of the present.

Some twenty years later and under very different social circum-stances, Shen Zhou adopted a very different visual mode of address in *Watching the Mid-Autumn Moon*, a handscroll in the Museum of Fine Arts in Boston (figure 4). Following the painting, there is a poem written by the artist to commemorate the specific occasion depicted in the work, the celebration of the Mid-Autumn Moon Festival with fel-low scholars of his own generation. The following is an excerpt from the poem:

> When young we heedlessly watch the mid-autumn moon,
> Seeing this time as all other time.
> With the coming of age respect has grown,

Fig. 3. *The Simple Retreat.* (ca 1370)
Wang Meng (Chinese, ca. 1308–1385)
Hanging scroll, ink and color on silk.
The Metropolitan Museum of Art,
Ex call.: C. C. Wang Family, Promised
Gift of the Oscar L. Tang Family
(L.1997.24.8) Photograph, all rights
reserved, The Metropolitan Museum
of Art.

> And we do not look lightly
> Every time we raise the deep cup to celebrate the feast.
> How many mid-autumns can an old man have?
> He knows this passing light cannot be held. . . . [18]

Fig. 4. Shen Zhou, Chinese, 1427–1509. *Watching the Mid-August Moon.* Chinese, Ming dynasty, Late 15th century. 30.4 × 134.5 cm. (11 15/16 × 52 15/16 in.) Ink and light color on paper, Museum of Fine Arts, Boston. Used courtesy of the Museum. Photograph © 2009 Museum of Fine Arts, Boston.

Shen Zhou alludes in his painting to the style of a work in his own collection by the scholar-painter Wu Zhen (1279–1354), another of the Four Masters of the Yuan dynasty. Entitled *Poetic Feeling from a Thatched Pavilion*, this handscroll, currently in the Cleveland Museum of Art, is dated 1347 and signed with the artist's *hao*, Meishami (Novice of the Plum Blossom) (figure 5).

In another section of Wu Zhen's hand scroll there is a seal and a most telling colophon by Shen Zhou:

> I love the Old Man of the Plum-blossom [Wu Zhen],
> Who inherited the secrets of Zhuran from heart to heart.
> In cultivating this "water and ink kinship"
> He was able to endow everything with a touch of aged mellowness.
> Trees and rocks seem to fall from his brush [so effortlessly]
> That even nature itself could hardly deny their emergence.
> So now, under the grove of the oak trees,
> I willing serve him with all my humility.
> —Shen Zhou, a later follower.[19]

In this inscription, Shen Zhou not only explicitly proclaims himself a follower of Wu Zhen, but also notes Wu Zhen's genealogical "water and ink kinship" to the tenth-century master Zhuran. This effectively establishes Shen Zhou's artistic lineage, via Wu Zhen once again, back to the "patriarch" of the literati tradition of Chinese painting, Dong Yuan (907–60), the teacher of Zhuran.

Wu Zhen, Maxwell K. Hearn observed, "developed a reputation as a recluse scholar who painted without regard to popular taste or monetary

Fig. 5. Wu Zhen. *Poetic Feeling in a Thatched Pavilion.* Dated 1347. Hand scroll, ink on paper, 23.8 × 99.4 cm. © The Cleveland Museum of Art, Leonard C. Hanna, Jr. Fund 1963.259.

reward, referring to his paintings as ink-plays [*moxi*], a term used by the literati to denote casual pictures done at leisure."[20] Wu Zhen's seemingly childlike depiction of human subjects and consciously naïve brush technique has a much admired, but difficult to emulate, unpretentious directness of expression. Shen Zhou, no doubt, deemed this style a most appropriate form of self-presentation in his own work, *Watching the Mid-Autumn Moon*, given the informality of the occasion commemorated and the intimacy of his personal relationship to its intended recipient, Xu'an, to whom it is addressed. This is revealed at the end of his poem:

> But let the floating clouds be jealous of us;
> There is wine in the jug
> And joy among ourselves.
> Shu-an [Xu'an] is my old friend;
> There is an order to the drinking;
> There is no clamor among guests.
> We recite Li Po's "Question to the Moon."
> And feel our white hairs are not one
> And so, draw in wave of wine and drink the moon.
> Shu-an [Xu'an] and I are sixty;
> And ask again of mid-autumn?
> Forty more.[21]

Let us now conclude by noting one last work by Shen Zhou, this time on a theme that he is little known for, a crab and shrimp, subject matter customarily considered "trivial" themes by scholar-painters. It appears within *Drawings from Life*, an album of nineteen leaves, dated 1495, in the National Palace Museum, Taipei. Although Shen Zhou occasionally painted these themes, James Cahill calls our attention to an apologetic inscription that accompanies this painting in which "Shen Zhou is careful . . . to inform the viewer that his purpose was not serious":

> In themes of things that wiggle and things that grow,
> By playing with my brush, I can still work transformations.
> On a bright day, by a small window, sitting alone,
> The spring wind in my face, this mind with subtle thoughts . . .
> I did this album capriciously, following the shapes of things, laying them out on paper only to suit my mood of leisurely, well-fed living. If you search for me through my paintings, you will find that I am some-where outside them.[22]

Who is Shen Zhou addressing? Unlike the former works, there was not a specific recipient, but rather one presupposed in the person of the social group to which the artist belongs. However, this is not something that we are able to infer from the very pictorial style of visual address. In fact, Shen Zhou's statement of self-denial concerning his interest in the "themes of things that wiggle and things that grow" is meant also to disown his descriptive use of broad wet brushstrokes and washes of ink. Scholar-painters deplored these brush techniques precisely because of their association with the much-maligned paintings of earli-er Chan Buddhist masters, such as the late-Song painter Muqi. As the disclaimer by the founder of the Wu school of literati painting tellingly proclaims: "If you search for me through my paintings, you will find that I am somewhere outside them."

It is here that we come to acknowledge the legacies of classical Chinese philosophical reflection that continued to inhabit, and are most salient to, a comprehension of the ever-changing historical develop-ments in traditional visual art. It represents an attempt to disclose some of the most fundamental premises about self and world essential to what it is we are to *attend to* in an appreciative understanding of traditional Chinese art. We learn how the selection of subject matter and the style of visual address are both indicative and productive of the artist-recipient relationship and the social orders they support, and how the creative appropriation of tradition within one's own aesthetic self-presentations—

allusions to the past recognized as appropriate to present circumstances—can be construed as a ritualized act of *reverence* and *deference* by which an individual attempts to relate authoritatively to others.

Notes

1. Richard Kearney, *Dialogues with Contemporary Continental Thinkers: The Phenomenological Heritage* (Manchester: Manchester University Press, 1984), 57.
2. M. M. Bakhtin, "The Problem of Speech Genres," in *Speech Genres and Other Late Essays,* translated by Vern W. McGee (Austin: University of Texas Press, 1986), 99.
3. Roger T. Ames and Henry Rosemont, Jr., *The Analects of Confucius: A Philosophical Translation* (New York: Ballantine Publishing Group, 1998), 112.
4. Ibid., 88.
5. Ibid., 46.
6. Roger T. Ames and David L. Hall, *Daodejing "Making This Life Significant": A Philosophic Translation* (New York: Ballantine Books, 2003), 16.
7. Ames and Rosemont, *Analects of Confucius,* 110.
8. Ames and Hall, *Daodejing,* 16.
9. Ibid., 17. For a discussion of the concept of *cheng* (commonly rendered "sincerity") in the *Zhongyong*, where it means "self-completing," or "truth," see David L. Hall and Roger T. Ames, *Thinking Through Confucius* (Albany: State University of New York Press, 1987), 57–62.
10. Although this merits further elaboration, it would take us beyond the limited aims of this essay. For a detailed discussion, see Eric Henry, "The Motif of Recognition," in *Harvard Journal of Asiatic Studies* 47, no. 1 (June 1987): 5–30; Martin W. Huang, *Literati and Self-Representation: Autobiographical Sensibility in the Eighteenth-Century Chinese Novel* (Stanford, CA: Stanford University Press, 1995), 80; and Huang, *Desire and Fictional Narrative in Late Imperial China* (Cambridge: Harvard University Asia Center, 2001), 76.
11. For a discussion of the notion of "cognitive environment," see Dan Sperber and Deirdre Wilson, *Relevance: Communication and Cognition,* 2nd ed. (Oxford: Blackwell, 1995), 38–46.
12. This was stated in his inaugural address, entitled *Discours sur le Style French*, delivered to the Académie Française, Paris, on August 25, 1753.
13. Bakhtin, "Problem of Speech Genres," 68.
14. Richard Edwards, *The Field of Stones: A Study of the Art of Shen Zhou (1427–1509),* (Washington D.C.: Smithsonian Institution, Freer Gallery of Art, Oriental Studies No. 5, 1962), 84.
15. Ibid.
16. For a reproduction, see James Cahill, *Chinese Painting* (New York: Rizzoli International Publications, Inc., 1985), 36.
17. Ames and Rosemont, *Analects of Confucius,* 109.
18. Cahill, *Chinese Painting,* 27.

19. Ibid., 134.
20. Maxwell K. Hearn, "The Artist as Hero," in *Possessing the Past: Treasures from the National Palace Museum, Taipei*, edited by Wen C. Fong and James C. Y. Watt (New York: Metropolitan Museum of Art), 1996, 306.
21. Edwards, *The Field of Stones*, 28.
22. Cahill, *Chinese Painting*, 95.

Suggested Readings

Ames, Roger T., and David H. Hall. *Daodejing "Making This Life Significant": A Philosophic Translation*. New York: Ballantine Books, 2003.

Ames, Roger T., and Henry Rosemont, Jr. *The Analects of Confucius: A Philosophical Translation*. New York: Ballantine Publishing Group, 1998.

Cahill, James. *Chinese Painting*. New York: Rizzoli International Publications, 1985.

Cleveland Museum of Art. *Eight Dynasties of Chinese Painting: The Collections of the Nelson Gallery-Atkins Museum, Kansas City, and the Cleveland Museum of Art*. Cleveland: Cleveland Museum of Art, 1980.

Fong, Wen C., and James C. Y. Watt. *Possessing the Past: Treasures from the National Palace Museum, Taipei*. New York: Metropolitan Museum of Art, 1996.

Hall, David T., and Roger T. Ames. *Thinking Through Confucius*. Albany: State University of New York Press, 1987.

Throp, Robert L., and Richard Ellis Vinograd. *Chinese Art and Culture*. New York: Harry N. Abrams, 2001.

PHILOSOPHY

Mary I. Bockover

Teaching Chinese Philosophy from the Outside In

Asian philosophy satisfies both "general education" and "diversity and common ground" requirements at many universities because there is an implicit belief in the value of comparative education. This "diversity and common ground" requirement was put into place to broaden students' exposure to cultural difference. The idea is that if we educate our students about views and ways that are quite different from their own, the understanding that results will create a more cohesive (although no less diverse) community. After all, America is very diverse; there is no one racial or ethnic standard that defines its culture. In particular, Chinese philosophy does not just inform students about China; it informs them also about much of the ethos that is still foundational to Americans of Chinese descent. The belief in comparative philosophy, then, goes hand in hand with the belief in education more generally: it increases understanding, and understanding increases communication and cooperation. A "diversity and common ground" requirement is one of the ways universities try to foster good citizenship by fostering comparative understanding. Studying the radically different systems of thought of ancient China is a perfect context from which to begin, for we can, and must, get outside of our own minds, if education is to proceed with significance.

Translation of the ancient primary texts poses another challenge. The texts were written in classical calligraphy. Character literacy was not widespread until Mao sanctioned the development of a simplified character system to enhance accessibility, and in ancient times the written language was known by only a select group of people, notably those who had the responsibility for documenting the history and philosophy of China. Such tasks were largely the province of those who served in government (or imperial dynasty), such as governing officials, military officers, teachers, scribes, and ministers. More recently, the spoken language too has been transliterated. The word, *daodejing*, which is used as the title of the book that is the focus of this essay and the text I use to introduce students to the more general worldview or "metaphysics"[1] of ancient China, is the pinyin transliteration of the characters 道 德 經. The characters are commonly translated, "The way and its power," but can be rendered more literally as "the way power book."

Chinese characters are picto-ideograms that represent actual processes or events found in the world. The main point to make in this connection is that the process of translation itself is highly interpretive. This is no truer anywhere than when translating from the ancient characters into a language that is syntactically structured like English. Chinese does not have a subject-verb-object format in either spoken or written form, and there are no cases or declensions. The meaning of characters can be highly ambiguous, and they must always be interpreted in context. The range of how literally or abstractly a character can be translated is wide indeed.

To demonstrate this difference, I require one text, such as Arthur Waley's traditional translation *The Way and Its Power*, and supplement it with a sample of chapters from other translations for the purpose of comparison, such as those by Jane English, John Wu, Michael LaFargue, or Roger Ames. Taking passages that focus on the central theme of Dao easily shows how much translation is an interpretive process. We start with the now relatively famous opening stanzas of Laozi's classic. Waley translates them as follows:

> The Way that can be told of is not an Unvarying Way;
> The names that can be named are not unvarying names.
> It was from the Nameless that Heaven and Earth sprang;
> The named is but the mother that rears the ten thousand
> creatures, each after its kind.[2]

Here is Wu's translation:

> Dao can be talked about, but not the Eternal Dao.
> Names can be named, but not the Eternal Name.
> As the origin of heaven-and-earth, it is nameless:
> As "the Mother" of all things, it is nameable.[3]

Notice that while Waley translates the character for *dao* as "Way," capitalized in the Western fashion to signify the importance of a metaphysical first principle, Wu leaves the term untranslated to bring out its ineffability. Indeed, the passage centrally expresses that no word can capture the fullness of 道, which may be translated simply as "way," "path," or even "road," but Dao is the dynamic unity of all being represented by a character or word (that is, a "name"). What we call Dao, how we conceive it, is not what it is. There is more to reality than what we could ever conceive, and it is "nameless" for this very reason. Dao is beyond "what is" and "what is not," beyond the full and empty, beyond ordinary human comprehension. However, the sage or shengren (聖人) has broadened his mind enough to commune with that ultimate reality. This reality is falsely characterized in affirmative terms—in any terms— because it includes what has come infinitely before, what has yet to be, and what will never be.[4] It is namable to the extent that it is "mother of all things," the progenitor who has "reared" them, but as the very origin of being itself Dao is incommensurable and so cannot be named.

One can see why Daoism is a religion, while the study of its principles is doing the *philosophy* of religion. Through conceptual analysis we can come to understand the working principles found in the Daodejing, but to really "know" Dao is to take our awareness beyond concepts and the ordinary experience they construct to the direct and undivided mystical experience of the "One"[5] itself. This is a *religious* experience of ultimate and ineffable reality, or as Laozi says, the "Mystery of mystery [that] is the Door of all essence."[6] No wonder such a "truth" is so often referred to in negative terms: "of what is not," "nothing," "nonbeing," "what is not had," "what is not known," or what is "empty." The most profound insight—into the greater miracle and mystery of life itself— must go beyond the usual framework that we have come to rely on for our understanding of the nature of things.

> "Look for It, you won't see It: It is called 'fleeting'
> Listen for It, you won't hear It: It is called 'thin.'
> Grasp at It, you can't get It: It is called 'subtle.'"

> *These Three lines*
> *are about something that evades scrutiny.*
> *Yes, in it everything blends and becomes one.*

> Its top is not bright
> Its underside is not dim.
> *Always unnamable, It turns back to nothingness.*
> *This is the shape of something shapeless*
> *the form of a nothing*
> *this is elusive and evasive.*[7]

This chapter is important, since there are always students who challenge the legitimacy of conceptually analyzing this great work because
of Dao's ineffability. Clearly, philosophy can never do justice to the
mystical wisdom of the sage who has insight into no less than the
dynamic unity of being itself. Dao is unknowable in the sense that any
concept of it must be distinguished from the direct mystical experience
of it. Moreover, Dao is in-finite, so any attempt to de-fine it will not
fully capture it. This very point can be used to distinguish philosophy
from religion: professors can only expect their students to learn about
ideas discussed in class, not expect them to have religious experiences.
Doing philosophy requires an open mind, so insight into principles can
be gained without the prejudice of preconception. Practicing religion
also requires an open mind that fosters insight into what those principles represent—Dao, God, Allah, Brahman, Jahweh, nirvana, *ren*, and
so forth are all words that name such a spiritual reality. Religious practice through its participatory nature tends to lead to a deeper communion with that ineffable spiritual reality, and supports a tradition consisting of people who engage in the same rituals or profess the same
commitment. To state the difference most simply, philosophy aims at
understanding through conceptual insight—or the analysis of *ideas*.
Religion aims at understanding through spiritual insight—or the ritual
practices used to grow closer to experiencing the sacred.

Although there can be considerable overlap, the philosophical study
of a religion does not require practice of or commitment to its principles. Students can gain insight into the principles of Daoism, or can
study its philosophy, without having to believe in the divine reality that
its principles represent. They gain such insight in part by analyzing the
central principle or theme of Dao and its attributes. After a casual and
enjoyable reading, I have students go through the text, to identify sys-
tematically what Laozi says about Dao—for example, that Dao is infinite, dark, mysterious, the mother of all things, unfathomable,

unchanging, like water, like an infant, actionless, nameless, like an uncarved block, paradoxical, incommensurable, and so forth. I ask them to list these attributes in conceptual clusters, or groups they think share philosophical affinity (with easily cited references). This is a creative exercise that allows students not only to develop *their own* concept of Dao, but places them directly in virtue of what Laozi says about it. Asking students to formulate their own definition of Dao after this reminds them that a good definition of anything must not be too broad if one wishes it to capture the concept, nor must it be too narrow unless one wishes it to end up being just an example (or attribute) of the concept instead of a definition of it. They must also explain what they think Dao means in writing; in other words, they must justify their definition, which I call an "interpretation," to allow the creative nature of the process to be appreciated more fully.

After analyzing Dao, my strategy is to move on to some other important themes of *de* (德), *wuwei* (無為), and *sheng* (聖) or sage. Looking at these main concepts, or themes, in light of their attributes ties the study to the text while allowing for creative thinking. This process leads naturally to an understanding of how the main themes are related. Understanding the conceptual connection between *dao* and *de*, for example, is critical to understanding Laozi's philosophy. This understanding depends on their ability to define the "undefinable" themes and to explain their significance in light of what Laozi says. The last critical part of doing Chinese philosophy, therefore, is to have students evaluate what they have studied. For philosophical purposes, this means they must explain what they find to be meritorious or problematic about the view, and even more importantly, why they think this is the case by giving reasons for their criticisms or positive appraisals.

To summarize, this method of studying the philosophies of ancient China is *interpretation* (or definition), *explanation* (or justification), and finally, *evaluation* (or critical appraisal) of the main themes in light of their attributes and connections. From this method, an understanding of Laozi's worldview and his ethics is gained for the purposes of general education.

This kind of critical analysis often involves a discussion of the easily misunderstood passages where Laozi encourages his readers to "discard knowledge" and "banish learning."[8] It is important not to gloss over that Laozi would probably tell students who are not interested in learning for its own sake to find something else to do so their lives have a greater sense of meaning.[9] But there is a more significant message here. The sage may be able to clearly distinguish ultimate reality from a more limited perspective, but until introduced to the difference most people will tend to take their experience of things as the same thing as reality. In other words, people must also unlearn what they think they know for a deeper understanding of the world to emerge. This is why the *paradox*, or apparent contradiction, is such an important tool for Chinese philosophy. Habitually, and by its finite nature, the mind sees things roughly as static, cohesive, and separate. Such "things" are seen as existing or not, constrained by the law of noncontradiction (where something and its negation cannot both be true). The *Daodejing* is full of paradoxes. This stops us in our mental tracks for the very reason that they do not make any sense. For Laozi, however, the paradox is a discipline that demonstrates that the nature of things is not reducible to logical analysis. One must discard preconceived notions in order to arrive at a greater vision. Struggling with paradox requires one to face what one does *not* know, that is, to embrace one's own ignorance in order to be open to an even fuller appreciation of reality. In the process, it becomes clear how the *mind* straitjackets reality into a vision that is far too narrow to do it justice (i.e., into logical p's and not p's). This habit of logic must be abandoned for long enough to gain insight into the ordinary, dichotomous way of perceiving that the mind far too quickly confuses with reality itself.[10] The paradox does not confirm that the nature of reality is contradictory; rather, it gets one to confront the limitations of one's own mind. One limitation is the very habit of believing that reality, and not just the mind, has a logical and dichotomous structure. Paradox is a mind trap that works to undo this habit—and it works for both philosophical and religious purposes.

It blunts all sharp edges,
It unties all tangles,
It harmonizes all lights,
It unites the world into one whole.[11]

The largest square has no corners,
The greatest vessel takes the longest to finish,
Great music has the faintest nodes,

The Great Form is without shape.

For Dao is hidden and nameless.

Yet Dao alone supports all things and brings them to their fulfillment.[12]

These passages are good places to draw a general comparative difference between the Chinese worldview and the mainstream Western one. The latter sees creation as conforming to Logos or the "Word," while the former characterizes Dao as going beyond human experience, beyond creation, and even beyond all of "being" (to include non-being or "what is not"). Here one could say that being and nonbeing are mutually entailing, but to be more in line with the basic Daoist insight into the nature of things, this just falsely dichotomizes the "One," Dao, that is beyond all distinction. Dao is incommensurable with word, thought, or precept; thus, sagely wisdom is about how things *really* are instead of how some human or anthropomorphic logos divides and depicts them. The paradox enables one to see that one must put the ordinary vision of things aside to arrive at this deeper wisdom. A "free" mind and a nonconforming orientation to life lead to greater spiritual insight into the divine nature of reality—often expressed in the *Daodejing* as being a way of perfect harmony. Daoists then can align themselves with that Great Way and learn to live in spontaneous communion with all things. What Laozi is condemning is society's frivolous values, which during his time of the warring states were unreflective and chaotic, because his world was full of self-serving people who only learned to the degree that it would lead to profit; they only learned about things by which they could "set their store." Such people would not achieve the kind of peace and tranquility experienced by the Daoist sage, who lives life for its own sake. Paradoxically, the sage lives life to the fullest by *wuwei* (無為) or by "doing nothing." In this context, it means just *being* alive and awake to the miracle and mystery of life itself, Dao. For the purpose of doing philosophy, paradox is only a tool to get one to see concepts as concepts. One must dispense with preconceived notions, must "unlearn" or "banish" them, in order to gain deeper insight into the "concept" of Dao, which is the most central idea of Laozi's metaphysics. In a philosophical context, Dao is recognized as an idea basic to the worldview that Laozi himself believed in, and evoked through poetry, allegory, and analogy.

A main feature of Dao in the *Daodejing* is that of interdependency.[13] All things are what they are only in relation to one another, and what is more, they are all actually aspects of the same "thing." The yin-yang cosmology of Daoism fully brings this message out. Any set of opposites such as light and dark, or creative and receptive, really refers to varying degrees of some larger quality.[14] For example, dark is just less light, and light is less dark.[15] In essence they are the same quality (of lightness or darkness, depending upon what one wants to name them) manifesting in varying degrees. The same is true of what is changing and what is changeless. The concept of *changelessness* that pervades the *Daodejing* must be read in the same way that actionlessness or any other negative term is: again, not as a logical negation, but as expressing a complementary relation between mutually entailing qualities that refer to the same larger process or reality. The changeless Dao does not falsify change any more than actionlessness falsifies action, or nonbeing (emptiness) falsifies being (fullness). Logic fails us, for Dao is the *essence of being*, and without it, quite literally, nothing could exist at all.

Dao is "less" only in the paradoxical sense of being more rarified; in fact, Dao is the most rarified aspect of being, so much so that it is beyond observation and description. It is the mysterious or secret essence that pervades all existence—that formless, shapeless, nameless "what is not," which gives all things their very being and guides them on their way. Expressed negatively, Dao is changeless in the sense that it is the only constant; all things have their being in and through Dao. Expressed positively, Dao is change itself, blending the "ten thousand" things together into one dynamic unity of Being so they can return to their "self so."[16] The paradox is this: what we call change really refers to the way Dao *affects* the myriad things, and this is what we can observe. More accurately, the way *is* change (*dao*), the unobservable changeless essence of existence that we see only in virtue of its mysterious power (*de*, 德) to affect things. "So, as ever hidden, we should look at its inner essence as always manifest, we should look at its outer aspects."[17]

Let us now consider the significance of another difference in translations: the Way or Dao is said to be "unvarying" by Waley and "Eternal" by Wu. Is there any difference in these concepts? Students consistently respond that "unvarying" seems to suggest a Dao rooted in time, that has not changed its course, and any idea we may have of what the future will bring is purely speculative and we must see it as such.

Students also reply that Wu's translation of the attribute of Dao as "Eternal" has metaphysical overtones not captured by Waley's. Eternal brings out that Dao is infinite or *always* existing, and especially when capitalized suggests a kind of transcendental quality, while something that is "unvarying" can be quite down-to-earth. While Dao is not an ordinary object of experience for most of us, it is ordinary (although no less mysterious and miraculous), especially for the sage whose life is pervaded by it. The sage has experienced the dynamic unity of all being directly—that is, the religious or mystical experience that the typical, unenlightened person does not have.

Students ultimately need to decide for themselves whether this unfathomable source and sustainer of all being has merit, at least to the degree that it allows for an interesting and cohesive worldview to emerge. Strictly speaking, for Daoists who believe *Dao* is real and woven into the very fabric of things, it is not a metaphysical principle removed from them (except insofar as it is an idea). Laozi may have clearly seen Dao in the way of the world, striking a perfect balance and "covering us like a garment," but he also suggests that we miss Dao and cannot see it because we no longer have the eyes of a child who experiences life in all its sublimity. We overlook Dao as we grow into adults, as we develop and get wrapped up in our ideas of self-worth and social standing. We get stuck in our own little lives, our own myopic *definite* existences, which shuts the window of awareness to our connection with all else and to the very "thing" that can give life its beauty. To this end, all any of us can do is interpret, explain, and evaluate what we read in the text. Since Daoist ideas are debatable, students should be asked what they think about them and asked to explain why they think what they do and what their reasons are for thinking whether or not the ideas found in the *Daodejing* have merit or not.

Often students find merit in Laozi's appeal to nature's awesome beauty and order and how he provides a picture of divinity without a human face and the fine examples for living a good life. Not surprisingly, many students also find the text problematic: that Daoism does not esteem properly the *natural* human tendency to think dichotomously; they argue that without this way of thinking society would lose cohesion altogether. To them, it seems contradictory that Dao would centrally endow us with a capacity that is worth condemning in the end. It also points to another contradiction: a key claim in the Daodejing is we cannot change Dao, the source and sustainer of all there is, then quite literally nothing is left to be done. Everything flows from Dao and is just where it ought to be metaphysically. Like water, Dao can never go amiss. On what grounds, then, can anything be criticized? Laozi himself was condemning conventional wisdom, after all, and was highly critical of the rulers and ways of his time for living in a manner that went against Dao. How can *anything* go against Dao, if it cannot be changed or affected?

This question brings us back to *de* (德), the mysterious power of Dao that brings things into being and causes them to pass from it without much ado. *De* is the power to act "actionlessly" (*wuwei*, 無為), and is seen most fluidly in its unselfconscious beauty and creativity in the spontaneous perfection of nature. In a human context, examples of *wuwei*, or great results achieved with minimum or *no* effort, abound in the text: consider all of the references to the best tailor, charioteer, warrior, ruler, or sage. Even after understanding the paradoxical nature of the *de* concept, students object that *wuwei* lends itself more to defeatism than to constructive social activism. They argue Daoist sages could never be social activists, since it is through *inactivity* that they accomplish their great feats and live completely tranquil and fulfilling lives.

Students who prefer philosophies about actively changing the world often declare that enlightenment is selfish, even pretentious, and leads away from the fight for social justice and political change. They think their actions really *can* make a difference, even in the greater scheme of things, and are hard-pressed to value removing themselves from the details of their active and purposeful lives. In short, many end up preferring Confucian principles,[18] but it is only through the study of both that this realization is possible.

At this point it is worth suggesting that Laozi was a social activist in his own way, which makes the claim that Daoism and social activism are at odds debatable. There is no reason to think that spiritual wisdom and social well-being must have inconsistent aims. But the Daoist *is* committed to the belief that the change one makes in the world cannot affect Dao and, moreover, that the effects cannot even be properly assessed from a human perspective. Humans are not the final arbiters when it comes to knowing the ultimate significance of things.

Perhaps it is best to focus on one's own life after all, free from the delusion that what we do will really make a positive difference to the "always so" and "self so" Dao. It makes for interesting discussion anyway, which is an immeasurable part of what teaching Chinese philosophy is all about.

Notes

1. The concept of "metaphysics," in being categorically distinguished from the physical world, may suggest a *dualistic* framework for understanding the nature of things. This concept is not really appropriate for many of the philosophies of China, where all aspects of reality are viewed more "monistically," as interconnected and mutually entailing. For example, *tian*, or heaven, was not viewed by the ancients so much as a different realm of being but as a more rarefied and more mysterious aspect of the world existing right here and now. This is one reason why ancestor worship as well as divination such as that practiced through the *Yijing* was (and still is) so important for the Chinese; *tian* was thought of as *interdependent* with the more tangible world ("the 10,000 things," *wan* or everything).

2. Arthur Waley, trans., *The Way and Its Power*, (London: Unwin Paperbacks, 1987).

3. John C. Wu, trans. *Tao Te Ching* (Boston: Shambala, 1990).

4. One way to understand the role of time in the Daodejing is to see it as the human measure of change. As such, it is a construct that attempts to "name" or quantify an unnamable reality that is constant. Both past and future are speculative, that is, or a function of the memory and anticipation that we too easily confuse with Dao, or reality itself.

5. From John Wu's translation.

6. Waley, *Way and Its Power*, chap. 1.

7. Michael LaFargue. *The Tao of the Tao Te Ching: A Translation and Commentary* (Albany: State University of New York Press, 1992), chap. 14.

8. See especially chapters 18, 19, 38, and 48.

9. This is not to deny Laozi's clear preference for learning in less-conventional ways (rather than getting a college education). Moreover, removing oneself from society and its institutions may be just what is needed to gain a fuller appreciation of life.

10. Religiously, the paradox is a tool for increasing awareness of this divine reality, a process often referred to as "enlightenment."

11. Wu, *Tao Te Ching*, chap. 4.

12. Waley, *Way and Its Power*, chap. 41.

13. I want to stress this aspect even though interdependency is more explicitly stated as central to later Buddhist thought.

14. Being receptive is *essential* to creativity—having a truly creative idea requires an open mind. These "opposites" in actuality are variations of the same larger, creative process that we refer to in positive (*yang*) language to make it appear more definite.

15. *Yin* was initially (and literally) the dark side of a mountain or river, while *yang* was by contrast the light. Yin and yang are now taken to represent the contrast of

any set of opposites at play: masculine/feminine, creative/receptive, life/death, and so forth. Because of their constantly changing nature (notice the paradox that change is a constant), it is better to think of yin/yang as varying qualities instead of more static things.

16. The quality itself that the "opposites" define and comprise is usually named in virtue of its yang principle—for example, light, creative, and life instead of dark, receptive, and death.

17. Wu, *Tao Te Ching*, chap. 1.

18. See my chapter "The *Ren-dao* of Confucius: A Spiritual Account of Humanity," in *Confucius Now*, edited by David Jones (LaSalle, IL: Open Court, 2006), 189–205.

Suggested Readings

Some Translations of (or Works on) the *"Daodejing"*

Ames, Roger T., and David L. Hall, trans. *Dao De Jing: A Philosophical Translation*. New York: Ballantine Books, 2004.

Chan, Wing-tsit. *The Way of Lao Tzu*. Indianapolis: Bobbs-Merrill, 1963.

Ch'u Ta-Kao. *Tao Te Ching by Lao-Tzu*. London: George Allen & Unwin, 1937. Quoted in *Dao—The Watercourse Way*, by Alan Watts. London: Arkana Penguin, 1992.

Gia-Fu and Jane English. *Lao Tsu—Tao te Ching*. [Place?] Wildwood House, 1991. (First published 1972.)

LaFargue, Michael. *The Tao of the Tao Te Ching: A Translation and Commentary*. Albany: State University of New York Press, 1992.

Lau, D. C. *Laozi, Tao Te Ching*. New York: Penguin Books, 1974. (First published 1963.)

Le Guin, Ursula K. *Lao Tzu: Tao Te Ching, A Book about the Way and the Power of the Way*. With Jerome P. Seaton. Boston: Shambhala, 1997.

Mitchell, Stephen. *Tao Te Ching*. New York: Perennial, 1992.

Waley, Arthur. *The Way and Its Power (The "Tao Te Ching" and Its Place in Chinese Thought)*. London: Unwin Paperbacks, 1987. (First published 1934.)

Watts, Alan. *Dao—The Watercourse Way*. London: Arkana Penguin, 1992. (First published 1976.)

Wilhelm, Richard. *Tao Te Ching (The Book of Meaning and Life)*. London: Arkana Penguin, 1990. (First published 1911, trans. H. G. Ostwald).

Wu, John C. *Tao Teh Ching*. Boston: Shambhala, 1990. (First published 1961.)

Other Suggested Readings

Allinson, Robert E., ed. *Understanding the Chinese Mind & The Philosophical Roots*. Oxford: Oxford University Press, 1989.

Ames, Roger. "The Chinese Conception of Selfhood." In *A Companion to World Philosophies*, edited by Eliot Deutsch and Ron Bontekoe, 148–54. Oxford: Blackwell, 1997.

Ames, Roger T., and Henry Rosemont Jr. *The Analects of Confucius: A Philosophic Translation*. New York: The Ballantine Publishing Group, 1998.

Chan, Wing-tsit. *A Sourcebook in Chinese Philosophy*. Princeton, NJ: Princeton University Press, 1963.

Cheng, Chung-ying, ed. *Journal of Chinese Philosophy*. Cambridge, MA: Blackwell.

Creel, Herrlee Glassner. *Chinese Thought from Confucius to Mao Tse-tung*. Chicago: University of Chicago Press, 1953.

de Bary, William Theodore. *East Asian Civilizations: A Dialogue in Five Stages*. Cambridge, MA: Harvard University Press, 1988.

de Bary, William Theodore, Wing-tsit Chan, and Burton Watson. *Sources of Chinese Tradition*. 2 vols. New York: Columbia University Press, 1964.

Fingarette, Herbert. *Confucius—The Secular as Sacred*. New York: Harper Torchbooks, 1972. (Reprinted by Westview Press.)

Fu, Charles Wei-hsun, and Wing-tsit Chan. *Guide to Chinese Philosophy*. Boston: G. K. Hall, 1978.

Fung, Yu-Lan, and Derk Bodde, eds. *A Short History of Chinese Philosophy*. New York: Free Press, 1948.

Graham, A. C. *Disputers of the Tao*. La Salle, IL: Open Court, 1989.

Hall, David, and Roger T. Ames. *Thinking Through Confucius*. Albany: State University of New York Press, 1987.

Herbert, Edward. *A Confucian Notebook*. London: John Murray Publishers, 1992. (First published 1950.)

Ivanhoe, Philip J. *Confucian Moral Self-Cultivation*. Indianapolis: Hackett, 2000.

Kohn, Livia, and Michael LaFargue, eds. *Laozi and the "Tao Te Ching."* Albany: State University of New York Press, 1989.

Koller, John, and Patricia Koller. *A Sourcebook in Asian Philosophy*. New Jersey: Prentice Hall, 1991.

Li, Chenyang. *The Tao Encounters the West: Explorations in Comparative Philosophy*. Albany: State University of New York Press, 1999.

Moore, Charles A., ed. *The Chinese Mind & Essentials of Chinese Philosophy and Culture*. Honolulu: University of Hawaii Press, 1967.

Rosemont, Jr., Henry. *A Chinese Mirror: Moral Reflections on Political Economy and Society*. LaSalle, IL: Open Court, 1991.

Schwartz, Benjamin I. *The World of Thought in Ancient China*. Cambridge, MA: Harvard University Press, 1985.

Smith, Huston. *The World's Religions*. New York: Perennial Library, 1991. (First published 1958 under the title *Religions of Man*.)

Waley, Arthur, trans. *The Analects of Confucius*. New York: Vintage Books, 1989.

Waley, Arthur. *Three Ways of Thought in Ancient China*. Garden City, NY: Doubleday. (First published in 1939.)

James Peterman

A Strategy for Integrating Confucius's *Analects* into a Typical Introduction to Philosophy Course

Anyone who has been trained in some version of Western philosophy—in my case, analytic philosophy—will find the task of integrating non-Western philosophy[1] into mainline philosophy classes daunting. The texts, beyond being unfamiliar, even upon sustained study, refuse to fit into familiar patterns of philosophical writing. Even if we could decode these texts, presenting them to students in, say, an introduction to philosophy, this would seem to take the class in a direction sufficiently different from the rest of the texts and issues under discussion that this project would tend to weaken the class. My ideal introduction to philosophy attempts to introduce students to a range of topics that build on and relate to one another in a way that allows students deeper insights into the texts and issues under discussion than would be possible by studying texts and issues in isolation. In this essay, I propose one way to integrate Confucius's *Analects* (*Lunyu*) into an introduction to philosophy that satisfies this criterion.

The introduction to philosophy that I am imagining begins with Socratic dialogues. Specifically, I will focus on *Euthyphro*.[2] I have chosen this text because it is often used both as an introduction to Socratic philosophy and to the dialectical method of doing philosophy. I have

I would like to thank my friend and colleague Jim Peters, who has influenced my views of Socrates and who was kind enough to provide me with suggestions for the secondary literature on Socrates that I have used in this essay. I also would like to express my debt to Henry Rosemont and Roger Ames, whose steadfast devotion in deed and writing to introducing philosophers in midcareer to Confucius and the Chinese tradition has had an indelible impact on both my professional and personal life.

also chosen to place the *Analects* in dialogue with this text, since both Socrates and Confucius stand in similar relation to their respective traditions: Both thinkers inspired the writing of founding texts, written during the Axial Age, that helped to define and inaugurate the path of their respective, quite different, traditions. Just as the Western tradition can be seen as a set of footnotes to Plato, and by extension Socrates, the Chinese tradition can be seen as a set of footnotes to Confucius.

I will begin by discussing the project of elenchus, or dialectical argument, that Socrates pursues in *Euthyphro*. I focus both on the Socratic method and on the principles that underlie it. Next, I will present an overview of the vocabulary and project of the *Analects*, along with some key passages that I will use to challenge the Socratic method. I will conclude with a reflection on the way in which an examination of the *Analects* and its distinctive approach to moral reflection and teaching can serve to deepen students' insights about the character and limits of Socratic reflection.[3]

Euthyphro begins with an encounter between Socrates and Euthyphro (4c–e). They exchange information about their respective legal situations. After describing issues arising in Miletus's indictment against him, Socrates inquires about Euthyphro's legal situation. He finds that Euthyphro is prosecuting his father for murder. The case against his father is not, however, straightforward. One of Euthyphro's laborers, while drunk, had killed a household servant. At the time of the killing, Euthyphro was away from the house, and his father by himself attended to the matter. He had the laborer bound hand and foot and left in a ditch and then sent a man to Athens to ask of the officials how he should proceed. While waiting for the man to return, the laborer died of cold and hunger. Euthyphro's family reasoned that Euthyphro's father did nothing wrong. After all, he himself did not kill the laborer, but even if he had done so, the killing would have been unproblematic, since the laborer was clearly a murderer. Nevertheless, Euthyphro insists that prosecuting his father is pious. His family, however, contends that Euthyphro's prosecution of his father is an act of impiety. In conflict with his family's assessment, Euthyphro insists on the piety of his action by arguing that "they [know] badly how the divine is disposed concerning the pious and the impious" (*Euthyphro* 4e).

While differing in detail and topic from the beginning of other Socratic dialogues, this beginning is representative. I will present this standard form of beginning as the first of six principles that define the basic commitments of Socratic (elenctic or dialectical) method:

   I. The beginning of Socratic inquiry is a specific moral judgment made by a particular person.

After this beginning, Socrates initiates an investigation of the sorts of moral knowledge implied in or presupposed by Euthyphro's specific moral judgment (4e, 5c–d). Socrates asks Euthyphro to tell him "what he has just now strongly affirmed that he *knows plainly*: what sorts of things . . . piety and impiety are" (5c–d). Even though this request initiates his questioning of Euthyphro's presuppositions, Socrates continues by making an even stronger claim about what Euthyphro's claim presupposes. He holds that not only does Euthyphro's claim presuppose plain knowledge of "what sorts of things piety and impiety are," it also presupposes knowledge of the sole *idea* of piety: "*Isn't the pious itself the same as itself in every action*, and again isn't the impious opposite to everything pious, while it itself is similar to itself, and *has one certain idea* in accordance with impiety—everything that is that is going to be impious" (5d). The term "idea" is a technical term, here not translated from the Greek. West and West explain the term as follows: "The *idea* . . . of a thing may be thought of as the look it has, in the mind's eye, *when it is truly seen for what it is*."[4]

Four crucial principles of Socratic method emerge in this passage:

   II. Any particular moral judgment about A being X, where X is a moral predicate, implies or presupposes plain moral knowledge about X.

  III. Plain moral knowledge about X requires knowing what the X itself is in every X action.

  IV. Knowing what the X itself is in every X action involves having the single *idea* of X.

   V. If one has the single idea of X, one sees it in one's mind's eye for what it truly is.[5]

Socrates conducts no investigation of these basic principles in *Euthyphro*. He states these presuppositions in eight short lines, but does not defend them.[6] For better or for worse, Euthyphro is quite willing to accept these ground rules for his and Socrates' inquiry, and he shows agreement with them in his refusal to question them and in his acknowledgment that principles II–V are "doubtless" (5d).

Principles I–V form the background for the investigation that follows and establish the principles by which Socrates corrects Euthyphro's false starts. Euthyphro responds to Socrates' request to say what piety is by giving a description of piety based on how he is proceeding now against his father.[7] Euthyphro attempts to justify his approach to his father's behavior by appeal to the example of Zeus, who is considered the best and most just god. He says Zeus bound his father, Kronos, after discovering that Kronos unjustly ate his other sons, and even Kronos himself castrated his own father, Ouranos, for similar deeds. Euthyphro reasons that if Zeus is the best and most just god, then his (Euthyphro's) own action, by analogy to that of Zeus, is also just. He argues that those who criticize him, but accept that Zeus is the best and most just god, are inconsistent (6a).

Socrates rejects Euthyphro's account of Zeus's behavior and his general acceptance of the Homeric tradition as irrelevant to his question about what piety is. He charges Euthyphro with just giving examples of various pious things (6d) and thereby avoiding the real question: What is the "*eidos* itself by which all the pious things are pious?" (6d). Euthyphro accepts Socrates' criticism and offers his first attempt at a definition of piety: "What is dear to the gods is pious, what is not dear is impious" (6e). Once Euthyphro has offered an account of piety that fits principles II–V, Socrates goes on to the next step of dialectical inquiry. In this next step, he reminds Euthyphro of his (Euthyphro's) beliefs that the gods quarrel (7b). After clarifying the source of disagreements between the gods, Socrates and Euthyphro agree that the very same things would be both hateful to the gods (that is, some gods) and dear to the gods (that is, other gods) (8a). The obvious conclusion, then, is that, given Euthyphro's definition of piety and impiety, the same things would be both pious and impious. Euthyphro's definition of piety and impiety, conjoined with his belief that the gods disagree about what to hate and hold dear, produces a contradiction.

This procedure indicates another principle of the Socratic project. Socrates examines other beliefs his interlocutors hold as a basis for determining the success of their account of some *idea*. This approach amounts to some form of coherence criterion for the justification of proposed accounts. This results in principle VI: A justified account of the *idea* of *X* offered by interlocutor A should be consistent with A's other beliefs.

As a matter of faith Socrates believes that by using this method, one can, in turn, examine and reject various accounts of an *idea* until one encounters an account that satisfies all of these criteria. Although this method does not produce divine wisdom, which demands absolute certainty and infallibility, it would produce a form of human wisdom.[8]

Can Euthyphro's initial account be developed in a way that would successfully fend off Socrates' criticisms? After all, as Socrates charges, Euthyphro does appeal to the example of Zeus in defending his action. So Socrates' charge that Euthyphro offers only examples, not an account of the idea of justice, may have some validity.[9] Euthyphro's initial account requires substantial development and perhaps even correction—his view that we stand in no different moral relation to our father than to a stranger seems wrong—but what is perfectly clear is this: Without a successful critique of the principles underlying Socratic method, no amount of elaboration and qualification will help. If knowledge of the truth of particular moral judgments requires knowledge of the *ideas* invoked in that judgment, then the type of account Euthyphro offers fails. It fails by not giving us what we need: an account of the *idea* of piety.

In opposition to Socrates' method, I would argue that the mode of moral reflection practiced by the authors[10] of the *Analects* presents a compelling alternative to that of Socrates. Confucian moral reflection and teaching provide a way to practice moral inquiry that would both serve to elaborate on and correct Euthyphro's initial account of piety and provide a way to critique the framework of principles that Socrates uses to dismantle it.

In order to understand the basic framework of the *Analects*, one needs to be familiar with its basic vocabulary.[11] The *Analects* describes Confucius's conversations with various interlocutors, many of whom are disciples seeking instruction on how better to follow the *dao* (way, path). Central to following *dao* is the most general moral virtue, *ren* (translated variously as "goodness," "benevolence," "humanity," "authoritative personhood," "kindness"), which both emphasizes the key notion that we are who we are as human beings in our relations to others and the related ideal of being good in maintaining those relationships (*Analects* 3.3, 4.3, 4.4, 4.5). One root of *ren* is the practice of *li* (ritual propriety), by which an internal pattern of moral behavior (*ren*) gets established (2.3, 12.1). Once established, however, one expresses *ren* through *li* (8.2, 4.5 in combination with 12.5). A second root of *ren* is *xiao* (filial piety) (1.2). By learning *li*, appropriate modes of ritual propriety and the forms of deference key to a harmonious family (1.13), one begins to learn to master *li* in its full generality. By mastering *li,* one is able to bring appropriate forms of *he* (harmony) into one's life and relationships (1.12) by doing what is *yi* (appropriate and fitting) (4.10).

The problem situation of Confucius's disciples differs from the situation of Socrates' interlocutors. Confucius's disciples most often present themselves as seeking guidance from Confucius because his mastery of *dao* is superior to their own.[12] Specifically, they seek instruction from him in order to improve their ability to follow the *dao* by improving their understanding of and proper performance of the constitutive ideals of *dao*: *li, xiao, ren* and *yi*. Confucius's approach to these problems is to give his interlocutors advice and ways of understanding themselves that will allow them to live better. He does not put them through the rigors of dialectic to show them that what they think they know they do not really know. The emphasis instead is on leading the disciples to change their lives. How might a Confucian, with this framework and goals, respond to Socrates' criticism of Euthyphro?

First, consider Socrates' criticism that Euthyphro gives only an example of a pious action. This criticism rests on the bedrock of Socratic principles II–V. But a Confucian would, at the very least, reject principles III–V. Again and again, in the *Analects*, a disciple asks (*wen*) Confucius about some component ideal of *dao*. Confucius presents himself as having answers to these questions, but he and his interlocutor never suppose that his "plain knowledge" about X involves knowing what X itself is in every action, having the *idea of X*, or seeing in one's mind's eye what X truly is. Instead of using this model, Confucius's approach emphasizes the practical situation of the disciple and shows no interest in definition.

Consider Confucius's responses in book 2 to a series of questions about filial piety or conduct.

Meng Yizi asked about filial conduct (*xiao*). The Master replied: "Do not act contrary. . . . While they are living, serve them according to the observances of ritual propriety (*li*); when they dead, bury them and sacrifice to them according to the observances of ritual propriety." (2.5)

Meng Wubo asked about filial conduct (*xiao*). The Master replied: "Give your father and mother nothing to worry about beyond your physical well-being." (2.6)

Ziyou asked about filial conduct (*xiao*). The Master replied: "Those today who are filial are considered so because they are able to provide for their parents. But even dogs and horses are given that much care. If you do not respect your parents, what is the difference?" (2.7)

Zixia asked about filial conduct (*xiao*). The Master replied: "It all lies in showing the proper countenance.[13] As for the young contributing their energies when there is work to be done, and deferring to their elders when there is wine and food to be had—how can merely doing this be considered filial?" (2.8)[14]

Note that in none of the answers does Confucius fulfill the Socratic demand to specify the *idea* of filial piety or conduct.[15] Instead, he offers a helpful insight. I call what he offers an "insight" insofar as what he says about filiality is put forth as a piece of plain moral knowledge. The insight is "helpful" insofar as it is designed to help the particular questioner in his own development into a person who embodies filiality. For example, Ziyou overemphasizes the formal side of Confucius's teaching, the precise following of ritual.[16] Consequently, Confucius's answer to Ziyou is designed to cause him to focus more on the "inward" aspect of filiality: Providing for parents, even if done according to all the appropriate rules, is not enough; it must be done out of a feeling of respect for them. His answer to Zixia is different. For someone who, like Zixia, focuses on book-learning, the tendency will be to think that by studying the classic texts, memorizing them, and being able to expound on filiality, he will be filial. But Confucius counsels him to focus on something else, something less intellectual—that is, his countenance.[17]

We, as philosophers, may wish to save Confucius from himself by thinking, as I once did, that these claims and others like them in this text could be organized into some sort of analysis of filial piety. I now doubt that this is so, but even if it were, it is clear that Confucius is not engaged in this sort of enterprise. His approach is not, however, deficient because of his lack of interest in definition of key concepts; rather, it represents an alternative to Socrates' way of thinking about moral reflection and clarification. At least, this is what I am prepared to argue.[18] In what follows, I will try to clarify this Confucian alternative.

All practical ideals are complex. For example, practicing filial piety requires balancing the following: providing for your parents, feeling respectful, keeping one's countenance, following ritual propriety concerning food and wine, reflection on the classical accounts of filiality, concern with the details of proper ritual behavior toward one's parents, and so forth. But when we ask the question, "Which of these phenomena really constitutes filiality?" the proper answer is that none of them do.[19] That is in part because being filial involves a complex that is not reducible to a subset or to anything more foundational than the complex practice itself.[20] Each of us will focus on the aspect most interesting and comfortable to us. But our real need is often just to incorporate other necessary aspects of the complex mix of things that make up filiality.[21] The Socratic focus on a single *idea* would not satisfy this basic need even if it were possible—which, if filiality is complex, it is not.

Training in filiality is not, however, completed by specifying elements of this complex. What it is to be filial—*pace* Socrates—depends also on specific examples of filial conduct. Consider, for example, Confucius's response to the governor of She, who asserts that in his village someone who is upright (a "True Person") reported his father when he took a sheep on the sly. To this assertion, Confucius replies: "Those who are true in my village conduct themselves differently. A father covers for his son, and a son covers for his father. And being true lies in this" (*Analects* 13.18).[22] This passage takes a piece of lore and offers it up as a paradigm of filial behavior of son to father and loyalty of father to son. The son must cover for his father by not reporting him. This behavior might seem outrageous to Euthyphro, but the sensibility Confucius articulates sees family bonds as paramount to the health of society in general and rejects appeals to a legal system and its forms of punishment and impersonal codes.[23]

These points indicate that for Confucius, teaching filiality requires teaching a complex set of practices that make up filiality, exemplars of filial behavior, along with insights about the importance of filial behavior in terms of its contribution to the common good. Teaching filiality is not, however, exhausted by these. Additional insights about unappreciated aspects of filiality might allow for an expanded understanding of filiality and the ways in which it is best pursued in particular contexts. Indeed, Confucius holds the general view that the *dao*, the ideal way of acting and living, is something that can be extended by human beings: "It is the person who is able to broaden the *dao,* not the *dao* that broadens the person" (*Analects* 15.29). The same holds for filiality, a component of *dao.* Confucius's attention to the differing needs of individuals, the complexity of filial practices, the importance of examples, and the open-endedness of *dao* arguably undermines any confidence we might place in the Socratic notion of a single *idea* of piety epistemically prior to any judgments or recommendations we make about piety.

Although adopting the methodology of the *Analects* would, if otherwise correct, undermine Socrates' critique of Euthyphro, Confucius's own call for covering for family members contradicts Euthyphro's position and represents a major difference between Euthyphro and Confucius. As mentioned, Confucius's view of the need for fathers and sons to cover for each other rests on his view of the centrality of filial piety in the family as the bedrock of social order generally. His view of the requirements of filial piety in the particular case of fathers and sons reporting on each other rests on this fundamental claim.

The Socratic method would require Confucius to forgo any appeal to this fundamental claim until he was able to provide an account of the *idea* of filial piety (or piety generally). But Confucius's method requires that he collect useful insights about filial piety in order to build up a rich sense of its elements, its central exemplars, its general importance, and a related proper sense of how best to encourage filiality in people with vastly different dispositions. If, indeed, Confucius's insights about filiality are worth preserving as the bedrock upon which ethical teaching takes place, the Socratic method is destructive of an important human enterprise.[24]

In pursuing the question of how a Confucian might critique the Socratic approach to moral inquiry, my primary concern has been to sketch out a way in which a discussion of Confucius's *Analects* could play a crucial role in an introduction to philosophy by way of presenting a key challenge to Socratic method. As I indicate above, my ideal introduction to philosophy attempts to introduce students to a range of topics that build on and relate to one another in a way that allows students deeper insights into the texts and issues under discussion than would be possible by studying texts and issues in isolation. By following a study of *Euthyphro*, or other Socratic dialogues, with an examination of the Confucian approach to moral teaching, students will be able to reflect on a possible problem in the Socratic demand to provide an account of moral ideas as the only possible basis for any moral judgment. By having both of these views in sight, they will be able to think better about the strengths and limits of Socratic moral inquiry. If that is not enough, here are two more benefits: students will also get exposure to another tradition and will get exposure to one of the most important texts ever written.[25]

Appendix: Preparing to Teach Confucius's *Analects*

For useful introductions to *Analects* for those who are teaching it for the first time, I recommend Ames and Rosemont (introduction), Fingarette, Graham, Hall and Ames, Jones, and Lau, all cited in "Suggested Readings."

For purposes of introducing the *Analects* to students, I highly recommend the approach offered by Jones. His list of passages that employ the basic terms from *Analects* make it easy to select representative passages from the *Analects* to introduce students to the text's central claims. I usually follow this approach. After that, I like to read selected chapters from the *Analects* in order to help students get a sense of the development of claims and tensions between earlier and later chapters. For the task of making a selection of chapters, I have relied heavily on Brooks and Brooks, who present a view of the development of the text. Once students get a feel for the *Analects*, I suggest turning to specific issues such as the one at hand: how to understand and clarify piety. One note of caution: It is matter of controversy how unified a text the *Analects* is. The sort of gloss I give of the basic views in the *Analects* rests on my weaving together strands that can be woven in this way. But this sort of gloss de-emphasizes tensions in the text. For example, the relation I assert between *ren* and *li* may only be part of the story. For the tensions, see *Analects* 9.1, along with the discussion in Brooks and Brooks, cited in their index under *ren* (or, as they transcribe it, rvn). For an evaluation of the general argument in Brooks and Brooks, see Slingerland's review.[26] My own approach is to present a simple overview at first and then read the text for complications and apparent tensions. In this way, I let students think through the possible inconsistencies and also encourage them to see the text as layered, with opening claims followed by developments and commentaries.

For extremely valuable introductions to the historical context of Confucius's thought and to the relation between Confucian thinking and more familiar Western views, I recommend Ames and Rosemont (introduction), Fingarette, Graham, Hall and Ames, and Schwartz.

For useful insights into the character traits and life circumstances of Confucius's disciples and his attitude toward them, I recommend Ames and Rosemont's notes and Lau's appendix.

I also recommend working with multiple translations. Classical Chinese texts have something of the character of Rorschach inkblots. The sentences are brief and suggestive. Very good translators often disagree about what the sentences mean in context. I have found it useful to determine the range of responsible translations and have, accordingly, recommended four translations.

Notes

1. I use the term "philosophy" with some hesitation, since the non-Western text I will discuss, the *Analects*, is not in any standard sense philosophical. What I mean is that the text does not, in any ways we are used to in the Socrates-Kant tradition, raise the questions philosophers have raised. But the *Analects*, like the Bible, can be put to philosophical uses. When so used, we could, in this extended sense, call the text philosophical.

2. Thomas G. West and Grace Starry West, *Four Texts on Socrates* (Ithaca, NY: Cornell University Press, 1984). Parenthetical references are to the Stephano page numbers.

3. In this essay, I am making this argument to an imagined audience that is already convinced of the wisdom of teaching Socrates to beginning philosophy students and that is open to adding Confucius. I do not mean to suggest that reading Confucius is important only because of the light doing so sheds on Socrates. For those already convinced of the wisdom of reading Confucius in an introduction to

philosophy, this argument would still serve to outline one way to bring Confucius and Socrates into dialogue in such a class.

4. West and West, *Four Texts on Socrates*, 46 n. 20, my emphasis throughout.

5. For a discussion of the various interpretations of this passage, see Henry Teloh, *Socratic Education in Plato's Early Dialogues* (Notre Dame, IN: University of Notre Dame Press, 1986), 32–34.

6. For a defense of the claim that Socrates does not seek indubitable foundations, but rests his case on getting others to agree with his methodological principles, see Gregory Vlastos, *Socratic Studies* (Cambridge: Cambridge University Press, 1994), 13.

7. For purposes of this essay, I accept Socrates' characterization of Euthyphro's view as correct.

8. For the argument that Socrates never defends his methodological principles, see Vlastos, *Socratic Studies*, 26.

9. Euthyphro presents this example as his central defense of himself. He also describes his treatment of his father as a basis for some other general principles of piety, but these are secondary to his appeal to the example of Zeus's treatment of his father.

10. For a detailed account of the history of the writing of the text and tensions within it, see E. Bruce and E. Taeko Brooks, *The Original Analects* (New York: Columbia University Press, 1998).

11. All translations of Confucius are from Roger T. Ames and Henry Rosemont, Jr., *The Analects of Confucius: A Philosophical Translation* (New York: Ballantine Books, 1998). Parenthetical references in the text are to the numbers of the *Analects* in this translation.

12. Confucius denies being a *ren* person (*Analects* 14.28), but he does claim to be a person who loves learning (5.28) and who also tirelessly teaches (7.34). See also 7.28 and 16.9 for different senses and levels of knowledge (*zhi*). Confucius, like Socrates, denies himself the highest level of wisdom. Like Socrates, he does admit to having a lower level of wisdom, though one different from Socrates'.

13. I argue against Ames and Rosemont's translation of this sentence below.

14. In addition to these passages, the other passages in which there is explicit use of the term *xiao* are *Analects* 1.2, 1.6, 1.11, 2.20, 2.21, 4.20, 8.21, 11.5, 13.20, and 19.18. Of course, other passages bear on the question of how to be filial.

15. Ames and Rosemont indicate that Confucius is engaged in the project of defining filial piety (*Analects of Confucius*, 52), but this claim seems in tension with their other basic insight that Confucius's response to questions differs from person to person. See *Analects* 11.22 for a clear example of the dependence of Confucius's answers on the questioner, and Ames and Rosemont, *Analects of Confucius*, 5 for their acknowledgment of this point. This pattern of not offering definitions is not restricted to *xiao*, but occurs throughout the text in the context of discussion of other key notions. For example, even the best possible examples of definitions of *ren* (12.1 and 12.22) appear to provide something else. *Analects* 12.1 gives a recommendation about how to become *ren,* and 12.22 appears, in analogy with the related question about knowledge (*zhi*), to clarify a feature of *ren*—that it involves one's relation to others. Even Fan Chi is confused by Confucius's response, and the subsequent clarification indicates nothing about a definition.

16. Ames and Rosemont, *Analects of Confucius*, 233 n.29.

17. From the references to young people it can be taken that Zixia's emphasis on book learning really is no different from young people's emphasis on doing the right thing at the right time. Both miss a key point: doing what you need to do while showing outwardly the right spirit.

18. It might be tempting to think, as Ames and Rosemont do, that at *Analects* 2.8 Confucius is claiming that proper countenance is part of the definition of filiality, but providing food is not. Their translation of 2.8 aims at this point. They translate 色難 *se nan* as "It all lies in showing the proper countenance." But this sentence literally means nothing more than this: countenance is difficult. (For this translation, see Arthur Waley's *The Analects of Confucius*.) If Confucius's answers are specific to the questioner, he may also mean that countenance is what is difficult for Zixia. But beyond these translation issues, the further question to ask is whether Confucius would hold that countenance is part of filial piety, but providing food is not. Imagine an interlocutor who, having heard Confucius's response to Zixia, decides to drop providing food, but work more on his countenance. This would not be an adequate expression of filiality. What we need is a proper balance of the range of elements of filiality. Of course, getting that is difficult, partly because the elements themselves present special difficulties. That seems to be Confucius's point to Zixia.

19. In making this argument, I am following a model for reading the *Analects* that is influenced by some parts of Wittgenstein's *Philosophical Investigations*, 3rd ed. (New York: Macmillan, 1958). I have in mind the passage in which Wittgenstein presents family resemblance (section 66) as an apt simile for understanding how general concepts have content (through a web of resemblances, not through the introduction of a single essence or idea). This particular argument also finds its home, however, in sections 168, 175, 176, 177, in which Wittgenstein rejects the idea that any of the phenomena we associate with some general concept can ever be essences of it.

20. Like Wittgenstein, Confucius rejects investigation of anything foundational. In his context, this meant rejecting any appeal to nature or heaven (*tian*) at the expense of a focus on life, culture, and matters more near to hand (*Analects* 5.13, 6.27, 7.21, 7.25, 11.12).

21. The notion that we need to mix the elements seems supported by the very idea that the point of behaving in ritually correct ways is to bring about a harmony (*he*). This notion is based on cooking and musical metaphors of mixing various elements to bring about either a proper blend of flavors, in the case of cooking, or notes in the case of music. See Ames and Rosemont, *Analects of Confucius*, 254, n. 216 for a passage on the cooking metaphor from the *Zuo Commentary to the Spring and Autumn Annals* and the use of this metaphor in ethical and political thinking.

22. But see *Analects* 16.13 for the claim that sons should not be treated as a special case.

23. See his comment on how being filial is itself government service (*Analects* 2.21). For a passage indicating his suspicion of legal systems for ensuring ethics of behavior, see also 12.13.

24. Seeskin thinks that Socrates' method is not so spartan. That view is hard to maintain, given Socrates' refusal to accept anything as known about *X* until *X* has been defined. Kenneth Seeskin, *Dialogue and Discovery: A Study in Socratic Method* (Albany, NY: State University of New York Press), 1987.

25. There are additional benefits to this coupling that I have not tried to pursue here; they will come from the comparison of the (a) different styles of these two texts and their related views of moral inquiry and deference to authority; (b) competing views of loyalty to family members offered by Confucius and Euthyphro; and (c) the distinctively different commitment to the use of explicit reasoning in fostering moral improvement.
26. Available online with an exchange with Brooks and Brooks at www.umass.edu /wsp/publications/books/original/index.html.

Suggested Readings

Ames, Roger T., and Henry Rosemont, Jr., trans. *The Analects of Confucius: A Philosophical Translation*. New York: Ballantine Books, 1998.

Brooks, E. Bruce, and E. Taeko Brooks. *The Original Analects*. New York: Columbia University Press, 1998.

Fingarette, Herbert. *Confucius: The Secular as Sacred*. New York: HarperCollins Publishers, 1972.

Graham, A. C. *Disputers of the Tao*. Lasalle, IL: Open Court Publishing, 1989.

Hall, David L., and Roger T. Ames. *Thinking Through Confucius*. Albany: State University of New York Press, 1987.

Jones, David. "Teaching/Learning through Confucius: Navigating Our Way through the *Analects*." *Education About Asia* 5, no. 2 (2000): 4–13.

Lau, D. C. *Confucius: The Analects*. New York: Penguin USA, 1998.

Schwartz, Benjamin. *The World of Thought in Ancient China*. Cambridge, MA: Belknap Press, 1989.

Slingerland, Edward. *Confucius Analects: With Selections From Traditional Commentaries*. Indianapolis: Hackett Publishing Company, 2003

———. "Why Philosophy Is Not 'Extra' in Understanding the *Analects*: A Review of Brooks and Brooks, *The Original Analects*." *Philosophy East and West* 50, no. 1 (2000): 137–41.

Waley, Arthur. *The Analects of Confucius*. New York: Vintage Books, 1989.

Contributors

ROGER T. AMES is professor of philosophy and editor of *Philosophy East & West*. His recent publications include translations of Chinese classics: *The Chinese Classic of Family Reverence* (2009), and the *Analects of Confucius* (1998) (both with H. Rosemont); *Focusing the Familiar: A Translation and Philosophical Interpretation of the* Zhongyong, and *A Philosophical Translation of the* Daodejing*: Making This Life Significant"* (both with D. L. Hall) (2001); *Sun Pin: The Art of Warfare* (1996), and *Tracing Dao to Its Source* (1997) (both with D. C. Lau); and *Sun-tzu: The Art of Warfare* (1993). He has also authored many interpretative studies of Chinese philosophy and culture: *Thinking Through Confucius* (1987); *Anticipating China: Thinking Through the Narratives of Chinese and Western Culture* (1995); and *Thinking from the Han: Self, Truth, and Transcendence in Chinese and Western Culture* (1997) (all with D. L. Hall). Recently he has undertaken several projects that entail the intersection of contemporary issues and cultural understanding. His *Democracy of the Dead: Dewey, Confucius, and the Hope for Democracy in China* (with D. L. Hall) (1999) is a product of this effort.

MARY I. BOCKOVER is professor of philosophy at Humboldt State University in California, and her scholarship is mainly in the area of comparative philosophy. Professor Bockover is editor of *Rules, Rituals, and Responsibility* (1991). Some of her articles include "Ethics, Relativism, and the Self" in *Culture and Self* (1997), "Confucian Values and the Internet: A Potential Conflict" in the *Journal of Chinese Philosophy* (2003), "Metaphors of Self in Confucius and Descartes" in *Religion East and West* (2007), "The Virtue of Freedom" in *Polishing the Chinese Mirror* (2008), and "The Ren-Dao of Confucius: A Spiritual Account of Humanity" in *Confucius*

Now (2008). She is also the founder and moderator of the Humboldt State University Ethics Forum, and has created a variety of practical and service learning courses for her students.

FRANCIS BRASSARD received his PhD from McGill University in religious studies. His research interests include Buddhist philosophy and psychology and comparative religions and philosophies. His book, *The Concept of Bodhicitta in Santideva's "Bodhicaryavatara,"* was published by the State University of New York (2000). Some of his other publication titles include: "Seeing the Good in Others: A Buddhist Perspective," "The Nature of the Buddhist Contribution to Environmental Ethics," (*Comparative Culture*), "The Significance of Buddhi in the *Bhagavad-Gītā*" in *Composing a Tradition: Concepts Teaching and Relationships* (Croatian Academy of Sciences and Arts, 1999), and "The Path of the Bodhisattva and the Creation of Oppressive Cultures," in *Buddhism and Violence* (Lumbini International Research Institute, 2006). He teaches religious studies at Miyazaki International College in Kyushu, Japan.

VRINDA DALMIYA is associate professor at the University of Hawai'i at Manoa, where she teaches courses in epistemology, feminist philosophy, and environmental philosophy. She was assistant professor at Montana State University, has been a visiting assistant professor at the University of Washington, and has also taught at the Indian Institute of Technology in Delhi. Dr. Dalmiya has co-directed summer institutes for college teachers on incorporating Indian philosophy into the undergraduate curriculum for the Asian Studies Development Program at the East-West Center in Honolulu. She has published in a wide range of journals such as *Environmental Ethics, Hypatia, Sophia, Journal of Social Philosophy, Journal of the Indian Council of Philosophical Research,* and *The Philosophical Quarterly.* In addition, she has contributed to a number of anthologies in comparative philosophy and epistemology and is currently working on care ethics and its connections with analytic and feminist epistemology.

JEFFREY DIPPMANN is associate professor of philosophy and religious studies, and former director of the Asia/Pacific Studies Program at Central Washington University. Having earned his doctorate at

Northwestern University, he specializes in Daoism and Chinese Buddhism. He has published in the areas of Daoism, Buddhism, and method and theory in the study of religion. His book, *Emptying Emptiness: The "Zhaolun" as Graduated Teachings*, is currently under revision for publication. His most recent work, "On Being a Civil[ized] Daoist," appears in *Polishing the Chinese Mirror: Essays in Honor of Henry Rosemont, Jr.* Along with Ronnie Littlejohn, he is co-editor of a volume on the *Liezi*, titled *Riding the Wind with Liezi: New Essays on the Daoist Classic* (SUNY, 2010).

STEPHEN J. GOLDBERG is associate professor of Asian art at Hamilton College. He received his PhD in the history of art from The University of Michigan. His specialty is in the history and aesthetics of Chinese calligraphy. He is currently concerned with the issues of identity, subjectivity, and voice in traditional Chinese painting, and history, memory, and forgetting in contemporary Chinese art. Among his recent publications are: "Modern Woodcuts and the Rise of a Chinese Avant-garde," in *Modern China, 1937–2008: Towards a Universal Pictorial Language* (Picker Art Gallery at Colgate University, 2009); "Art and the Authority of Excellence in Traditional China," in *La question de l'art en Asia orientale* (Paris: Presses de l'Universite Paris-Sorbonne, 2008); "The Primacy of Gesture: Phenomenology and the Art of Chinese Calligraphy," in *Metamorphosis: Creative Imagination in Fine Arts Between Life-Projects and Human Aesthetic Aspirations, Analecta Husserliana* LXXXI (Kluwer Academic Publishers Dordtrecht, The Netherlands, 2004); "Recognition of the True Self: Zen Buddhism and Bokuseki Calligraphy," in *Zen no Sho: The Calligraphy of Fukushima Keido Roshi* (Clear Light Publishers, 2003); "Chinese Calligraphy in an Age of Globalization," in *The International Symposium: Words and Writing*, Taiwan Museum of Art, Taichung, Taiwan, Republic of China, 2001; and "Tradition and Authorial Identity in Chinese Calligraphy: Three Works From the Elliott Collection," in *Oriental Art* Vol. XLVI No. 5 (*Oriental Art Magazine*, 2000).

HARRIETTE GRISSOM is adjunct professor of Humanities at the University of North Carolina in Asheville, where she also works as a freelance writer and editor and studies Chinese medicinal plants. She was formerly a professor and head of liberal arts at Atlanta College of

Art. Her research focuses on the psychology of art-making across cultures with particular interest in the mind-body connection. Her recent publications include "The Haiku as a Catalyst for Modernist Poetry" in *East-West Connections*; "The Tanka Poetry of Akiko Yosano: Transformation of Tradition Through the Female Voice" in *Japan Studies Review*; and "Animal Forms and Formlessness: The Protean Quality of Buddha Nature" in B*uddha Nature and Animality* (David Jones, ed.). She has also written reviews for *Art Papers*. She received her doctorate from the Graduate Institute of Liberal Arts at Emory University in psychology and literature.

XINYAN JIANG is associate professor of philosophy and director of Asian studies at the University of Redlands. Her interests are primarily in Chinese philosophy, comparative philosophy, and ethics. She has published in the *History of Philosophy and Logic, Philosophy East and West, Journal of Chinese Philosophy, Philosophical Inquiry, Hypatia: A Journal of Feminist Philosophy*, and in several anthologies. She is the editor of *The Examined Life: Chinese Perspectives* (Global Publications, 2002). She received her BA and MA from Beida (Peking University) and taught there before she went overseas. She earned her PhD in philosophy from the University of Cincinnati. She was the first chair of the Committee on the Status of Asian/Asian American Philosophers and Philosophies of the American Philosophical Association (1998–2002) and is currently deputy director and treasurer of the International Society for Chinese Philosophy.

JOHN M. KOLLER is professor emeritus of Asian and comparative philosophy at Rensselaer Polytechnic Institute and adjunct professor of philosophy at SUNY Stony Brook. His research areas include Buddhism and psychoanalysis, philosophy of religion, mind and self identity, and cognition and the self. A frequently invited lecturer at universities throughout the world, Professor Koller is the author of more than fifty journal articles and chapters in edited books as well as five books. His books currently in print include: *Asian Philosophies* (Prentice Hall, 2007); *The Indian Way* (Pearson Prentice Hall, 2005); and *A Source Book in Asian Philosophy* (Macmillan & Co., 1991). He is a graduate of the University of Chicago and the University of Hawai`i where he was an East-West Center Fellow.

GEREON KOPF received his PhD from Temple University and is currently associate professor of Asian and comparative religion at Luther College. As a research fellow of the Japan Foundation and the Japan Society for the Promotion of Research, he conducted research in 1993 and 1994 at Obirin University in Machida and at the Nanzan Institute for Religion and Culture in Nagoya from 2002 to 2004. He is currently working on a non-dualistic philosophy based on the work of Nishida Kitarō and others of his circle including Takahashi Satomi, Tanabe Hajime, and Mutai Risaku. He is the author of *Beyond Personal Identity* (Curzon, 2001) and the co-editor of *Merleau-Ponty and Buddhism* (Lexington, 2009). In addition, he has published numerous articles on the religious philosophies of Dōgen and Nishida Kitarō.

RONNIE LITTLEJOHN is chair and professor of philosophy at Belmont University where he also is director of Asian Studies. His doctoral training at Baylor was in early modern philosophy and the work of Ludwig Wittgenstein, but his recent work is in comparative and Chinese philosophy, especially classical and contemporary Daoism. He is author of *Daoism: An Introduction* (London: I.B. Tauris, 2009) and *Confucianism: The Life, Teachings, and Influence of the Uncrowned King* (forthcoming from I.B. Tauris, March 2010). Littlejohn is the general editor of the new *Blackwell Encyclopedia of Asian Religions and Philosophy* (Oxford: Wiley-Blackwell). He is co-editor of *Riding the Wind: New Essays on the Daoist Classic The* Liezi and *Polishing the Chinese Mirror: Essays in Honor of Henry Rosemont, Jr*. He has published over 25 articles in journals including *Philosophy East and West, Dao: A Journal of Comparative Philosophy,* and *Ching Feng*. He has contributed over a dozen essays to various anthologies and collections. In 2003, he received the *Award for Innovative Excellence in Teaching, Learning and Technology* at the *14th International Conference on Teaching and Learning* and was consulting author for the Asian traditions script of episode 13 in the *Religions of the World* series developed by Greenstar Television and narrated by Ben Kingsley.

SHIGENORI NAGATOMO received his PhD in philosophy from the University of Hawai`i where he studied comparative philosophy focusing on Asian and European traditions. He has been interested in the mind-body problem with a particular emphasis on Yoga, Buddhist (Zen), and Daoist meditation methods, while supplementing them with Jung's psychology and research on *ki*-energy. He is the co-author of *Science and Comparative Philosophy* with David E. Shaner and Yuasa Yasuo (Brill Academic Publishers, 1989) and author of *Attunement through the Body* (SUNY, 1992), *A Philosophical Investigation of Miki Kiyosh's Concept of Humanism* (Edwin Mellen Press, 1995), and *The Diamondsutra's Logic of Now and a Critique of Katz's Contextualism* (Edwin Mellen Press, 2006). He has also translated several books: Yuasa Yasuo's *The Body: Toward an Eastern Mind-Body Theory* (SUNY Press, 1987) with Thomas P. Kasulis; Motoyama Hiroshi's *Toward A Superconsciousness: Meditational Theory and Practice* (Asian Humanities Press, 1990), with Clifford Ames; Yuasa Yasuo's *The Body, Self-Cultivation, and Ki-Energy* (SUNY Press, 1993), with Monte Hull; Motoyama Hiroshi's *Religion and Humanity for a Global Society* (Institute for Human Science, 2001), with David Shaner; and Yuasa Yasuo's *Overcoming Modernity: Synchronicity and Image-Thinking* (State University of New York, 2008), with John Krummel. He teaches in the Department of Religion at Temple University.

JAMES PETERMAN received his PhD in philosophy from the University of California, Berkeley, where he studied ethics and philosophy of language. He is now professor and chair of philosophy at Sewanee: The University of the South. His book, *Philosophy as Therapy: An Account and Defense of Wittgenstein's Later Philosophy* (SUNY, 1992) examines the way in which the acceptance of forms of life plays a central role in Wittgenstein's later philosophical project. Since 1998, he has been exploring the comparative relationships between Wittgenstein, Zhuangzi, and Confucius and the ways in which each thinker's views can be amplified and complemented by appeal to the others' work. In addition to his recent work, which appears in *Philosophy East & West* and *Dao: A Journal of Comparative Philosophy*, he is completing a monograph, tentatively titled, *Confucius and Wittgenstein: The Project of Ethics without Philosophy*. He sees his interest in Confucianism as informing his research in medical ethics, his work on local hospital ethics committees, and his involvement in education on end-of-life issues.

THOMAS PYNN is assistant professor of philosophy and coordinator of the Peace Studies Program at Kennesaw State University. Trained primarily in continental philosophy, he also works in the area of comparative philosophy, particularly in the area of East-West Studies (Yoga, Daoism, Buddhism, and the Chinese and Japanese philosophical traditions), indigenous philosophy, and aesthetics. Some of his recent work appears in *Buddha Nature and Animality* (David Jones, ed.), *East-West Connections, The Journal of Adolescent Research*, and the *Southeastern Review of Asian Studies*.

BRIAN SCHROEDER is professor and chair of philosophy and director of religious studies at Rochester Institute of Technology. He is the author of *Altared Ground: Levinas, History and Violence* (Routledge, 1995) and *Pensare ambientalista. Tra filosofia e ecologia* (Paravia, 2000). He is co-editor of: *Thinking Through the Death of God: A Critical Companion to Thomas J. J. Altizer* (SUNY, 2004); *Contemporary Italian Philosophy: At the Threshold of Ethics, Politics, and Religion* (SUNY, 2007); *Levinas and the Ancients* (Indiana, 2008); *Between Nihilism and Politics: The Hermeneutics of Gianni Vattimo* (SUNY, forthcoming 2010); and with Bret Davis and Jason M. Wirth *Japanese and Continental Philosophy: Conversations with the Kyoto School* (Indiana, forthcoming 2010). Schroeder has also published essays in English and Italian on Zen and the Kyoto School. He is presently writing a book titled *Atonement of the Last God*.

JOHN A. TUCKER is professor of history at East Carolina University. He is the author of two translation-studies, one titled, *Ogyū Sorai's Philosophical Masterworks: The Bendō and Benmei* (University of Hawaii Press, 2006), and *Itō Jinsai's Gomō jigi and the Philosophical Definition of Early Modern Japan* (E. J. Brill 1998). A specialist in Tokugawa Confucian thought, he has published articles in *Philosophy East & West, Journal of Chinese Philosophy, Asian Philosophy, Sino-Japanese Studies*, the *Japanese Journal of Religious Studies, Japanese Religions*, and the *Journal of the Royal Asiatic Society*. He is a past editor of *Japan Studies Review*, published by the Southern Japan Seminar. Professor Tucker received his PhD from Columbia University.

JASON M. WIRTH is associate professor of philosophy at Seattle University. His books include a translation of Schelling's *The Ages of the World* (SUNY Press, 2000), *The Conspiracy of Life: Meditations on Schelling and his Time* (SUNY Press, 2003), and the edited volume, *Schelling Now* (Indiana, 2004). He is currently finishing a book on Milan Kundera and an edited volume with Bret Davis and Brian Schroeder on the interface between Continental Philosophy and the Kyoto School. He is associate editor of the journal *Comparative and Continental Philosophy*, and he publishes in the areas of continental philosophy, Buddhist philosophy, aesthetics, and Africana philosophy.

ROBIN (RONGRONG) WANG is the director of Asian and Pacific studies and associate professor of philosophy at Loyola Marymount University. She regularly teaches undergraduate and graduate courses on comparative ethical theory, classics of Chinese philosophy, Chinese philosophy and images of women in philosophy West and East. She was voted the Outstanding Professor of the Year in 2003 by the LMU Students Association. Her publications include: *Internal Alchemy: Self, Society and the Quest for Immortality*, co-edited with Livia Kohn (Three Pines, 2009); *Chinese Philosophy in an Era of Globalization* (SUNY Press, 2004); *Images of Women in Chinese Thought and Culture: Writings from the Pre-Qin Period to the Song Dynasty* (Hackett, 2003); *Reason and Insight: Western and Eastern Perspectives on the Pursuit of Moral Wisdom* (Wadsworth, first edition, 1996; second edition, 2002); and essays in *Philosophy East & West*, *Journal of the History of Ideas*, *Chinese Philosophy*, and *Journal of the American Academy of Religion*. She is a board member for several international and national academic associations and has been a philosophy consultant for Hollywood movies. She has degrees from Beida (Peking University), Notre Dame, and received her PhD from the University of Wales, Cardiff.

Editors

DAVID JONES is professor of philosophy, editor of *Comparative and Continental Philosophy* (Equinox) and *East-West Connections*, director of the Atlanta Center for the Development of Asian Studies, and has been visiting professor of Confucian Classics at Emory. His publications are in the areas of Chinese, Japanese, Buddhist, comparative, continental, and Greek philosophies. His current books include *The Fractal Self and the Evolution of God* with John L. Culliney and *Zhu Xi Now: Contemporary Encounters with the Great Ultimate* (SUNY), co-edited with He Jinli. His recent edited books include: *Confucius Now: Contemporary Encounters with the* Analects (Open Court, 2008); *Buddha Nature and Animality* (Jain, 2007); and *The Gift of Logos: Essays in Continental Philosophy* with Jason M. Wirth and Michael Schwartz (Cambridge Scholars, forthcoming 2010). A past president of the Southeast Regional of the Association of Asian Studies and present president of the Comparative & Continental Philosophy Circle, he received his PhD in comparative philosophy from the University of Hawai`i at Manoa and was the East-West Center's Distinguished Alumnus in 2004–2005.

E. R. KLEIN is an unaffiliated scholar who resides in Washington, DC. She was an NEH recipient for Asian studies at the East-West Center in Honolulu and a Fulbright Scholar in Residence in Bosnia/Herzegovina. She served as a congressional fellow for the House International Relations Committee's Sub-committee for the Middle East and Central Asia. Dr. Klein has been published in several anthologies in the area of political and social philosophy, and has authored dozens of articles and three monographs, including *Undressing Feminism*. She earned her PhD in philosophy from the University of Miami.

Index